W9-CLU-022

DISCARD

FAITH AND WORLD

CONTEMPORARY ISMAILI SOCIAL AND POLITICAL THOUGHT

MOHAMMAD N. MIRALY

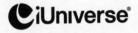

FAITH AND WORLD
CONTEMPORARY ISMAILI SOCIAL AND POLITICAL THOUGHT

iUniverse books may be ordered through booksellers or by contacting:

iUniverse
1663 Liberty Drive
Bloomington, IN 47403
www.iuniverse.com
1-800-Authors (1-800-288-4677)

Because of the dynamic nature of the Internet, any web addresses or links contained in this book may have changed since publication and may no longer be valid. The views expressed in this work are solely those of the author and do not necessarily reflect the views of the publisher, and the publisher hereby disclaims any responsibility for them.

Any people depicted in stock imagery provided by Thinkstock are models, and such images are being used for illustrative purposes only.
Certain stock imagery © Thinkstock.

ISBN: 978-1-4917-8973-5 (sc)
ISBN: 978-1-4917-8974-2 (hc)
ISBN: 978-1-4917-8972-8 (e)

Library of Congress Control Number: 2016902496

Print information available on the last page.

iUniverse rev. date: 09/29/2016

TO MY
FATHER AND MOTHER

CONTENTS

A HISTORICAL NOTE ON ISMAILISM

Islam, like other faiths, is divided in opinion. Sunni and Shi`i Islam are the two main branches of interpretation, but Shi`ism has always been in the demographic minority. Ismailism is a sect of Shi`ism, which affirms that the Prophet Muhammad publicly designated `Ali—his cousin and son-in-law—as his successor.

After the death of the Prophet Muhammad in 632 CE, the Muslim Community (Ummah) was divided over the issue of succession to the Prophet's authority. The period immediately following the Prophet's death was tumultuous and violent, and a few close companions of the Prophet asserted themselves as his successor. The group who supported `Ali as the Prophet's designated heir came to be known as the Shi`a. `Ali thus became the first Imam (spiritual leader) of the Shi`a.

Imamate—the foundational doctrine of Shi`i Islam—is an institution of hereditary leadership. Because of its hereditary nature, there were often multiple claimants to the Imamate. After the death in 765 of Jafar al-Sadiq, the fifth Imam in the modern Ismaili chronology, three major groups of Shi`is formed. The followers of al-Sadiq's uncle Zayd came to be known as Zaydis; the followers of al-Sadiq's son Musa al-Kazim came to be called Ithna`asharis (or Twelvers) and now form the majority of the world's Shi`a population; and the followers of al-Sadiq's son Isma`il came to be known as the Ismailis. Later, in 1094, a split occurred among the Ismailis following a dispute over the succession of the Fatimid caliph-Imam al-Mustansir. Those who followed his younger son Must`ali came to be known as Must`ali Ismailis and are currently headed by representatives of their occulted Imam. Those who followed al-Mustansir's elder son, Nizar, came to be known as Nizari Ismailis.

By the fifteenth century, the Nizari community had itself split into two main factions, the Muhammad-Shahis and the Qasim-Shahis. While the former group's line of Imams became discontinued by the nineteenth century, the latter group's line continued, and they are currently headed by their forty-ninth Imam, His Highness Prince Shah Karim al-Husayni—Aga Khan IV—who claims descent from the Prophet Muhammad through the progeny of his daughter, Fatima, and his son-in-law, 'Ali. The honorific title "Aga Khan" ("Chief of Chiefs") is the hereditary title of modern Nizari Imams, given to the title's first bearer by the Shah of Persia in the early nineteenth century. It is to the followers of the Aga Khans and their ancestors, the Nizari Imams, to whom the terms "Nizari" and "Ismaili" shall refer.

The Nizaris form the largest branch of the world's Ismailis, and they are the only Muslim community that claims a present and living Imam as their leader. The most prominent and prosperous group of contemporary Nizaris are the South Asian "Khojas"—Indian converts to Nizari Ismailism from the thirteenth century onward—who are located primarily in the Indian subcontinent and the Western countries of Europe and North America. Their culturally-specific practices and interpretations of Ismailism tend to shape the implicit normative profile of the Ismaili diaspora. The second major group of contemporary Nizaris are the Central Asians – located mostly in Tajikistan, Afghanistan, and Uzbekistan – who are now emerging and integrating into the wider Ismaili diaspora. All the groups of today's approximately fifteen million Nizari Ismailis, residing in over twenty-five countries—whether in the West, the Middle East, the subcontinent, or Central Asia—are bound in fraternity by their allegiance to their Imam, Aga Khan IV.

I

Opening

Being popular is the most important thing in the world!
　　　　　　　　　　　　　—Homer Simpson, *The Simpsons*

Truth always rests with the minority.
　　　　　　　　　　　　　　　　—Søren Kierkegaard

The world was entranced in 1957 when a young Harvard undergraduate became Aga Khan IV, inheriting his grandfather's spiritual obligations to millions of Ismailis worldwide—in addition to his numerous sports cars, private yacht and plane, Swiss chalet, Riviera chateau, Parisian mansion, and so many valuable racehorses. Contrasting the image of the studious Harvard senior that adorned the cover of *Life* magazine in 1958, the young Aga's public image—whether rightly or not—quickly became that of a gallivanting prince with a taste for fast horses, cars, and women, and as someone who could afford all three.

Though he claimed no penchant for nightlife and was not seen to be linked with multiple women—asserting "I am not a social butterfly or a salon lion"[1]—the jet-set lifestyle of Aga Khan IV in the second half of the twentieth century became the stuff of popular legend. His name conjured images of fantastic wealth and opulent orientalist lifestyles and was repeated not only in tabloids and weeklies like *Paris Match*, where he made regular appearances, but also across the spectrum of popular culture. In Ian Fleming's 1963 novel, *On Her Majesty's Secret Service*, James Bond is informed that "Everybody who is anybody" is present at a particular ski lodge: "We have quite taken the international set away from Gstaad

1

and St. Moritz [...] Why, we only need the Aga Khan ... and we would have everybody, but everybody!" Peter Sarstedt warbles in his 1969 song "Where Do You Go To (My Lovely)?" to a girl that her clothes are made by Balmain and she summers in Juan-les-Pines and "Your name is heard in high places / You know the Aga Khan / He sent you a racehorse for Christmas," referencing the Aga Khan's renown as a racehorse breeder. As well, any mention of Sardinia warrants mention of the Aga Khan, as attests Michael Dibdin's 1990 novel, *Vendetta*: "By 'Sardinia,' of course, one meant the Costa Smeralda on the northern coast of the island, which the Aga Khan had bought for a pittance from the local peasant farmers and turned into a holiday paradise for the super-wealthy."

At the same time, however, there was little exposure in the European media of the 1960s and '70s about the actual function of the Aga Khan as the forty-ninth Imam of the Ismailis. Partly, this was due to the mixed feelings of an essentially Christian society—used to seeing men of wealth as frivolous and men of religion as divorced from everyday life—toward the Aga Khan, whom it perceived as a wealthy young man that seemed to combine in himself the roles of *pontifex maximus*, head of state, racehorse owner, and real estate developer. For his own part, however, the Aga Khan understood the Islamic institution of the Imamate as one that combined the spheres of faith and world, realizing thereby the central Islamic ethic that humankind must work toward success in both the material and the spiritual realms.

This ethic, he says, is the undergirding element of the Imam's mandate to ensure the upliftment of his followers—which, in his opinion, is best achieved in modern times through institutional means. To this end, he established various institutions in the 1970s, such as the Aga Khan Development Network (AKDN) and the Institute of Ismaili Studies (IIS), to tend to the material and psychological needs of his community. On the one hand, the AKDN—one of the world's largest private development networks—works to ensure that the countries in which Ismailis live have stable political, civic, educational, and health institutions. On the other hand, the IIS was established as an academic institution with a mandate to recover and analyze key historical Ismaili texts as well as to engage contemporary Muslim scholars and the contours of contemporary Muslim thought.

The current Aga Khan, through his efforts to modernize both the lives and minds of contemporary Ismailis, is thus the driver of contemporary Ismailism. It is this "aga-khanienne"[2] project of modernization that we are delving into here. Specifically, we are attempting to explore the current Aga Khan's intellectual engagement with modernity: his advocacy of liberal values like democracy, pluralism, and education, which he says are also essential Islamic ethics deriving from the Qur'an; and also the way in which he guides the contemporary Ismaili academic machine to develop a historical self-narrative that locates these contemporary liberal values in Ismaili history.

Through the work of the IIS, the contemporary Ismaili tradition has developed a historical self-narrative that connects contemporary liberal values with certain Islamic values, which it says have guided the tradition since the time of the Qur'anic Revelation. In effect, this narrative creates a sense of continuity that provides the contemporary Ismaili tradition with a strong sense of historical and ethical identity, which in turn enables it to engage the modern world with an ethical framework that allows itself to be at once both liberal and Muslim, navigating smoothly the rocky confluence of old and new that is the hallmark of our times—captained throughout by its Imam, Aga Khan IV.

THE AGA MYTH

The Aga Khans have been no strangers to the European press, whose fascination with royalty abounds. The hereditary title "Aga Khan"—which translates loosely as "Chief of Chiefs"—was given to the first Aga Khan (1804–1881) by the Shah of Persia in the early nineteenth century, along with the hand of one of his daughters in marriage. Later, the British recognized the princely status of Aga Khan I and his heirs, making them the only religious leaders in British India to be granted a personal gun salute. Since then, the title "Aga Khan" has been the hereditary title of the Imam (spiritual leader) of the Shi`a Ismailis, an office held currently by the fourth bearer of the title.

Just as the paparazzi followed the European exploits of Aga Khan IV's grandfather and predecessor, the lavish Indian prince Aga Khan III (1877–1957) (a two-time president of the League of Nations who was given his weight in gold by his followers at his Golden Jubilee ceremony) and the "playboy lifestyle" of his father Prince Aly Khan (1911–1960) (a former vice president of the United Nations General Assembly who famously married Hollywood starlet Rita Hayworth), so do they follow the peregrinations of the current Aga Khan (b. 1936) from Longchamp to Klosters to St. Barth's.

Typically, tabloid writing on Aga Khan IV's life and reputation gives little attention to the Ismaili community he leads, making mention only of its pecuniary anxieties or its historical secrecy and twelfth-and-thirteenth-century practice of political violence. Indeed, the group known as the Assassins is a particularly popular aspect of Ismaili history that has provided fodder for theorists of the clandestine as well as inspiration for works of both nonfiction and fiction, such as Vladmir Bartol's famous 1938 allegory to Mussolini's fascist state, *Alamut*—the name of the Assassins' primary Persian fortress—as well as more romanticized fare, such as Judith Tarr's 1989 novel of the same name, James Boschert's 2010 novel *Assassins of Alamut*, and the highly popular 2007 video game *Assassin's Creed*.

In the same fashion, tabloid writing about the Aga Khan tends to focus less on his extensive diplomatic and development efforts, in favor of more whimsical reporting about his expensive and drawn-out divorce[3] or even more expensive super-yacht.[4] Admittedly, books like A. U. Pendragon's 2008 *Aga Khan's Billions and the Assassins: Ismailis—The Next Islamic Threat? (Sex, Money and Power: An Insider's Account of the Secret World of the Aga Khan)*, which connect the Aga Khan to vast international conspiracies of power that include groups like the Freemasons, are taken less seriously by the academic community, but they are indicative nonetheless of the mythological stature the Aga Khan holds in the popular imagination.

An Ethical Bifröst

The Ismailis, on the other hand, have never been popular. Persecution tints their history as a persistent theme: from initial phases of *taqiyya*—dissimulation of one's beliefs under duress—a practice so recurrent among early Shi`is that it became doctrine; to Genghis Khan's planned destruction of the Ismailis' Persian mini-state of Alamut in 1256 CE. Even when the Ismaili Imams ruled North Africa as caliphs of the Fatimid Empire from 909 to 1094, the community remained a minority—rulers, yet subject to the brutalities of demography. But despite the community's physical marginalization, they have had—from post-Prophetic doctrinal scuffles, to expressions of philosophical rationalism, to mediaeval mystical bouts— an intriguingly disproportionate influence on Islamic thought and the Muslim imagination.

Seyyed Hossein Nasr, that doyen of Islamic studies, makes a potent statement about the status of the Ismailis in Islam's history: "there is hardly an aspect of the Islamic community, especially in its earlier period, which was not touched in one way or another by the presence of Isma`ilism."[5] Fatimid Egypt, he affirms, was one of Islam's most artistically and scientifically creative periods, where the caliph-Imams institutionalized space for Muslim intellectuals to flourish by founding the world's first university, al-Azhar in Cairo. Nevertheless, he concludes, Ismailism's great intellectual impact passes largely unnoticed: "Isma`ili philosophy, still not fully appreciated as a major element in the intellectual life of the Islamic community, stands as one of the richest schools of thought in early Islamic history."[6]

So we arrive at the natural question: why, if the Ismailis' intellectual influence suffuses the Islamic zeitgeist, have they been—as IIS Co-Director Farhad Daftary puts it—"almost continuously treated as heretics by the Sunni and most Shi`i Muslims," and "been among the most ruthlessly persecuted minorities of the Muslim world, being frequently subjected to massacre"?[7] Historian Michael Brett suggests that it was Ismailism's entrenched avowal of the doctrine of Imamate that put it outside the Islamic mainstream. Specifically, the revolutionary aims of the early/ middle Ismaili missionary machine, the *da`wa*, to fulfill the typically Shi`i goal of establishing the Imam as the head of the entire Muslim community. Though Imamate gave the tradition "its peculiar strength and endurance," Brett opines, the failure of that doctrine to gain footing among the various schools of Islam left the tradition "increasingly isolated and ultimately vulnerable," causing its "own version of its history to be disregarded."[8]

Understanding the contemporary Ismaili conception of that history is the goal here. The primary creators of the contemporary Ismaili self-narrative are the scholars at the IIS, an Imamate institution founded in 1977 by Aga Khan IV, who heads the boards of governors of all Imamate institutions and thus captains their direction. Contemporary

Ismaili self-history is constructed on a trident-shaped thematic matrix: persecution, adaptability, and intellectualism are the arms, while Imamate is the leg that supports the frame.

The Imam is Ismailism. In the Shiʻi interpretation of the Qur'an, the Imam is invested with the "special knowledge" (*ʻilm*) to interpret the faith, making him the legitimate successor to Prophetic authority—a divine blessing that allows continual guidance for humankind. According to Azim Nanji, a former director of the IIS, all Shiʻi groups believe the Imamate is a divinely mandated institution "through whose agency Muslims are enabled to contextualise the practice of their faith and to understand fully the exoteric and esoteric dimensions of the Qur'an."[9] In Ismaili interpretation particularly, the Imam is the "speaking Qur'an" and must be physically present in the world in order to interpret the faith in changing times and to guide followers accordingly. This dual mandate embodies the Islamic principle of *din wa dunya*—the unity of "faith and world"—the two dimensions of life that, in the Ismaili conception, are balanced by the existence of the Imam and his guidance.

Aga Khan IV, who succeeded his grandfather as Imam in 1957 while he was still an undergraduate at Harvard University, reiterates this notion and explains his function:

> In both Sunni and Shia Islam, the Imam is responsible for the quality of life of those who look to him for guidance and for overseeing the practice of the faith. There is no division as there is, for example, in the Christian interpretation, between the material and the spiritual. The Imam's responsibility covers both domains. Hence, his first concern is for the security of his followers; his second is for their freedom to practise their religion; his third is for their quality of life, as I have just mentioned. I repeat, the Imamat is an institution whose two-fold mission is to guarantee quality of life and to interpret the faith.[10]

That the Ismailis conceptualize Imamate as an institution becomes extremely relevant in the modern global context. According to anthropologist Jonah Steinberg, "the institution of imamate has allowed

Isma'ilis to adapt their practices to new social realities."[11] Adaptability, again, appears as a central theme for the modern Ismaili community. The rhetoric of the current Aga Khan reflects Ismaili adaptability; he seeks to fulfill his mandate by institutionalizing modern liberal values like democracy, pluralism, and education, all of which he says are fundamentally Qur'anic ethics that the Ismailis have avouched and supported throughout their history.

Thus he is returning to the Qur'an as the font of Ismaili ethics, thereby establishing the vertical history supported by contemporary Ismaili scholarship in its presentation of certain themes as essentially and eternally Ismaili. For contemporary Ismailism, then, tradition is of utmost relevance. The present is reflected in the past, linked via an ethical bridge—or, to appropriate the allegorical "rainbow bridge" of Norse mythology connecting the transcendent realm of the divine with the immanent realm of the world—an ethical Bifröst.

The ethical Bifröst is reflected in the way contemporary Ismailism appeals to its tradition of esoteric authority and mysticism in order to articulate its support for liberal values like democracy, pluralism, and education. In the view of contemporary Ismailism, these are primal Ismaili values and form the best basis for engendering social justice and an environment of freedom for diverse intellectualisms in the modern context. Indeed, Steinberg notes that "in the last century Isma'ili religious discourse has been deeply concerned with modernity and with responding to its perceived social exigencies."[12]

For the Aga Khan, these concerns are of direct relevance to the impoverished and persecuted Ismaili communities around the world, to whose assistance the Aga Khan Development Network is directed. The IIS defines the AKDN as "a contemporary endeavour of the Ismaili Imamat to realise the social conscience of Islam through institutional action."[13] Thus, in this conception, the AKDN institutionalizes the bridge between the practical modern and the eternal ethical: "the institutions of the Network derive their impetus from the ethics of Islam which bridge the two realms of the faith, *din* and *dunya*, the spiritual and the material."[14]

Importantly, Steinberg observes that the official photographs of the AKDN "focus on the values of the Enlightenment and modernity: individualism, democratic political participation and cooperation, 'progress' and 'development,' virtuous leadership, health, education, and the benefits of capitalism."[15] To be a modern Ismaili, then, is to uphold liberal values—not only because they are practical for human survival, but also *because they are Ismaili values*, connected via the ethical Bifröst to fundamental Qur'anic ethics.

The liberal state seems to provide the necessary space for Ismailism's unique interpretation of Islam. The contemporary globalized context, too, seems essential for modern Ismaili flourishing—what one Ismaili scholar calls their "phoenix-like renaissance"—and its transnationalism, whose organizational structure with its multiple international and local councils and various institutions reflects the corporate model. Indeed, for Steinberg, the community's organizational dynamics alone make it worthy of study, as "they present a basic challenge to theoretical and popular understandings of the state, of globalization, and of Islam" and thereby "represent a new possibility for transnational social organization, for socio-political participation beyond the nation-state, for citizenship without territory."[16]

It is in the liberal West, then, where Ismailism seems to find a concordance of thought and values, where the community is not brutalized—as in Pakistan and Afghanistan—and where a former governor general of Canada can remark that "with the Aga Khan and what he represents, we are a better country" because "he embodies the values that we Canadians most cherish, and the actions that have created the country that we are."[17] Curiously, Canada seems to be contemporary Ismailism's success story. Indeed, the community thrives in Canada, where it counts among its members the country's business and political elite, including some of its wealthiest citizens as well as the first female Muslim senator and first Muslim mayor of a major North American city. In Canada, the community is welcomed and the country's immigration minister makes public pronouncements to the effect that "Canada has benefited greatly from members of the Ismaili community who have made, and continue to make, great contributions to Canada's heritage, culture and society."[18] Here, in a country hailed as a benchmark for global liberal multiculturalism, Ismailism is celebrated as an integral component of that success story. Here, in this global moment, Ismailism is finally popular.

CONTEMPORARY ISMAILISM IN CONTEMPORARY ISLAM

Much of the community's contemporary popularity can be attributed to the respect garnered by Aga Khan III and IV among the international community, which is perhaps why the current Aga Khan and his Ismailis are welcomed so readily by political and economic leaders all over the world. To be sure, while Ismailism is not well understood in popular Islam, on the global stage it is viewed as an important player, perhaps as a result of the Aga Khan's political clout. Nevertheless, the fact that this historically marginalized and persecuted tradition is now internationally well respected is noteworthy, as it speaks to the increased salience of the Ismaili community's position in modern global society.

After centuries of being maligned, the tradition is now welcomed into the fold of Islam even by some of its most important representatives, such as King Abdullah II of Jordan. Abdullah included the Ismailis—represented by the Aga Khan—in his 2005 Amman Conference, which brought together the diversity of global Muslim leaders and scholars to define "*what Islam is and what it is not*" and "to clarify to the modern world *the true nature of Islam and the nature of true Islam*."[19] In his Letter to the Amman Conference, the Aga Khan affirmed the unity of the Muslim Ummah (Community) and applauded the attempt to "search for the answers to the issues of a rapidly evolving modernity which Muslims of the world face" using "the knowledge that Islam is Allah's final message to mankind, the Holy Quran His final Book, and Muhammad, may peace be upon him, His last and final Prophet."[20] These values are common to all Muslims, he says, including Ismailis:

> These are the fundamental principles of faith enshrined
> in the Shahada and the Tawhid therein, which bind the
> Ummah in an eternal bond of unity. With other Muslims,
> they are continuously reaffirmed by the Shia Ismaili
> Muslims of whom I am the 49th hereditary Imam in direct
> lineal descent from the first Shia Imam, Hazrat Ali ibn
> Abi Talib through his marriage to Bibi Fatimat-az-Zahra,
> our beloved Prophet's daughter.

Here, he asserts (1) his role as the legitimate successor to the Prophet and (2) that the unity of the Muslim Ummah is grounded in shared ethical principles. The Imam is thus presented as a moral and spiritual leader within the transnational Muslim Ummah—united in the ethical realm; needing no physical realm—which fulfills, in a postmodern, global way, Shi`ism's perennial preoccupation with the recognition of the Imam's leadership within the Ummah.

The Aga Khan continues in his Letter to situate Ismailism within the historic tradition of Shi`a Islam, which, he says, affirms the validity of personal search, the necessity for balance between faith and world, and the authority of the hereditary Imam:

> Our historic adherence is to the Jafari Madhab [legal school] and other Madhahib of close affinity, and it continues, under the leadership of the hereditary Ismaili Imam of the time. This adherence is in harmony also with our acceptance of Sufi principles of personal search and balance between the zahir [exoteric] and the spirit or the intellect which the zahir signifies.

The authority of the Imam to interpret the faith remains a central and defining doctrine of Shi`ism and, thereby, Ismailism. The Aga Khan confirmed this principle when he drafted in 1986 the Constitution of the Shia Imami Ismaili Muslims, whose preamble affirms the key doctrinal principles of Shi`a Ismailism.[21] It begins by iterating the central Islamic principles of *Tawhid* ("Oneness of God") and Muhammad's role as Last Prophet, then proceeds to avow the central Shi`i principle of hereditary Imamate and the complete authority of the Imam over Ismaili doctrine. It also ratifies the Imam's responsibility to ensure the spiritual and material upliftment of his followers as part of the historically continuous Ismaili tradition. Finally, it makes clear the distinction between allegiance to the Imam and to the state.

Article E states:

> From the time of the Imamat of Hazrat Mawlana Ali (a.s), the Imams of the Ismaili Muslims have ruled over

territories and peoples in various areas of the world at different periods of history and, in accordance with the needs of the time, have given rules of conduct and constitution in conformity with the Islamic concepts of unity, brotherhood, justice, tolerance and goodwill.[22]

The ethical principles listed in Article E are presented as values upheld continuously by the Ismaili tradition from its origins. Building on this conception, the Aga Khan focuses on modern liberal values as the core of contemporary Ismaili social and political thought. This is revealed in his public pronouncements, some of which he chose to publish in a collection of speeches entitled *Where Hope Takes Root: Democracy and Pluralism in an Interdependent World* (Vancouver: Douglas & McIntyre Ltd, 2008). The collection "sets out the principles that inform his vision," namely: democracy, pluralism, and education.[23]

In short, while the Imam's authority is strongly reasserted in contemporary Ismaili thought, it is also wedded to liberalizing commitments to democracy, social justice, and multicultural diversity. To be sure, most commentators concede that the Ismaili tradition is one of the more progressive and liberal strands in Islam, though its significance is often dismissed within the academy and beyond as marginal, at best, or, at worst, eccentric, irrelevant, and even heretical. Furthermore, the minority status of the Ismaili community has fostered an internal tradition of discretion that makes it reluctant to draw attention to its own contributions. Thus, for a variety of external and internal reasons, there is currently no significant body of scholarship that examines the contemporary contours of this understated and largely overlooked tradition of Islamic social thought.

Some appreciation of the significance of contemporary Ismaili social and political thought can be gauged from Akbar Ahmed's study *Journey into Islam: The Crisis of Globalization* (Washington, DC, 2007). Ahmed explores three broad approaches to modernity, secularity, and the West in contemporary Islam. His "models" are named after major Islamic educational centers: Ajmer, Deoband, and Aligarh. The Ajmer model refers to "all those Muslims inspired by the Sufi and mystical traditions within Islam," of which the Gülen movement is an important example. The Deoband model comprises the modern neo-orthodox movements within

Islam, specifically the Wahhabis in Saudi Arabia, the Muslim Brotherhood, and Hamas in the Middle East. This form of fundamentalism argues that modernity poses significant challenges to Islamic identity that can be critically engaged only by a return to origins and a reaffirmation of the teaching of the Qur'an and the example of the Prophet.

The Aligarh model represents "a broad but distinct modernist Muslim response to the world" that argues for the convergence of Islam with contemporary commitments to human rights, democracy, secularity, and pluralism. Named after the site of the first modern Muslim college founded in India, representatives of this model include nineteenth-century reformers like Syed Ahmed Khan (d. 1898) in India and Muhammad Abduh (d. 1905) in Egypt, as well as diverse liberal, socialist and modernizing voices in the Middle East. Ahmed argues that Aligarh University played a decisive role in fostering this modernist voice within Islam.

Contemporary Ismaili Islam clearly fits within this modernizing trajectory of Islam. However, the distinctive character and significance of its contribution has not been a focus of research. For example, Ahmed's study overlooks the fact that the educational movement that gave its name to the Aligarh model benefited greatly from the work of Aga Khan III, who spearheaded the establishment of the Aligarh Muslim University in the 1920s by going from door to door to ensure the Muslim community's full participation in its funding. In short, the Ismaili tradition has fused itself to the evolving movement of Islamic modernism and has proved to be its most durable and devoted advocate.

HISTORY AS IDENTITY

In a sense, contemporary Ismailism's reconstruction of its history is an example of the modernizing efforts undertaken by traditional groups attempting to revivify and undergird their senses of identity in the modern context. According to Aziz Esmail, a former dean and present governor of the IIS, history fortifies a sense of identity because it reinforces a sense of continuity.[24] For Steinberg, the IIS is the hub for the creation of a new Ismaili metaculture, part of which is "the *creation* of Isma'ili images and discourses of the past, and the selective emphasis on certain elements of this past,"[25] such as the Fatimid era, which he says Aga Khan III deliberately recalled as a foundational image in his pan-Ismaili identity-creation project. Differently, and practically, Esmail argues that "in periods of rapid or fundamental change, the search for the past is a vital spiritual necessity."[26] Thus, in his conception, the attempt to reconstruct and recapture an historical narrative is an essential component of the ability of a religious community to survive, modernize, and adapt. Indeed, says Steinberg, "for the Isma`ilis history has become a central motif or emblem of contemporary identity."[27] Going a step further, Esmail explains that "by acquiring a vital self-image through assimilation of one's historical past, energies for future adjustments and modifications are set free."[28] For Ismailis, he concludes, this need has never been as acute as it is today.

Esmail is speaking both about and to the Ismaili community. In an article titled "The Role of the Institute of the Ismaili Studies," appearing in an Ismaili community publication, he argues that the need to understand both the faith and the contemporary world are critical. He presents an argument that makes clear the impetus and goals of the contemporary Ismaili project of identity construction, whose reconstruction of history is also an engagement with modernity: "If our articulation of the faith was unattuned or unintelligible to the world outside, we would be opting in effect for a ghetto, which is the very antithesis of the policies of our late and present Imams. Our articulation must be at once primordial and modern. It must be rationally comprehensible, and spiritually satisfying."[29]

He believes, thus, that contemporary Ismailism must articulate itself using the parlance of the times, while simultaneously recovering and reformulating its "primordial" spiritual tenor. In his view, the need "to recognise the historical dimension *within* religion and, conversely, the religious imagination *within* history"[30] is the key to navigating the challenges of contemporaneity. Any Islamic thought or theology that would seek to master those challenges, he says, must "discover its past anew, not as a legacy, not as a deposit, not even as a body of tenets and principles, but as a vision of which the principles were in their time and place an expression."[31] This is, in effect, the project in which the IIS and the contemporary Imamate are engaged.

THE ISMAILI MODERNITY
In Esmail's view, the venture to connect with the world rather than retreat from it is the only means of survival, and a pluralistic point of view seems

to be the only one suited to address the challenges of the modern world.[32] While this "does not necessitate the abdication of particular viewpoints and commitments,"[33] he says, a culture becomes isolated if it locks itself up in itself. "Escape from introversion," he concludes, "lies not in the obliteration of specific memory but in an enlargement of its intellectual horizons."[34]

For Amyn Sajoo—a frequent IIS collaborator—there is no alternative to the pluralist worldview. It is a central theme of modernity, which itself has no alternative, considering humankind's current stage of history and political economy. Writing in an IIS volume entitled *Muslim Modernities*, he argues that "it is the idea of *plural modernities* that holds promise."[35] We must admit the "founding" influences of Eurocentric narratives, he says, but the promise of plural/multiple modernities is its offer to be "aware of the ethical and practical limits of the hegemonial narrative."[36] Multiple modernities "insist on the plurality of ways in which to construct the key themes of the modern, within the broad nexus between past and present."[37]

Exemplifying the reality of multiple Muslim modernities is the fact that diverse Muslim groups grappling with key themes of modernity—such as secularism, human rights, democratic governance, and globalism— produce different solutions about how to engage with the world. While contemporary militant, revivalist, or literalist forms of Islam are types of Muslim modernities, their desire to *restore* the past runs both parallel and contrary to that of liberal Muslim groups, like the Ismailis, who seek to *invoke* the past in their engagement with contemporary challenges. For Esmail, writing on Islam and modernity, the modern tradition of reinterpretation means "on the one hand to be selective about the modern world, and on the other hand to revivify loyalty to their past."[38]

The contemporary Ismaili embrace of pluralism goes to the heart of its understanding of Islam and modernity. Following this pluralist worldview, the tradition is attempting to situate itself as one of an array of possible contemporary Muslim responses to modernity, rather than *the* essential Muslim modernity. Contemporary Ismailism has selected a particular engagement with modernity—one that engages Western liberal values of democracy, pluralism, and education—which it sees as concordant with its conception of its own ethical history. Unlike other transnational expressions of modern Islam like the Muslim Brotherhood, or forms of extremism like al-Qaeda, Ismailism is happy to dance with Western liberalism. Steinberg sees this as Ismailism's most enduring contribution, because it is a Muslim modernity that belies typical media images of "global Islam"—"The Isma`ili self-representation as the 'Modern Muslims,' has the potential to disturb and destabilize popular (mis)representations of just what Islam *is* and to complicate and problematize uncritical constructions of a homogeneous, univocal 'Islamic World.'"[39]

Ultimately, he says, Ismailism's imagining of itself as progressive, adaptive, and liberal is, in a sense, true. The particular trajectory of Western liberalism that Ismailism engages, though, is closer to the Taylorian conception of communitarian, multicultural liberalism, as opposed to the more Rawlsian conception of comprehensive liberalism or procedural liberalism. The Ismaili tradition gravitates toward Canadian and American liberal pluralists (Christian and Jewish) like Charles Taylor, William Kymlicka, James Tully, Michael Walzer, and William Galston, who support a more communitarian view attentive to the dilemmas of minority status.

The contemporary Ismaili engagement with these Western thinkers in critical debates on secularism, pluralism, and democracy is an exercise in social and political thought. Through this engagement, Ismaili scholars and public figures have been participating also in an interpretive engagement with contemporary Ismaili thought. There are some distinctive features of this modernizing trajectory within contemporary Islamic social and political thought that warrant investigation.

First, the Ismaili movement is unique in that Ismailism is the only Islamic sect to acknowledge a line of living and present Imams who claim direct lineal descent from the Prophet Muhammad. The social and political teaching of the Aga Khan carries a "magisterial" weight and authority within the community that is analogous, in a sense, to the magisterial authority of papal teaching in the Catholic tradition. What role has the Imamate played in shaping and directing the Ismaili commitment to modernism? There are analogous expressions of modernism within Muslim thought among other strands of Sunni and Shi`i Islam, but these modernist approaches typically have faced an uphill battle in light of more powerful neo-orthodox or fundamentalist movements. The effortless way that the Ismaili tradition seems to embrace and sustain a commitment to a modernist trajectory of Islamic social and political thought may be a function of this magisterial voice within the tradition.

Second, the modernist vision of the Ismaili tradition is rooted in a particular conception of the continuity of its Islamic modernism to history and tradition. The Aga Khan contends that the social philosophy he espouses is a continuation of a longer tradition of ethical and social thought that reaches back to the Prophet Muhammad (570–632) and the Imams who followed. This conception of intellectual and historical continuity is a central feature of Ismaili teaching and is critical to its interpretation of the evolving tradition of Islamic social and political thought. In particular, contemporary Ismaili thought typically presents its commitments to pluralism and democracy as universal features of the Islamic tradition, rather than keynote features of its own unique sectarian stance.

For example, the tradition's commitment to pluralism could be viewed as a functional necessity arising out of its own minority status within Islam. However, contemporary Ismaili social and political thought argues that the commitment to pluralism is deeply rooted in Islamic history and tradition. Indeed, the Aga Khan chose pluralism as the theme for his Golden Jubilee in 2007 and selected verse 4:1[40] of the Qur'an to surround his emblem, bringing attention thereby to a "universal" Islamic message of divinely created diversity that exists within the unity of humankind. Contemporary Ismaili social and political theorists, following the Aga Khan's lead, emphasize the centrality of the role of pluralism in their exegesis of Qur'anic ethics.

Contemporary Ismaili thought also points to the Prophetic example of consultation as an example of early democratic governance in Islam. The Aga Khan said: "I am a democrat ... primarily because of principles that go back 1400 years. These principles, cemented 14 centuries ago, are consistent with democratic models that exist around the world today."[41] In short, contemporary Ismaili thought is striving to make the case that the principle of democracy is a deeply entrenched ethical form of governance within Islam.

A third feature of Ismaili social philosophy is the conviction that faith must be actualized and embedded in institutional expressions. In his only American television interview, the Aga Khan notes that "it is better that the work should speak" rather than the religious leader.[42] For the Aga Khan and contemporary Ismailism, modernist commitments to pluralism and democracy arise from within the Islamic tradition, but they are to be promoted more by concrete forms of social action rather than disputation and debate. Social development is seen as a practical implementation of the Qur'anic call for social justice, pluralism, and democracy.

In this view, the institution of Imamate "ensures the balance between the *shariah* [legal] or the exoteric aspect of the faith, and its esoteric, spiritual essence."[43] This balancing of the exoteric (*zahir*) and the esoteric (*batin*) coalesces in the person of the Imam, through whom the inseparable nature of faith (*din*) and world (*dunya*) in Islam is realized. Thus, it is the Imam's principal function to interpret and make relevant the ethics of the faith in accordance with the needs of the day, thereby enabling the believers to go beyond the outward form of revelation in search of its spiritual and intellectual realities.[44]

This conception of theory/praxis, faith/world, *batin/zahir, din/dunya*, is a core element of Ismaili thought and finds expression in the array of institutions established by the Ismaili Imamate to give substance to the principles to which it adheres. The Global Centre for Pluralism in Ottawa concretizes its commitment to pluralism, while the network of educational institutions and the Aga Khan Academies concretize its commitment to education. The current work of the AKDN in Afghanistan provides the most striking example of its holistic approach to democracy, education, pluralism, and development—what it calls Multi-Input Area Development (MIAD), the notion that simultaneous work on several fronts spurs progress on other fronts.[45]

SPEAKING WITH ISMAILISM

Considering that no major work has been undertaken to map the contemporary intellectual landscape of the Ismaili community, we may question where to begin. The Ismailis themselves would start with the Imam, since the Imamate is their central doctrine and it informs their activities and forms their identity. "One of the particularities of Ismailis," says the Aga Khan, is that "the Community always follows very closely the personal way of thinking of the Imam."[46] Thus, to focus on the role and thought of the Imam as the starting point for Ismaili thought in general is consistent with the tradition's approach to its history and development.

In some ways, the rationale for this approach would be analogous to the rationale for focusing on the magisterial social teaching of the Catholic Church. However, whereas the magisterium of the Catholic Church tends to view itself as a somewhat freestanding authority in faith and morals, the Ismaili Imamate tends to view itself as an authority that utilizes a consultative cultural matrix.

According to Quentin Skinner, one of the leading historians of early modern social and political theory, engaging the thought of a political theorist requires situating oneself within that thinker's distinctive discursive community.[47] Following this, we may identify four circles of discourse around contemporary Ismaili social and political thought.

First, the Ismaili tradition does not see itself as disconnected from the larger Islamic tradition; rather, it sees itself as part of a tradition that finds its foundation in the Qur'an and the teachings of the Prophet and the Imams. In this way, a sense of intellectual continuity is part of the Ismaili doctrine, and the Imamate represents the nexus of that continuing tradition that turns back to its foundational sources. Thus, the Aga Khan portrays himself as an interlocutor with the universal Islamic discourse embedded in the Qur'an.

Second, the Imam actively fosters and engages in dialogue with a contemporary community of Ismaili scholars. The current Imam has revived the Ismaili tradition of cultivating intellectual life through the establishment of major intellectual institutions such as the transnational Aga Khan University (AKU) and University of Central Asia (UCA), as well as the Institute of Ismaili Studies in London (UK) and the Global Centre for Pluralism in Ottawa. Some of the most engaged contemporary Ismaili social and political theorists include Amyn Sajoo, Ali Asani, Azim Nanji, and Karim Karim, among others.

The IIS is itself a hub for the third circle of discourse, namely contemporary Muslim scholars who are not Ismaili but whose thought resonates in significant ways with the nexus of concerns that drive contemporary Ismaili social thought. The IIS therefore produces publications not only on Ismaili intellectual history, but also on the contemporary intellectual landscape of the Muslim world, such as *Civil*

Society in the Muslim World (2004) and *Modern Muslim Intellectuals and the Qur'an* (2004). The Ismaili intellectual institutions thus provide a home for contemporary Muslim scholarship in general, creating space for partnerships—which is perhaps emblematic of the Aga Khan's emphasis on intellectual pluralism as being a touchstone of Ismaili history. Sunni and Shi`i social and political theorists who have been drawn into this Ismaili circle of dialogue include Abdou Filali-Ansary, Reza Shah-Kazemi, Mohammed Arkoun, Abdulaziz Sachedina, Tariq Modood, Abdolkarim Soroush, and others.

Fourth, there is a non-Muslim circle of discourse involving the dialogue between Ismaili political thought and contemporary Western political theory. Ismaili theorists such as Amyn Sajoo and Karim Karim are actively engaging contemporary theories of pluralism, multiculturalism, and democratic citizenship. Contemporary social and political theorists of liberal multiculturalism (Charles Taylor, John Rawls, William Kymlicka, et al) have thus become a fourth circle of discourse for Ismaili social and political theory.

However, because of the unique role of praxis with Ismaili tradition there is another circle that needs to be included in this analysis, namely the ways in which social and political thought are embodied in action. The major social action arm of the Ismaili community, the Aga Khan Development Network, provides a concrete expression of the Ismaili commitment and approach to democracy, pluralism, and education. Currently, the most significant outreach of the AKDN is its development work in Afghanistan, the "failed democracy"[48] at the center of global attention. It is worthwhile to look at the AKDN's work as an example of the implementation of Ismaili social and political philosophy, as well as a concrete articulation of the role of the core interconnected principles of democracy, pluralism, and education in socioeconomic development.

Our study seeks to examine these issues outlined above. Most notably, it seeks to examine the way in which contemporary Ismaili institutions articulate their social and political ideas as, on the one hand, connected to Ismaili history and Qur'anic ethics, and, on the other hand, wedded to the notion of faith and world by institutionalizing the ethics of justice/democracy, equality/pluralism, and knowledge/education through the Imamate institutions and the AKDN. Our goal here is to map the architecture of contemporary Ismaili self-understanding. One understandable misreading might be that this is an attempt to *argue for* contemporary Ismaili approaches to its core modernizing values as well as to *argue for* its account of how these commitments are anchored in its history. This study is, however, an attempt to (1) elucidate the normative form of the current modernizing construction of the Ismaili tradition, and (2) problematize it by highlighting the ways in which it reads contemporary commitments back into history.

The book begins with a review of both popular and academic literature about the Aga Khan and the Ismailis. As mentioned, there is no study that investigates contemporary Ismaili thought. Thus, the chapter surveys the major Ismaili institutional players who are involved in the creation of contemporary Ismaili thought. The premise of the chapter on the contemporary Ismaili historical narrative is that contemporary Ismailism relies heavily on its past to provide both legitimacy and impetus for its present. The chapter thus navigates the work of contemporary Ismaili historiographers, which tend to locate the ethics of justice, pluralism, and learning in the defined periods of Ismaili history: Early, Fatimid, Alamut, Modern. The chapter on Ismaili approaches to the Qur'an explores and explains the essentially Ismaili approach to Qur'anic exegesis, which is to uncover allegorical interpretation from the Scripture, an approach they argue is the way to understand the essential meaning of the Qur'an. The following chapter surveys the work of the AKDN in Afghanistan, which serves as the basis to explore the Aga Khan's stated ethical impetus for the existence and work of the network. The first part of the chapter explores the Aga Khan's argument that the AKDN institutionalizes the essential Islamic concern for social justice as well as his mandate as Imam to ensure the upliftment of his followers. The second part looks at the work of the AKDN in promoting the values of democracy, pluralism, and education. Part II of the book explores the core liberal commitments that inform contemporary Ismaili thought: democracy, pluralism, and civic education. The closing chapter examines the emergence of the transnational Ismaili community, and the role of the Imamate in fostering an overarching sense of loyalty and unity among the diverse ethnocultural Ismaili communities. It looks at the growing significance of Canada as a central site for the working out of contemporary Ismaili identity and its commitments to pluralism, education, and multiculturalism.

CREATING A GLOBAL ISMAILI IDENTITY

Perhaps the central objective of contemporary Ismailism—and the reason it engages a particular sort of political liberalism—is to create a more unified and secure global Ismaili community out of persecuted and impoverished minority Ismaili communities in developing or underdeveloped states. The Aga Khan has stated that such practical concerns have undergirded his support for pluralist democratic values from the beginning of his tenure. He has sought to ensure, he says, that the countries in which his followers live are stable and have "clear development horizons," and to this end he has sought to "underwrite the integrity of the State and to contribute to improving the quality of life for all communities, not just my own."[49] On this view, support for liberal values is directly connected to practical notions of freedom from oppression and poverty. This idea concorded with his early view of the Imamate's developing conception of the management of global Ismaili communities: "This aspiration, I felt, was particularly appropriate to the Imamate because of its commitment to broad social objectives without political connotations, save in its concern for the fundamental freedom of its followers to practice the faith of their choice."[50]

Today, the Ismaili institutions are the key players in the creation and encouragement of a uniform global Ismaili identity. Through the refinement of Ismaili images and history, they are attempting to create a unified ethical and spiritual identity that binds the various Ismaili global communities, transcending their cultural idiosyncrasies. The institutions serve as the locus for interaction between the various Ismaili communities, which brings to light the stark differences between the affluent and Western-integrated diasporic Khoja Ismailis[51] and their scattered and isolated brethren in Central Asia, toward whose development much of the institutions' work is focused.

Importantly, many of the diasporic Ismaili elite work in the institutions, which Steinberg recognizes as symptomatic of the high value placed among them on serving their less-privileged brethren. He sees this widespread practice as a "pilgrimage," a rite of passage not unlike organized journeys to Israel for Jewish youth, but which is nevertheless "crucial in the construction of transcultural (but intra-Isma`ili) sharedness."[52] Because of their wealth and education, the Khojas lead the Ismaili institutional structures and, therefore, the institutional globalization of Ismailism. As a function of their leadership role, they tend to introduce their view and version of Ismailism to the Central Asian communities, which leads to a degree of resentment over the infringement on indigenous religious practices and autonomy.[53]

The provenance of the Khojas is the Satpanth tradition, the form of Ismailism that abounded in the Indian subcontinent from the thirteenth century onward, and whose particular identity is tethered to a heritage of devotional poetry known as *ginan*s. The *ginan*s were part of the larger musical and poetical culture of the subcontinent, which offered open space for a community like the Khojas, who were culturally Indian but were now being exposed to the most basic Islamic and Ismaili ideas through an indigenous cultural and religious tool. Through the *ginan* tradition, the Khojas were able to learn Ismaili ideas while simultaneously embedding themselves into the almost syncretic Indic religious milieu for hundreds of years, until the arrival of the Aga Khans in the nineteenth century from Iran.

The Aga Khans concretized the religious identity of the Khojas, who began to differentiate themselves as a Shi`a Muslim community amid the various religious communities in the region. Unlike their Middle Eastern or Central Asian brethren, the Khojas were not persecuted, and thus their conception of *taqiyya* had been more acculturation than dissimulation. Perhaps this relative freedom—offered first by the syncretic Indian religiocultural milieu and later the legal culture of British colonialism—was the reason the Aga Khans chose to reside in Bombay, to solidify the tenets of modern Ismaili Shi`ism among the Khoja community first, to educate them in Western ideas and mores, and eventually to send its British-acculturated members across the world to settle in other British colonies.

Until recently, Ismailism was secretive and the Khojas were unaware of their hidden, persecuted brethren. But, as a result of the tides of globalism and changing political realities, other Ismaili communities have in recent decades come into the open, and the new cross-cultural encounters have created the need for an Ismaili identity that takes into account both the local cultures of the various Ismaili communities and a more universalizing discourse and doctrine to unite them all. Most pivotal to this project have been the efforts of Aga Khan IV to create a pan-Ismaili narrative based on Qur'anic and Islamic tenets rather than particular cultural derivations of the tradition.

The Khoja community holds a definitive place in this project, since their material success, their acculturation to Western norms, and their well-defined religious practices have made them the normative Ismaili community. To a degree, then, the Khojas are essential to understanding the contours of modern Ismailism. Our focus, however, is on the contemporary construction of the pan-Ismaili identity, which is buttressed on the concept of shared values across the various Ismaili communities, and though it supports the plurality of various Ismaili cultures, it seeks to establish an ethicohistorical narrative to unite them.

To be sure, the Satpanth tradition is unique among modern Ismaili traditions because of its history of pluralistic engagement and interreligious interface. While acculturation may be seen as akin to dissimulation, the Satpanth tradition represents a more creative application of *taqiyya*, in that it embedded itself into the culture and engaged with it. While it did not have a radically distinctive Ismaili character—in the sense that it was part of a shared symbolic and poetical heritage and was not noticeably different from other cultural groups in the Indic context—it was not pretending to be not Ismaili. This can perhaps be seen as postmodern dissimulation, similar to the Canadian experience of working with the currents of cultures rather than hiding from them. This Ismaili conception of dissimulation by engagement may have global implications, since all communities today seek to maintain their identities, engage with their wider societies, and not be fingered as a problematic minority tradition but rather as a cooperative one.

THE ISMAILI IDIOM

Why have the Ismailis been so successful at integrating into the modern world, unlike so many other Muslim groups? The contemporary Ismaili scholar might answer that it is due to a tradition of adaptability, undergirded by unfailing loyalty to the institution of Imamate, whose persistent goal has been to interpret the faith in accordance with changing times.

Part of that is true. Strong, adaptive leadership is the sextant that guides the traveller through the seas of life. Another part—perhaps the esoteric or *batini* part—is the firm belief of the Ismailis throughout history in the truth of their doctrines. As a persecuted minority, they must have held tightly to a sentiment similar to that expressed by Kierkegaard above: "truth always rests with the minority."

The sentiment speaks to more than mere self-affirming self-preservation, though. Kierkegaard contends that the strength of majority opinion is illusory because it is not based on knowledge, while the truth, battered by gangs of the uninformed, moves quietly from minority to minority, where knowledge informs opinion. This is the history of gnostic knowledge—the esoteric teachings aimed at abolishing the distance between man and God—and the unfailingly persecuted groups who passed on its secrets, from the ancient mystery religions to Manicheanism and Valentinianism. In some Islamic interpretations, the kernel of esoteric knowledge passed later from John the Baptist to Jesus of Nazareth and onward from his brother, James the Just, down to Bahira the Monk, who whispered to the youthful Muhammad prognostications of his future prophetic career.

Ismailism sees itself as the successor to Prophet Muhammad's esoteric knowledge, which it perceives as foundational to the religion.

Frithjof Schuon, the twentieth-century authority on comparative religions, argues that esoteric knowledge—man's knowledge of divine wisdom—"is reserved, by definition and because of its very nature, for an intellectual elite necessarily restricted in numbers."[54] This is not because the knowledgeable minority keeps esoteric knowledge hidden; rather, it is hidden because the truth to which they are privy is embedded so deeply within that it is not convincingly communicable to the exoteric majority. This is the paradox of the Shi`a Ismaili gnosis: the permanent challenge of man is to penetrate the hidden aspect of religion and surpass it, yet the outward form of religion must persist so that man might exceed it.

That is the crux of the entire Ismaili adventure.

PART I

2

SPEAKING ABOUT ISMAILISM

The only thing worse in the world than being talked about is not being talked about.

—Oscar Wilde

Beyond the slew of newspaper and magazine articles in recent years discussing the work of the Aga Khan and the AKDN, there is no significant body of literature assessing the sociointellectual contribution of the modern Ismaili community. Although some relevant scholarly and journalistic articles and books have appeared sporadically over the decades, the focus of analysis in this project is the evolution of contemporary Ismaili social and political thought, about which no significant study exists. Indeed, the historical and institutional features of the modern Ismaili tradition have only begun to be engaged more deeply over the last year, evinced by a handful of recent scholarly works.[1]

Considering the relatively new ground covered, the body of literature relevant to this project is confined to the scholars working in the fields of Ismaili history and historiography as well as those who probe the confluence of contemporary Islamic and liberal political ethics. The main source of contemporary scholarship about the Ismailis is the Institute of Ismaili Studies (IIS), an Imamate institution that produces works on Ismaili history and thought. The main interpreter, however, of the work of the Ismaili Imamate and, by extension, the Ismaili community, is the Imamate itself. While there is a lack of scholarly material about the work of the Imamate, there is an implicit historiography in the work of the Aga Khan himself—his speeches, interviews, and direction of the

Imamate institutions—which highlights the themes that he and the Ismaili community consider relevant to their conception of the lived ethic of Islam in the modern world.

The primary focus of contemporary Ismaili thought is the issue of pluralism, which is at the forefront of the Aga Khan's concerns. This is shown in the discussion below, which begins with a survey of modern writing on the Aga Khan and the Ismailis that provides a perspective on the journalistic writing about the Imam and the community from the mid twentieth century to the present. The lack of present-day academic scholarship about the history and doctrines of the Ismailis is, as previously mentioned, somewhat compensated by the growing corpus of literature produced by the IIS.

Since the IIS plays a central role in the intellectual construction of contemporary Ismailism, determining the major players in this global educational institution also serves a critical role in determining the interlocutors relevant to this study. This identification of the key players is based on examining a range of formal and informal participations in the work of the IIS: Ismaili and non-Ismaili scholars who are members of the Institute; Ismaili and non-Ismaili scholars who are regular participants in activities of the Institute; and non-Ismaili Muslim and non-Muslim scholars who are regularly cited as important intellectual interlocutors. The discussion below will focus on the work of scholars currently shaping the contours of contemporary Ismaili thought.

THE MEDIA AND THE MESSAGE: MODERN PERSPECTIVES ON THE AGA KHAN AND THE ISMAILIS

In recent decades, the focus of much journalistic coverage of the Aga Khan and the Ismaili community has been their social work, albeit with introductory paragraphs that expound on the Aga Khan's lifestyle, which has been a subject of keen interest to the press for much of the second half of the twentieth century.

Books like Anne Edwards's *Throne of Gold: The Lives of the Aga Khans*—which celebrate the extravagant lifestyles of the Aga Khans—get more purchase and are sometimes quoted by the press, despite this particular text's surprising inaccuracies on both historical and contemporary details, which should raise doubts for the academic reader of the text's general validity.

Edwards appears to be careless with detail: she has Aga Khan IV born four days late, on December 17, 1936,[2] and attributes the 1967 establishment of the Aga Khan Foundation to his then-deceased grandfather.[3] Her depiction of Muslim history seems also to be slightly irresponsible: her presentation of the beliefs of the early Ismailis reflects that of mediaeval anti-Ismaili polemicists, and she misrepresents the Assassins as hashish users. Beyond the technical aspects, however, the book suffers from subtle inconsistencies. For example, on page 130 the author writes that the tithe collected from the community "was responsible for [the Aga Khan's] enormous wealth," but she states elsewhere that it accounted for only 2 percent of his wealth.[4]

In any case, Edwards's book was not intended to be scholarly. Indeed, *Publishers Weekly* describes it as "engrossing gossip" about "the third-richest man in the world, the late Aga Khan III."[5] Nevertheless, it had an effect on the Ismaili community at the time of its publication, raising fears that its sensationalist nature would shake the faith of young Ismailis, leading to its ban in many Ismaili households. To be sure, for those Ismailis weaned on an unquestioning approach to their religion and the sanctity of its leader, the representation of Aga Khan III as a frivolous millionaire playboy and sycophant-to-the-British would certainly be dangerous.

The *Publishers Weekly* account of the book continues:

> His fabled wealth derived not from the pursuits of ordinary robber barons but from the generous tributes of his millions of followers. Twice in his lifetime, in a legendary ceremony, they matched his hefty weight with gold. Although he committed much of his wealth to bettering their lives through education, housing and health care, enough remained to support his own fabulous lifestyle, which included wives, mistresses, offspring and champion horses. Sincerely devout, he spent an hour every day in meditation and study of the Koran. He despaired of his playboy son Aly Khan, husband of Rita Hayworth, and he never married or divorced without observing Muslim precepts. A devoted Anglophile, he used his influence to keep the British in India as long as he could.[6]

Europe today has retained its fondness for gossip about royals, and the British and French presses remember the Aga Khan's family as lavish members of that set, so the "Prince of Chantilly"[7] remains of interest in contemporary tabloids.

On the other hand, the focus and content of media coverage in recent years has shifted. The work of the AKDN is increasingly recognized throughout Europe, where the Aga Khan's development activities and pluralist outlook are celebrated, as testify various interviews in publications like *Le Monde*[8] and *Der Spiegel;*[9] the conferment of honors like Le Nouvel Economiste Philantropic Entrepreneur of the Year 2009 Award in Paris in 2009;[10] and invitations to lecture, such as at the Nobel Institute on Democratic Development, Pluralism and Civil Society in Oslo in 2005,[11] the Academy of Sciences in Lisbon in 2009,[12] and the London Conference on Afghanistan in 2010.[13]

In East Africa, the Aga Khan is viewed as a key player in national development. Ugandan president Museveni said that "institutions like the Aga Khan Schools, Diamond Trust and Jubilee Insurance Company have not only offered services to Ugandans but also availed employment,"[14] and "the story of the Serena [Hotel] is the story of the recovery of Uganda. The fact that you can have such a world-class hotel in Uganda is proof that Uganda is recovering."[15] In Afghanistan and Pakistan, the AKDN is also recognized as a vital development partner—especially for its leading work in education[16] and health[17]—but the Ismaili community is often attacked and vilified as irreligious.[18] While he has detractors in the US,[19] the Aga Khan has a longstanding relationship with that country and has enjoyed friendships with many US presidents, such as Kennedy[20] and Reagan,[21] and more recently with Governors Arnold Schwarzenegger and Rick Perry, with whom he launched a program to educate Texas schoolchildren about Islamic culture and history.[22]

Canada, however, is the Ismailis' success story. In that country, both the community and the Aga Khan are highly respected, and profiles in local and national newspapers focus on the community's financial and political success as well as their humanitarian work, always remarking that this model Muslim minority group takes its cue from the thought and work of its leader. The first major group of Ismailis arrived in Canada in 1972 after Idi Amin's program of expulsion in Uganda. About this ingress,

Michael Valpy of the *Globe and Mail* writes: "Reportedly, Canada decided to admit the Ismailis after a telephone call from the Aga Khan to then-prime minister Pierre Trudeau, a personal friend of 30 years."[23] Another thirty years later, he writes, "the Aga Khan was an honorary pallbearer at Trudeau's funeral."[24]

In 2005, the Aga Khan was invested as an honorary Companion of the Order of Canada by then-Governor General Adrienne Clarkson, who spoke highly of him five years later at the LaFontaine-Baldwin Symposium in Toronto:

> He embodies the values that we Canadians most cherish, and the actions that have created the country that we are. He not only celebrates diversity, he also honours the differences between people that can paradoxically give them their greatest bond. He has two roles in this world; one which he has inherited as an extraordinary charge, and the other that he has built upon and recreated, that now involves all of us. He manifests the creative relationship of spiritual values and material concern, which is unique in the world today, and is a model for all of us. [...] We could have no finer citizen and we could have no finer bearer of the motto of the Order of Canada: 'they desire a better country.' With the Aga Khan and what he represents, we are a better country.[25]

In 2006, he established the Global Centre for Pluralism in Ottawa in collaboration with the Government of Canada, reflecting in his LaFontaine-Baldwin Lecture in Toronto in 2010 that his interest in launching the center was because "there was yet no institution dedicated to the question of diversity in our world, and that Canada's national experience made it a natural home for this venture."[26] His respect for Canada's pluralist culture is expressed explicitly in a 2002 *Globe and Mail* interview:

> Canada is today the most successful pluralist society on the face of our world. Without any doubt in my mind. You have created the perfect pluralist society where minorities,

generally speaking, are welcome, they feel comfortable, they assimilate the Canadian psyche, they are allowed to move forward within civil society in an equitable manner, their children are educated. So Canada has succeeded in putting together a form of pluralist society which has been remarkably successful. I'm not the one who's making a judgement. Look at the international evaluation of Canada as a country and the way it functions.[27]

To be sure, the Ismailis have indeed assimilated the Canadian psyche, making Canada their home, following the 1978 *farman* (directive) of their leader, echoed at the establishment of the Ismaili Centre in Burnaby, B.C., in 1985. Today, writes Valpy, Canada's forty-five thousand Ismailis are a close-knit community known for their business acumen, educational attainments, and philanthropy—so much so that "Prime Minister Jean Chrétien once joked that what his hometown of Shawinigan, Que., lacked was a dozen Ismaili entrepreneurs."[28] Indeed, a 2006 *BCBusiness* article by Adriana Barton titled "Ismaili Success: Made in Vancouver" waxes laudatory on these "modern-thinking Muslims" with a "Midas touch": "In the last three decades they've built some of B.C.'s biggest companies, raised stacks of cash for good causes, and quietly joined the golf and country club set."[29]

Barton takes the domed and dramatic but deliberately hidden Ismaili Centre in Burnaby as a metaphor for the local Ismaili community, "whose low profile belies its tremendous impact on the B.C. economy."[30] She lists among its members Larco Group of Companies owner Aminmohamed Lalji and kin as among the one hundred richest families, with wealth estimated by *Report on Business* magazine at $884 million; Abdul and Shamim Jamal, owners of Retirement Concepts seniors facilities; and property holders Noordin and Farida Sayani, owners and founders of Executive Hotels and Resorts.[31]

Unlike *Vancouver Sun* reporter Douglas Todd, who bemoans the community's secrecy,[32] Barton found the Ismailis she approached to be open about their beliefs, lives, and success. "Ismailis," she says, "tend to be charming, well dressed and extremely gracious; they might insist on giving you a lift or pick up the tab for lunch."[33] She describes the travails of the

Canadian Ismaili community, who left East Africa penniless following the Ugandan expulsion of 1972, and marvels at how they "didn't lose their Midas touch after their exodus from East Africa."[34] She surmises this is because their role model is a multibillionaire. "The Aga Khan," she writes, "owns a bank in Pakistan, plantations in Kenya and a chain of luxury hotels, not to mention his own jet, stables of racehorses and an estate outside Paris. In all, his holdings generate an estimated US$1.36 billion in sales annually, according to a November 2005 Bloomberg.com article."[35]

The Ismailis' conception of Islam as complementary of both faith and world is part of their success, she postulates. "For Ismaili Muslims, the Aga Khan's riches do not detract from his role as their spiritual leader," and thus, "Ismailis follow in his philanthropic footsteps."[36] She writes: "In Vancouver, the annual Ismaili Walk for Kids raised $200,000 last year for a United Way children's program. The 2005 annual World Partnership Walk, a countrywide Aga Khan Foundation Canada event, raised over $4 million for development initiatives in Asia and Africa."[37]

Some commentators take a different view of the Ismailis, however. An article published in June 2010 on the IslamicInsights website with the faintly provocative title "Why Canada Doesn't Need an Islamic Art Museum" presents the collaboration between the Government of Canada and the AKDN as a colonialist project in which the AKDN-CIDA partnership in Afghanistan has been "central to the invasion and occupation of Afghanistan ... encouraging collaboration with the occupiers by conditionally distributing aid to those who assist the forces, and skewing public opinion in support for the war."[38]

The author of the article, Sumayya Kassamali, argues that not only is the $300 million museum an unnecessary extravagance that smacks of indirect corporate financing, but that it "is also happening in the context of significant state repression of the Muslim community in Canada."[39] She cites as evidence "just the better-known examples":

> [T]he legitimization of the invasion of Afghanistan by claiming the need to "save" oppressed Afghani women; the controversies around Shari`a Law in Ontario; Herouxville and the Reasonable Accommodation debates in Quebec; the five Muslim security certificate detainees, all but

one now released (on strict conditions of house arrest) after years of later-deemed unconstitutional detention; the refusal to bring home Omar Khadr, Guantanamo Bay's youngest prisoner and only Western citizen despite global calls to do so; the ongoing trials of the Toronto 18, charged with allegations of terrorism despite a paucity of publicized evidence and the revelation of an RCMP informant heavily compensated to incite the young men involved; and the government's explicit instruction to Syria and Egypt to torture numerous Muslim Canadians, of which Maher Arar is the most famous.[40]

For Kassamali, the Ismaili community in Canada has nothing to do with the realities of other Muslims. She disparages the community for being "notorious for its secrecy" and describes Ismailis in Canada as "among the richest in the country," including among its ranks former Conservative MP Rahim Jaffer and then-CEO of Rogers Nadir Mohamed as well as "luxury hotel owners, mineral resource developers, real-estate moguls and more, many worth hundreds of millions of dollars."[41]

She aligns herself against the Ismailis as a member of those Muslim communities "on the other side of this celebratory moment," whose mosques are vandalized, whose religious scholars are interrogated, whose youth groups are infiltrated by informants, and whose charities are banned from operating.[42] She has a strong message for the Aga Khan, whom she ties up with the political power players: "And to Stephen Harper and the Aga Khan: we reject your glorification of a state that does not exist for our protection, and your pride in the close cooperation between your two institutions of power."[43]

Kassamali appears here as representative of the disenchanted Western Muslim angered by a lack of perceived justice. Against this, she presents the Ismaili community as somewhat traitorous for endearing itself to unjust holders of power (a representation that recalls so many portrayals of Aga Khan III's relationship with the British). She writes of the community's diverse socioeconomic status and its subversive hypocrisy in presenting a public face "dominated by an elite all too willing to position themselves as model minorities."[44]

Kassamali appears, like many Muslims in the postcolonial period, disillusioned by the lot of Muslims around the world and, more importantly, with the inability of its leaders to improve that lot.[45] The Ismaili Muslims—a financially and politically successful group of Muslims—are very different from the Muslims with which she and so many others around the world are familiar. Whereas in the West her frustration takes the form of articulate acrimony, in other parts of the world the criticism against the Ismailis for their integration into Western culture takes on a bloody hue.

In Pakistan, the Ismailis are persecuted—despite Aga Khan III's role in that country's formation and Aga Khan IV's extensive development work there. In 1982, sixty Ismailis were reportedly killed in northwestern Pakistan, and their community buildings burned down. In recent years, employees of the Aga Khan Foundation have been attacked in Karachi. In January 2005, Sunni extremists shot and killed a prominent Ismaili leader and scholar in Gilgit, ostensibly in an attempt to stoke sectarian tension in the region.

In March 2005, an alliance of Sunni religious organizations proposed to have the Ismailis declared infidels.[46] An *Asia Times* article writes that "while the 'Western' lifestyle and the 'blasphemous beliefs' of the Ismailis might have provoked to some extent Pakistan's Sunni hardliners, their anger appears to have more to do with concern over the Ismailis' growing secularizing influence in the educational arena in Pakistan."[47]

In 2002, the government of Pakistan signed an order inducting the Aga Khan University Examination Board (AKUEB) into the national education system, allowing affordable access to the British O-level and A-level system of education. Pakistan's educational system had hitherto been dominated by the *madrasa* education offered by Sunni institutions, which reacted angrily to the announcement that schools would now be allowed to offer the AKUEB system. They argue that it would secularise the country despite the AKUEB's insistence that it would follow the national curriculum. "The battle," concludes the *Asia Times* article, "is for control of the minds of young Pakistanis. And the Sunni extremists ... feel threatened that [the AKUEB system] would shrink the size of the turf over which they wield influence [and] are fighting in the only way they know—violence, death threats and intimidation."[48]

Persecution appears to be a recurrent theme in Ismaili history, unshakeable to this day, despite their highly public promotion of humanitarianism and pluralism. Doubtlessly, though, the lot of the Ismailis has improved drastically, in the West at least. Nevertheless, in Asia especially, much of the community is impoverished, though they are beneficiaries of the energetic work of the AKDN, itself spurred by the time and resources of their better-off brethren in the West.

Though for some Ismailis little has changed in terms of their lot or their perception by others, for others the difference is spectacular. In the thirty years since leaving Africa, the *baana*s—as they are not entirely affectionately called by their Asian brethren—have achieved an unthinkable level of success, reflected in the way they are written about in the press. Whereas in Pakistan the Ismaili community earns begrudging acceptance due to the development work of the Aga Khan, they are persecuted for their seeming lack of Muslim-ness. In the liberal West, the minority has thrived, especially in Canada. There, they are the Muslim darlings of the press, known more for their distinctive green jackets worn as 2010 Olympic ambassadors in Vancouver than for their doctrines, and their leader is extolled as the epitome of Canadian values, leaving behind his hat at Ascot and his skis in St. Moritz.

Toward an Informed Ismaili Engagement with the Public Sphere: A Background to the IIS

Without a doubt, the Aga Khan's liberal outlook, emphasis on civic participation, and practical interpretation of Islam—which he has transferred to his followers—affords him the respect of key Western players, making him and his followers not only welcome in liberal societies but also able to integrate into those societies with ease. To be sure, the Ismaili community takes its cue in all matters from its Imam, and the thought and direction of the Imam is the font of Ismaili practice and intellectualism. Just as with all the agencies of his network, he sits at the head of the boards of governors of the various intellectual institutions he has established, such as the Aga Khan University (AKU) and the Institute of Ismaili Studies, which is perhaps the chief Ismaili vehicle for critical and informed engagement with the public sphere.

Since its founding in 1977, the Institute of Ismaili Studies has been the primary institution for furthering contemporary Ismaili scholarship. It has produced numerous books on a selection of subjects, revealing its outlook on what Ismaili scholarship ought to be. Covering five publication series, the publications of the IIS include translations of historical Ismaili texts; studies on historical Qur'anic commentaries and contemporary commentators; investigations of Ismaili intellectual and cultural history; examinations of the Epistles of the Brethren of Purity, a tenth-century Muslim (apparently Ismaili) group that produced an encyclopedic corpus of available human knowledge; and, lastly, explorations of themes in Islamic civilizations, such as religious authority, ethics, social justice, and civil society. The subjects chosen for research by the IIS reveal a liberal bent with a staunch respect for Ismaili tradition as well as for variety of interpretation among the spectrum of Islamic thought, both historical and contemporary.

The work of the Imamate institutions necessarily reflects the concerns of the Imam, an example of which is the IIS's articulation of itself, which reflects the prevalence of pluralism in the Imam's thought. The website of the IIS articulates its goal as "promoting scholarship and learning" about contemporary and historical Muslim societies, in order to gain "a better understanding of their relationship with other societies and faiths."[49] Certainly, the Ismailis have an interest in studying their own history, but when articulated this way, the study of Ismaili history becomes a bridge by which to connect the community with the larger world of Islamic scholarship and contemporary thought.

Indeed, according to Paul E. Walker, an historian of Fatimid thought and frequent IIS collaborator, the institute's mission is to promote the investigation of historical and contemporary Muslim societies and cultures in order to "explore the interaction of religious ideas within the broader aspects of modern life, but to do so with special attention to often neglected fields that contain the intellectual and literary expressions of esoteric Islam, including Shi'ism in general and Ismailism in particular, in the full richness of their diversity."[50] Importantly, the emphasis on the interaction of religion in modern life and the advocacy of diversity are two intertwining issues that are central to the Imam's conception of successful pluralist coexistence in the modern world.

The contemporary Ismaili scholar may argue, however, that pluralism has been evident in and central to Islamic history and Ismaili history from the time of the Prophet onward. As well, among modern scholars of Islam there is growing attention to and celebration of the internal diversity and pluralism of the Muslim community. Further, modern historians highlight the existence of multiple and simultaneous understandings of Islam in mediaeval Muslim societies, and also give credence to the theory that a society's success or failure depends largely on its ability to manage its internal pluralism. Nevertheless, Ismaili scholars may argue that while these themes do recur in Ismaili history, to explain them using the sociological terminology of the twentieth century is simply to use the language of the time to articulate eternally existing ethics and doctrines, much in the way mediaeval Islamic and Ismaili thinkers used Aristotelian or Neoplatonic philosophical language or, indeed, in the way the Qur'an used Arabic poetic language to make itself intelligible to its historical audience.

Almost all of the articulation of contemporary Ismaili thought and history comes from scholars working with the IIS. The current codirectors of the IIS are Farhad Daftary and Karim H. Karim, both well-established scholars. The institute is home to a number of renowned Ismaili and non-Ismaili scholars, such as Faquir M. Hunzai, Arzina R. Lalani, Shainool Jiwa, S. J. Badakhchani, Hermann Landolt, Wilferd Madelung, Eric Ormsby, Mohammed Arkoun, Reza Shah-Kazemi, and Nader el-Bizri, to name a few. As well, the IIS has strong connections to important scholars of Ismailism and Islam who, though not housed permanently at the IIS, collaborate with the institution regularly. Some of these scholars include Amyn B. Sajoo, Ali S. Asani, Shafique Virani, and Azim Nanji (the former director of the IIS), as well as Paul E. Walker, Heinz Halm, and Abdou Filali-Ansary, the former director of the Institute for the Study of Muslim Civilisations, Aga Khan University in London.

The Institute of Ismaili Studies has had a strong historical connection with McGill University's Institute of Islamic Studies (in fact, many of the scholars now connected with the IIS in London were at one time connected with McGill) and continues to collaborate with that university as well as several other institutions of learning, such as the University of London's Institute of Education, the School of Oriental and African Studies (SOAS), the University of Jordan, and faculty members of a number of universities in the United Kingdom and elsewhere.

A major component of the IIS's work is research and publications; its focus is on translating classical Ismaili texts, translating Qur'anic commentaries of classical Muslim scholars, and publishing the work of contemporary Qur'anic scholars from across the world. The IIS has an impressive library, housing one of the most comprehensive collections of manuscripts and books relating to Ismaili studies.[51] Importantly, the IIS is also a teaching institute: the Graduate Programme in Islamic Studies and Humanities (GPISH) is a three-year postgraduate program that "combines intellectual training with exposure to practical and field issues in the contemporary context."[52]

ACADEMIC ENGAGEMENT WITH KEY THEMES IN CONTEMPORARY ISMAILI SOCIAL AND POLITICAL THOUGHT

It is reasonable to assume that the work of scholars within the orbit of the IIS concords with the institute's Weltanschauung. The institutionalization of education seems to be a perennially motivating conviction of the Ismailis, with today's AKU and IIS perhaps recalling the Fatimid al-Azhar university and the Dar al-Hikma research institute. The IIS scholars are the institutionally recognized players, which perhaps evokes a parallel to the *da'wa* system of the Fatimid period, in which select scholar-missionaries (*da'is*) were the official mouthpieces of the Ismaili doctrine.

While the age-old ideal remains, the focus of contemporary scholarship has changed. Typically, mediaeval Muslim thinkers of all denominations used Greek philosophical language to explain Qur'anic ideas. Today, many Muslim thinkers, including the Ismailis, are using liberal theory to frame their conceptions of the modern lived Islamic ethic. Whereas Fatimid scholars engaged Greek philosophers to articulate their interpretations of Qur'anic eschatology, contemporary Ismaili scholars engage liberal political theorists to articulate their interpretations of Qur'anic ethics. The engagement with non-Ismaili thinkers remains, but Plato and Aristotle have been replaced by Rawls and Taylor. The sort of liberalism these theorists espouse holds a measure of concordance with the way in which the contemporary Ismaili intellectual machine articulates its version of pluralist democratic society.

Contemporary historiographers, too, find liberal themes in Ismaili history. While it may be argued that Ismailism's interpretation of Islam is one that has consistently found liberal themes in the Qur'an—which is a possibility, considering that Ismaili treatises tend to discuss the same Qur'anic themes and verses throughout history—it is clear that contemporary Ismailism uses the language of liberal theory to articulate its conception of Islam, which nevertheless appeals to Qur'anic ethics as the foundation of its doctrines.

In any case, contemporary scholars like Farhad Daftary, Reza Shah-Kazemi, Nader el-Bizri, Arzina Lalani, Shainool Jiwa, Heinz Halm, Amyn Sajoo, and Shafique Virani see certain politico-ethical themes arising in Ismaili history—such as justice, pluralism, and education—and construct the Ismaili identity around these motifs. Showcasing the community's continued history of intellectualism, they highlight its habit of institutionalizing education. Recalling the language of liberal multiculturalist theory, the Ismaili community is presented as a minority group that promoted pluralist policies and a universalizing interpretation of the Qur'anic ethic. Part of that ethic, it is argued, is a commitment to justice, in turn giving rise to a commitment to ethical governance and the protection of vulnerable parties, such as ethnic and religious minorities.

The contemporary Ismaili construction of its own historical narrative paints a picture of an intellectually influential minority that buttresses its commitments to institutionalized education and ethical governance on an unshakeable dedication to the ethic of pluralism, supported by the strength of the interminable Imamate, which leads the community through the vicissitudes of recurring persecution. This theme of persecution is the fulcrum on which Virani's book rests. He opens his book, *The Ismailis in the Middle Ages: A History of Survival, A Search for Salvation*, with a quotation from Genghis Khan ordering the massacre of all Ismailis during the attack on the mountain fortress of Alamut in 1256: "None of that people should be spared, not even the babe in its cradle."[53] Using various sources of information, Virani's book is an important reconstruction of the post-Alamut period of Ismaili history, which is obscured by a dearth of information and has been the focus of only a handful of recent books. He suggests that the primary reason for the Ismaili community's survival—after what medieval history records as their total extermination in 1256—is their devotion to the ideal of the Imamate, with which they had little or no contact after the destruction of Alamut until the modern period.

Daftary, in his expansive corpus of work on Ismaili history, also emphasizes the Ismailis' history of persecution and their resultant periods of obscurity, which he says pose obvious difficulties for the historian. The Ismailis were, he writes, "coerced into what may be termed an underground existence,"[54] limiting much of the study of the Ismailis to anti-Ismaili sources. In his comprehensive book, *The Isma`ilis: Their History and Doctrines*, he writes:

> Some of the research problems in this complex field of study stem from the very nature of the Isma`ili movement, while others have been due to the fact that at least until recent times, study of the Isma`ilis was limited mainly to anti-Isma`ili sources. The Isma`ilis have been almost continuously treated as heretics by the Sunni and most Shi`i Muslims. As a result, they have been among the most ruthlessly persecuted minorities of the Muslim world, being frequently subjected to massacre. In such hostile surroundings, the Isma`ilis have been obliged from the earliest times in their history, to adhere rather strictly to the Shi`i principle of *taqiyya*, the precautionary dissimulation of one's true belief in the face of danger. Consequently, the Ismai`ili movement, in particular its important religious hierarchy and propaganda organization, evolved under utmost secrecy.[55]

The history of early Shi`ism—before the genesis of Ismailism as an independent movement in the eighth century—is, however, preserved. Lalani, in her book, *Early Shi`i Thought: The Teachings of Imam Muhammad al-Baqir*, appraises the evolving doctrine of Imamate in early Islamic history through an examination of the teachings of Imam Muhammad al-Baqir (d. 733), whose ideas were foundational for later Shi`i doctrine. Lalani's approach in this study is to examine al-Baqir's conception of the

Imamate, which he bases in the Qur'an and the Hadith, and from which he develops key theological points. Most notable of these is the notion of the Imamate as a hereditary office—the Imam explicitly designates (*nass*) his successor—and that the authority of the Imam is based on a special knowledge (`*ilm*) exclusive to the holder of the office. According to Lalani, "Al-Baqir maintains that knowledge, which was granted to Adam, is never taken away; rather it is always inherited, passed on from generation to generation ... The imams, according to al-Baqir, are the treasurers of Allah in the heavens and on the earth; they do not guard gold and silver, but divine knowledge."[56]

Thus, she concludes, "the doctrine of the imamate put forward by al-Baqir was based primarily on knowledge, not on political rule, although the imams were also entitled to the latter."[57] Knowledge thus appears early in Shi`i thought as a foundational aspect of Shi`i doctrine, since it is the cardinal condition for Imamate.

As well, the centrality of education and intellectual engagement emerges as a central theme in contemporary Ismaili thought and historiography. Indeed, Halm writes that "teaching and learning are the very essence of the Ismaili mission," and that the *da`i*, the teaching missionary, was the central figure of the community after the Imam.[58] In his book, *The Fatimids and their Traditions of Learning*, Halm explores the various teaching institutions of the Fatimid period, from the intimate "Teaching Sessions" (*majalis al-hikma*) of the *da`is* to the public university of al-Azhar. In the attempt to explain the importance of knowledge and learning in Ismaili doctrine, he quotes an old Ismaili text called "The Teacher and the Pupil," in which knowledge is allegorically compared to life: "I was a dead man," it says; "God turned me into a living being, a learned man." This, writes Halm, is the entire Ismaili idea of knowledge, learning, and teaching, and he concludes dramatically: "Knowledge means life."[59]

The focus by the IIS on studying and publishing the encyclopedic efforts of the Brethren of Purity (*Ikhwan al-Safa*) is revealing here. Although el-Bizri—the editor of the IIS publication series on the Brethren's Epistles—writes that "it is ultimately unclear whether [the group] can be definitively classified as Ithna`ashari (Twelvers) or Ismaili,"[60] Ismailis have often claimed the group's comprehensive corpus as their own. Regardless of whether the IIS as an academic institution views the Brethren as Ismaili, they identify with its work strongly enough to allocate to it an entire publication series. The following words by el-Bizri may shed light on why this could be:

> Marked by a perceptible receptivity to otherness, and eschewing fanaticism, the *Rasa'il Ikhwan al-Safa* seems to embody a form of diversity in Islam that can accommodate miscellaneous ancient and monotheistic traditions. Encountering 'veracity in every religion', and seeing knowledge as 'pure nourishment for the soul', the Ikhwan associated the attainment of happiness and the *soteriological* hope for salvation with the scrupulous development of rational pursuits and intellectual quests. They also promoted a 'friendship of virtue' amongst their brotherhood, and venerated the liberal spirit in Islam.[61]

If one were to substitute the name "Ikhwan" with "Ismaili" above, it would not appear out of place. El-Bizri's comments seem to reflect the IIS's interpretation of the Ikhwan, and though it may concord with general scholarly opinion, it is telling that the IIS has chosen to expend so much effort on translating the work of the Ikwhan, which it likely wishes to showcase as an early Muslim group with this twin obsession for knowledge and pluralism.

Pluralism, as stated many times already, is the central theme of contemporary Ismaili thought. Jiwa seeks to show that it was a paramount ethic for the Fatimids as well. In her article "Religious Pluralism in Egypt: The Ahl al-Kitab in early Fatimid Times," she argues that much of the success of the Fatimids was due to their ability to manage a society that was multiethnic and multireligious. Daftary, too, makes this claim. He notes that the Fatimids had a "special talent for utilizing the services of capable individuals and groups, regardless of their race and creed," and concludes that "the successes of the Fatimids were in large measure due to the remarkable ethnic and religious tolerance of the dynasty and the administrative stability of the Fatimid state."[62]

Jiwa's paper continues in this vein, arguing that the Fatimids had to develop strategies to govern each of the distinctive elements of the Egyptian populace while maintaining the "truly pluralistic"[63] communities under their direct authority and administration not only as caliphs, but also as Imams. "The early Fatimids," she writes, "actively tapped the experience and expertise of the *ahl al-kitab* in Egypt based on the merit of individuals from these communities."[64] Furthermore, while they safeguarded and promoted the rights of the *ahl al-kitab* (People of the Book), "they assertively maintained clear boundaries concerning what was permissible to them and what was not."[65] She argues that the humane and inclusive policies implemented by the Imam-caliphs toward the *ahl al-kitab* were undergirded by Qur'anic principles, and she critiques the view of Western historians who argue that such policies were a matter of political tact rather than religio-moral conviction.

Beyond the practical policies of the Fatimids, pluralism is also promoted by the IIS as a theme rooted in the Qur'an itself—a Qur'anic fact, so to speak. Shah-Kazemi's paper, "The Metaphysics of Interfaith Dialogue: A Qur'anic Perspective," constructs an argument in favour of a Qur'anic basis for pluralism. He presents the Qur'an as a source of dialogue among different belief systems and argues that it is imperative for Muslims to bring to light that which unites peoples in their various belief systems in order to enter into constructive and inspired dialogue with others. Through an exegesis of various Qur'anic verses, Shah-Kazemi argues that the Qur'an not only supports, but also wholeheartedly encourages the pluralism of faiths in today's world while vehemently opposing religious nationalism and fanaticism. He writes:

> One sees, then, that it is not so much "religious pluralism"
> as "metaphysical unity" that establishes a deep-rooted and
> far-reaching tolerance, one that is not so much formulated
> as a rule, to be obeyed or broken as one will; rather, what
> emerges is a mode of tolerance that is organically related
> to an awareness of the divine presence in all things, an
> apprehension of the inner holiness of all that exists.[66]

The presentation of his analysis here is not intended to characterize this work as apologetic. Shah-Kazemi's exegesis of Qur'anic pluralism is thoughtful and philosophically sophisticated, and his understanding of the esoteric doctrines of Shi'ism is subtle and complex. However, this intellectual and historiographical work does reflect deep convictions within the evolving modern Ismaili tradition.

A further example is Shah-Kazemi's book, *Justice and Remembrance: Introducing the Spirituality of Imam 'Ali*. In this book, he examines the ethics of justice and governance as articulated by the first Shi'i Imam, which became foundational for early Shi'ism in particular and all of Shi'i ethics in general. He argues that Imam 'Ali's "ethical orientation toward justice is ... linked to the spiritual precepts of the Islamic faith,"[67] illustrating that the Imam's letter to his Egyptian governor is not only a lesson in just governance, but also expresses the Imam's belief that all of life's actions must be suffused with the Qur'anic ethos of justice. Shah-Kazemi says about the letter:

> It is as much a statement of ethics as of politics—not a discursive "system" or theory of ethics, to be sure, but an inspiring expression of the spiritual ethos which the Imam embodied and radiated, an ethos that flows directly from the sources of the Islamic revelation, and which therefore discloses the roots of virtue and ethics in a climate governed by the all-embracing principle of revelation.[68]

Ethics is Sajoo's ultimate object of inquiry. The Prophetic example, he writes, shows that "the pursuit of ethical ideals is not an abstraction but a practical matter."[69] In his insightful essay on pluralist governance in his book, *Muslim Ethics: Emerging Vistas*, he posits three propositions:

> First, that pluralist governance is a quintessential prize for the public sphere, and requires a rule of law that is favoured by an ethos of separation of Religion and State (a proposition which is neither alien to Muslim theology nor civilizational experience). Second, that the rule of law in all its potency still requires an engagement with ethics to deliver a meaningful pluralism [...] Finally, that the interplay of social ethics and the law can make the encounter of Islam and the West profoundly enriching

in facing the shared critical challenge of civic pluralism, again not only in the Muslim world but also in the Western diaspora.[70]

Sajoo is among the more percipient Muslim scholars in the West. He is also one of the Ismaili institutions' most notable interlocutors with Western liberal thought. He is the editor of the IIS publication series dealing with Islam and contemporary society (including *Civil Society in the Muslim World: Contemporary Perspectives* [2002] and *Muslim Modernities: Expressions of the Civil Imagination* [2008]), as well as the general editor of the Muslim Heritage Series (including *A Companion to the Muslim World* [2009] and *A Companion to Muslim Ethics* [2010]), a series intended for the general reader, whose mandate, written on the inside of each publication, is telling of the IIS's Weltanschaaung: "In keeping with the Institute's mandate, the series will be informed by the plurality of communities and interpretations of Islam, as well as their locus in modernity and tradition."

In his work, Sajoo writes as a witty political commentator and intertwines commentary on the global political and economic climate with an impressive engagement of both Western and Muslim political theory and history. He advocates strongly the role of ethics in upholding Western institutions, such as the rule of law and civil society, and argues that religious ethics offer a strong impulse that can be harnessed. In his introductory remarks to the conference "The Good Society: An Ethical Perspective" held at the IIS in April 2001, he argues that philosophers as diverse as Confucius, Plato, Aristotle, Augustine, Spinoza, Farabi, Miskawayh, and Tusi have all claimed that ethics is a primary element of political as well as personal existence. He thus argues that "we need to bridge personal and social ethics." Furthermore, he asks, "if civil society is about building social capital, then what could be more congenial than Muslim ethical values relating to communal solidarity, charity and volunteerism, personal and institutional accountability and integrity, and non–violence? Are these not indispensable for a critique of the public sphere in transitional Muslim contexts?"[71]

Sajoo lists an array of Muslim intellectual activists whom he articulates as "striving for secular spaces while invoking ethical as well as human rights critiques of the failings of their governing elites and institutions."[72]

They include Mohsen Kadivar and Abdolkarim Soroush in Iran, Nurcolish Madjid and Abdulrahman Wahid in Indonesia, Sadiq Al-Azm and Mohammed Shahrur in Syria, Saad Eddin Ibrahim and Nawal Sadawi in Egypt, Daulat Khudanazarov in Tajikistan, Chandra Muzaffar and Farish Noor in Malaysia, Sima Samar in Afghanistan, and Ayesha Imam in Nigeria.[73]

"Penetrating the Roots": Seeing the Past in the Present

The world that Sajoo inhabits—in which Muslim intellectuals are influenced and stimulated by an interconnected web of thinkers spread worldwide—would certainly have been unimaginably grand for mediaeval lifeworlds. But this is the characteristic stamp of a modern world made small in the wake of colonial tides, the sociopoliticoeconomic processes of which are recalled by and encapsulated in that most modern of words: globalization.

Jonah Steinberg summons those processes in his assertion that "the current shape of the global Isma`ili community is a product of empire."[74] He means, of course, that the Indian Ismailis (Khojas) were subject to (1) the imperial obsession with legally classifying social groups and (2) the global migrations that attended imperial expansions. The British did not invent the Ismailis, he clarifies, but through their construction of community in colonial law, the British certainly created the boundaries by which the Khojas came to see themselves as a "distinct, separate, and internally cohesive 'community'"[75] of Ismailis.

He argues that the 1866 Aga Khan court case in Bombay defined the Khojas as a *community* and institutionalized the role of the newly arrived Persian Aga Khan I, who he says had until then been "a symbolic figure of some religious importance for the Khojas, but not their supreme and authoritative leader."[76] In his 2011 book, *Isma`ili Modern*, he writes that "the special position, sealed by the court case, of the Aga Khan in the Isma`ili community fundamentally emerges largely out of the interaction and alliance between the Khojas and the British administration."[77] He argues that "it was that colonial moment—and not some distant past or essentialized cultural characteristic—that thus crystallized the role of the Aga Khan and set the stage for the construction and consolidation of a global community centered around him."[78]

47

The title of Steinberg's book sets up his colonialist contention: the descriptor is "Isma`ili," the noun is "Modern." For Steinberg, the modern, translocal Ismaili community is teleologically free-floating, a colonial construct with no historical ties to an earlier period—a child of the "colonial moment." Steinberg here represents a non-Ismaili reading of the tradition, which nevertheless helps illuminate the Ismaili reading.

The Ismailis expend immense intellectual effort to establish a historical narrative that connects contemporary Ismaili experience with history. Emphasizing the tradition's historical adaptability and multivalence, Ismaili scholarship sees modern developments as an enrichment of a longer, historical tradition. Steinberg adopts a colonialist perspective, a constructivist anthropological approach that does not view groups as having long historical traditions, and he thus sees 1866 as the modern community's birthdate. For Asani, however, the 1866 case is certainly a watershed moment in modern Ismailism, but not its birth.

In his chapter in *A Modern History of the Ismailis: Continuity and Change in a Muslim Community*—a 2011 IIS publication whose title reveals its perception of change as part of a continuum—Asani argues that the community's multivalence is due to its ability to adapt to different contexts. "The impulse to acculturate is innate to the ethos of Ismailism," he concludes. In his view, "a distinctive element contributing to this ethos is the strong emphasis on the *batin* (the spiritual and esoteric) over the *zahir* (the physical and exoteric)," and that "the motivation to integrate, reformulate and acculturate to different environments is hence part of the Ismaili legacy."[79]

In this conception, the past is the present's buttress, upon which the community's ability to adapt relies—that ability is itself treated as a symptom of an inherited, timeless doctrine. This is a vastly different narrative than Steinberg's historical frame, which contrasts starkly with the Ismaili effort to explain the historical arc in a way that creates a sense of coherence from the Qur'an onward.

The role of Qur'anic doctrine in the tradition's historical narrative is evident—certain themes and motifs highlighted in the history are argued to be consonant with a doctrine that has remained consistent since its initial articulation. This endeavor supersedes time to construct a vertical history that concords with the contemporary Ismaili tradition's conception of itself.

But, says Sajoo, building a connection to the Qur'an is an attempt to create an ethical unity, and it is not a solely Ismaili endeavor. "Delving into the primary sources for renewed inspiration," he writes, is "an exercise in *rational* historical retrieval that aims to grasp an ethical unity beyond 'isolated commands and injunctions.'"[80] He notes that this effort contrasts with "fundamentalist" or "Islamist" revival, as it is "firmly anchored in historicity and context," and recognizes that "the past is not for imitation (*taqlid*) but part of a continuum in which texts, narratives and experience are shared by a diverse *umma*."[81] Sajoo presents a short list of scholars at the forefront of this endeavor: Abdolkarim Soroush, Khaled Abou El Fadl, Mohammed Arkoun, Sohail Hashmi, and Ebrahim Moosa, all of whom recall the pioneering work of the late Fazlur Rahman.[82]

Primarily, Rahman approached Islam and the Qur'an with a renovative eye, suggesting a reinterpretation and rethinking of the Scripture. Rahman's method was to analyze the historical processes Islam has undergone and excoriate the religion's essential principles, then determine how to implement those principles in the present time. British researcher Yahya Birt says that Rahman moved away from the inherited Islamic tradition to "abstracting general ethical principles which could be extracted from the Qur'an." In this way, he concludes, "it is the Qur'an that judges not only the Muslim past but adjudicates its present and presents the model blueprint for its future."[83]

For a variety of reasons, Rahman's hermeneutical approach is perceived to be coherent with the contemporary, and even historical, Ismaili approach to the Qur'an. California State University professor Diana Steigerwald, in her article "Ismaili *Ta'wil*," writes that the Ismaili method of approaching the Qur'an is intellectual: "the Ismailis seek to understand the Qur'an by penetrating to the roots, and then retrieving and disclosing that which is interior or hidden."[84] This technique of "delving into the primary sources for renewed inspiration" can be seen as representative of the contemporary Ismaili method of interpreting both their history as well as the lived ethic of Islam, which they undertake with the aid of their official interpreter, the "speaking Qur'an"—their Imam. Steigerwald writes, "Even when the Isma'ilis lived in difficult times, they were still the champions of *batin* (the 'inner meaning' of revelation) because they, especially the Nizari Isma'ilis, remain attached to the necessity of a 'speaking' (*natiq*) Qur'an, accessible in this physical world and whose main function is to update the interpretation of the Qur'an for the present time."[85]

To be sure, Qur'anic exegesis is a key focus of the IIS. In addition to its publications of mediaeval Ismaili exegeses, one of its publication series is focused on the exegeses of non-Ismaili historical and contemporary Muslim thinkers. The first chapter in a key volume from this series, *Modern Muslim Intellectuals and the Qur'an* (I.B. Tauris, 2004), is devoted to Rahman, with other chapters discussing the work of thinkers such as Nurcolish Madjid, Amina Wadud, Mohammed Arkoun, Mohamed Talbi, and Mohamad Shahrour, all of whom approach the Qur'an as a source for "renewed inspiration" in navigating the seas of modernity.

This approach to the Qur'an culminates in contemporary Ismaili thought with the articulation of Qur'anic ethics in the language of liberal theory, emphasizing the Aga Khan's core themes of pluralism, education, and governance. For example, Nanji argued in his 2003 Peterson lecture for the need to "rethink" our world in terms of education, especially regarding the notion of pluralism. Providing historical examples of how pluralism emerged as a powerful force in relation to religious stereotypes, he argues that this knowledge could be used to great effect within an international curriculum, concluding that there has always been a strong link between pluralism and internationalism. Education, he concludes, must anticipate the shifting boundaries of the contemporary global economic, political, and theological contexts and encourage "seeds of avoidance."[86]

Education, says the Aga Khan, is crucial. "Pluralism is a process and not a product," he says, and thus education in pluralism is critical to reducing conflict, since "pride in one's separate identity can be so strong that it obscures the intrinsic value of other identities."[87] In his 2010 LaFontaine-Baldwin Lecture in Toronto, the Aga Khan presents pluralism as a critical requisite for humanity's survival and states that democracy and education help to provide the necessary framework to engender that goal.

He further says that pluralism is an issue of "immense importance" to him, since the role and responsibility of an Imam, he says, is not only to interpret the faith but also to do everything possible to improve the life and security of the community.[88] He concludes his lecture by "emphasising the urgency" of the pluralist challenge:

> Responding to pluralism is an exercise in constant re-adaptation. Identities are not fixed in stone. What we imagine our communities to be must also evolve with the tides of history. As we think about pluralism, we should be open to the fact that there may be a variety of "best practices," a "diversity of diversities," and a "pluralism of pluralisms." In sum, what we must seek and share is what I have called "a cosmopolitan ethic," a readiness to accept the complexity of human society. It is an ethic which balances rights and duties. It is an ethic for all peoples.

Steigerwald defines the Aga Khan as the only exegete of contemporary Ismailism,[89] providing a spiritual exegesis suited for modern times, which "emphasizes an intellectual approach to the Qur'an and favors the use of intellect (*'aql*) to acquire knowledge."[90] Thus, the articulation by the Imam of pluralism as a central Qur'anic ethic and a primary goal of the AKDN becomes a key concern for the entire Ismaili community, influencing thereby its intellectual output as well as its development work, since a core component of Ismaili doctrine is that faith and action go one with the other.

WHITHER VERACITY?

The Imam is the beginning and end of Ismailism, its *alpha* and *omega*. Though the tradition's adherents are far-flung and various, he remains the authoritative interpreter of doctrine and prime historiographer. In the present day, Aga Khan IV has institutionalized both Ismaili doctrine (through the 1986 Ismaili Constitution) and Ismaili history (through his direction of the IIS).

For contemporary Ismaili scholarship, however, doctrine and history are inextricable. For example, Asani argues that the Ismaili tradition of esotericism—which viewed different creeds as undergirded by a single spiritual reality—inspired the "surprising intellectual flexibility" which now motivates contemporary Ismaili support for pluralist policy as well as their ability to acculturate to new environments, a skill that he says is "part of the Ismaili legacy."[91] Indeed, adaptability appears as a defining feature of Ismailism, as articulated by its previous *paterfamilias*, Aga Khan III, who observed that "Ismailism has survived because it has always been fluid. Rigidity is contrary to our whole way of life and outlook. There have really been no cut-and-dried rules."[92]

There do seem, then, to be some key normative elements in the Ismaili narrative arc. Fluidity, for example, seems to be a crux. Intellectualism seems to be another, and the tradition today is doing serious work on itself, freed by the twentieth century from obscurity and persecution (in half the world, at least) to construct a re-presentation of itself in the contemporary period. Their historical construction—which emphasizes an ethical unity based on appeals to the Qur'an—displays some of these normative elements in the themes it chooses to highlight, which feeds into its contemporary engagement with liberal values and the cluster of outside players that appear to be partners in dialogue.

The observer might ask now: Is it legitimate to find liberal themes in Ismaili history? Further, is it legitimate for the tradition to argue that those themes have been a part of their unchanged interpretation of Qur'anic ethics, and that they now simply articulate them in the contemporary sociological vernacular? Put bluntly, is this work merely apologetic? This "normative" question is, for our purposes, misplaced. The focus here is to map out the complex set of normative elements that contemporary Ismaili scholarship is "discovering" within its own tradition and history.

The aim here cannot be to judge or justify the tradition's claims, but rather to present a critical account of the tradition's self-conception in a period in which its spokespersons are engaged in the serious inquiry of excavating its own normative claims. In the tradition's articulated self-perspective, its history is undergirded by a doctrinal and intellectual coherence that informs its contemporary contours, which views itself as an evolving tradition informed by its deep connection to the past. To misappropriate Wilde's wit, narratives of self cannot be deemed true or false; they are simply well written or badly written. That is all.

3

THE CONTEMPORARY ISMAILI
HISTORICAL NARRATIVE

Legend is historical, just as history is legendary.
      —Alexandre Grandazzi, *The Foundation of Rome*

The past is a wilderness of horrors.
      —Anthony Hopkins, *The Wolfman* (2010)

Everyone who has got far from his source
harks back for the time
when he was one with it.

           —Rumi

"Not one of that people should be spared," decreed Genghis Khan, "not even the babe in its cradle."[1] This edict of the Great Khan, ordering the total annihilation of the Ismailis, features as the opening epigraph in Virani's acclaimed account of Ismailis in the Middle Ages. For Virani—who uses British historian E. G. Browne as endorsement—the thirteenth-century Mongol invasions were unprecedentedly savage and "inflicted more suffering on the human race than any other event in the world's history."[2] While the upshot of the Mongol warpath was a Baghdad sacked and an Abbasid caliph murdered, the famous Sunni historian 'Ata-Malik Juwayni, eyewitness to this litany of horrors, dedicates the concluding one-third of his account to a different event: the obliteration of the mini-state of the Shi'i Ismailis, centered at the fortress of Alamut in Persia. For the modern historian, says Virani, the division of Juwayni's text in this way indicates a religiopolitical prominence for the Ismailis that was disproportionate to their size, belying their minority status.[3]

Virani's emphasis on what he calls "one of history's most lurid examples of mass extermination"[4] brings to light a noticeable current running through contemporary Ismaili historiography, whose thematic plinth seems to be: remarkable adaptability in the face of persistent persecution. In the 2011 IIS publication on Ismaili history, Asani contends that "the Ismailis rank among the most frequently persecuted minorities of the Muslim world,"[5] a claim confirmed by Daftary—the most prolific producer of Ismaili history—who writes elsewhere that the Ismailis were "coerced into what may be termed an underground existence."[6]

Calling itself the "first scholarly attempt" dealing with modern Ismaili history, the volume in which Asani makes his comments is thus one of the most valuable representations of Ismaili self-history available. The book's subtitle—*Continuity and Change in a Muslim Community*—is perhaps reflective of a conception of the Ismaili tradition as a Muslim community that, although in a state of flux, is bound in time by a coherent continuum. Asani certainly seems to reflect this notion when he comments that the tradition's multivalent nature has inspired a "remarkable ability to adapt to different contexts and circumstances," exemplified by the tradition's habit of expressing its central doctrines in the terminologies of various theological and philosophical frameworks, depending on historical and geographical circumstances.[7]

His essential point, crucial for the observer, is that Ismailism's adaptability is a function of its doctrine: "the impulse to acculturate," he writes, "is innate to the ethos of Ismailism."[8] The contributing element to this ethos, he contends, is the strong emphasis on the *batin* (the spiritual and esoteric) over the *zahir* (the physical and exoteric), which has meant that "externals of culture, such as language or dress, have not been considered essential to Ismaili articulations of faith and identity."[9] The result of Ismaili traditions of esotericism, he concludes, is that the tradition has been able to "respond to cultural diversity by tolerating"[10] what Walker calls "a surprising intellectual flexibility and leeway."[11] Asani's articulation here deftly ascribes the tradition's adaptability to the quintessential Ismaili doctrine of esoteric Qur'anic interpretation, a theory he brings into the present by using the language of liberal political theory to signify Ismailism as a minority group that supports pluralist policies because of its historical success in tolerating cultural diversity.

Like Asani, other scholars of Ismailism—such as Farhad Daftary, Reza Shah-Kazemi, Nader el-Bizri, Arzina Lalani, Shainool Jiwa, Heinz Halm, Amyn Sajoo, and Shafique Virani—see certain themes arising in Ismaili history that define the nature and identity of the group and that resonate with contemporary themes in Ismaili thought. Their telling of the Ismaili narrative is constructed around critical motifs, emphasized in history, they argue, by the Imams and *da`is* (missionary-scholars). In this conception, pluralism—the ethic at the center of contemporary Ismaili discourse—is paramount and undergirds the Ismailis' historical emphasis on open and ethical governance as well as its foundational commitment to learning and education—an ethic they argue is at the core of Ismaili doctrine, as it is through didactic instruction that the disciple gains access to the Imam's teachings.

This conception of the Ismaili tradition cuts across time's boundaries to create a vertical history based on an ethical and doctrinal unity, grounded in an esoteric hermeneutic, which supports and inspires its self-view as an intellectually powerful yet physically persecuted Muslim minority. Steinberg, on the other hand, argues that "the real connection between those pasts and the present is tenuous."[12] He also argues that the effort to construct connections is revealing, and he describes the IIS's efforts to create and institutionalize the academic discipline of "Ismaili Studies" as "an effort to gain public legitimacy and recognition," thereby "bestowing upon Isma`ilism a special epistemological status that reinforces the view that it has objective historical significance."[13]

He uses an IIS children's publication, *Murids of Imam az-Zaman* (Disciples of the Imam of the Time), to show how the Ismaili institutional machine conveys and promotes key Ismaili themes, the most notable of which are "[C]ommonality across the diversity of the Isma`ili community, modernity and progress, membership and citizenship, liberal modes of plurality and unity in multiculturalism, disciplines of loyalty to the imam (through following the *farmans* and attending *jama`at khana*), and the importance of the past in the present."[14]

That these liberal themes appear in Ismaili educational programs at all levels demonstrates their significance to contemporary Ismaili thought in general. It seems, then, that the observer cannot discount their inclusion in the tradition's self-narrative as apologetic. The tradition seems to take seriously its claims to an ethical unity that cuts through time and remains as virile today as at its origins, though couched in a new vernacular. Using the vernacular is itself a practice that they see as an adaptive endeavor informed by their eternal and unchanged doctrine.

Considering the defining role that the contemporary tradition gives to its past, it also seems that an examination of its historical narrative is essential to understanding its contemporary contours. The contemporary Ismaili construction of its own historical narrative uncovers a history that gives prominence to a pluralism of thought and practice that provides support for its commitments to ethical governance and a culture of learning, all of which are focused through the lens of the critical role of the Imamate in guiding this oft-oppressed minority community through the perils of a turbulent historical experience.

For Virani—reconstructing this historical narrative—it was Ismailism's indispensible and essential notion of the Imamate that allowed the tradition to survive its near annihilation in 1256, a trauma that can be said to have had immense influence on the development of the modern Ismaili tradition. Historically, it is a tradition whose intellectual output directly impacted Muslim thought from the time of the Prophet onward, which established the Fatimid caliphate—the longest sustained Shi`i contender to Sunni authority—and which from Alamut garnered enough power to exact tribute from European kings and Muslim caliphs, but which, all of a sudden, disappeared for some five hundred years and then seemed miraculously to reappear, its doctrines intact and its communities revitalized. Its conception of its history as definitive of its present allowed the tradition to survive what thirteenth-century Persian historians celebrated as the silencing of a politicointellectual threat and a "powerful voice of Shi`i Islam" into the modern period, which contemporary historians like Virani see as their "phoenix-like renaissance."[15]

EARLY

The period following the Prophet's death was tumultuous and violent, and the dispute over his succession is one of the seminal issues in Islam. While the Shi`a supported the claims of their first Imam, `Ali ibn Abi Talib, Abu

Bakr was declared caliph in a spur-of-the-moment election on the day of the Prophet's death.[16] Nevertheless, 'Ali eventually became the fourth caliph of the Muslims in 656 and was assassinated in 661. During his life, however, he wrote extensively and provided a model of ethical governance for his contemporary and future followers.

According to Shah-Kazemi, 'Ali's most paradigmatic statement on the subject comes from a letter addressed to his governor in Egypt.[17] Imam 'Ali writes: "Incline your heart to show clemency, affection, sympathy, and beneficence to your subjects ... after all, they are either your brothers in religion or your equals in creation."[18] 'Ali's exhortation is meant to recall the Qur'anic idea of humankind's inherent unity (such as in Q. 4:1), which reminds humans that though they be different in form they are single in fact.

Cyril Glassé, writing in *The New Encyclopedia of Islam*, says that 'Ali is "highly revered" as the "fountainhead of esoteric doctrine,"[19] and is remembered as one of the four "rightly-guided" caliphs; as the champion of Muslims on the battlefield and the model for Islamic chivalry; and as the Cicero of Arabic, having laid down its rules of grammar and being its most eloquent writer.[20] For the Shi'a, however, 'Ali has deeper significance.

Imamate, they argue, was an essential component of the Prophet's message, without which the Revelation would be incomplete (Q. 5:67).[21] 'Ali, as the first Imam, was endowed thus with spiritual knowledge (*'ilm*) of the Qur'an's proper interpretation (Q. 3:7)[22] that afforded him the right to the community's leadership (Q. 4:59),[23] which was to be passed hereditarily to his descendents by explicit designation (*nass*). They argue that the Prophet designated 'Ali as his successor at the oasis of Ghadir Khumm during the return journey from the Prophet's final pilgrimage to Mecca before his death.[24] The "canonical" sources of Prophetic tradition (*hadith*) relate that on March 10, 632, the Prophet took 'Ali's hand and uttered the famous phrase "He whose *mawla* (Lord) I am, 'Ali is his *mawla* (Lord)," subsequently ordering the congregation to congratulate 'Ali and offer him their *bay'a* (allegiance).[25] According to L. Veccia Vaglieri, writing in the *Encyclopedia of Islam*, this was "thus a *nass* [designation] nominating 'Ali as *imam* of the Muslims after the death of the Prophet."[26]

Some commentators, basing themselves on the historical sources, argue that 'Ali's political decisions both before and during his caliphate were impolitic and lacked cunning.[27] Shah-Kazemi, however, offers a historical reconstruction that presents the Imam's decisions as consistent with ethical governance.[28] For example, Shah-Kazemi sees ʿAli's refusal to confirm his predecessor's corrupt governors—even as a tactical maneuver—as an example of the Imam's commitment to justice, as well as disdain for momentary ease at the cost of essential principles. For Imam ʿAli, "religion without justice is not religion,"[29] and installing corrupt governors would have been tantamount to renouncing a part of his religion.

Justice, says Shah-Kazemi, is at the core of Imam ʿAli's conception of good governance, exemplified in his letter by a statement that Shah-Kazemi says is "indispensable for any discourse on good governance in Islam": "The subjects will not be righteous except through the righteousness of the rulers, and the rulers will not be righteous except through the uprightness of the subjects."[30] Justice through equity thus appears at the heart of Ismaili understandings of good governance.

Shah-Kazemi outlines some of Imam ʿAli's key principles regarding his conception of justice as they are articulated in the letter. There is a recognition and respect for local traditions: the Imam cautions against setting up "some new practice which is detrimental to the already established traditions," which could disrupt carefully established unity and harmony.[31] Also, he advises placing restrictions on the market: just as the Messenger of God prohibited hoarding, writes the Imam, so should "trading be carried out with propriety and fairness," according to prices that are not burdensome to either party.[32]

As well, he discusses the ethics of war and advises the reader to be humane. "Never reject any call to peace made to you by your enemy," he writes, "for truly in peace lies repose for your soldiers, relaxation of your concerns, and security for your lands."[33] On the other hand, he very practically intimates that one must remain vigilant of the enemy's intentions even after brokering peace, "for it is possible that the enemy is only making peace with you in order to lull you into a false sense of security."[34]

One of the Imam's major concerns, argues Shah-Kazemi, was the need for social welfare. He draws attention to certain parts of the letter which prescribe that the ruler must take care of the ruled, paying particular attention to "the lowest class, those who have no wherewithal, the destitute, the needy, the afflicted, the disabled."[35] The Imam reminds the reader of his duty: "Be mindful of God in regard to their rights, for He has entrusted these rights to your care."[36]

That Imam ʿAli wrote extensively about ethical governance was a natural consequence of the fact of his times. His management of the caliphate would establish for posterity a prototype of the caliph-Imam model of rule. On the other hand, the fact that his immediate successors to the Imamate did not rule established the legitimacy of alternate models of governance in Islam, also communicating the principle that the office of Imamate need not be tied to that of the caliphate.

Following the death of Imam ʿAli's son at Kerbala in 680, the theology of the Imamate became systematized. In this period, argues Lalani, the emphasis shifted to intellectual authority as the Imam's province, above political authority. According to Lalani, the period of Imam al-Baqir (d. 743) represents an important chapter in the evolution of the Ismaili tradition. Al-Baqir's insistence on the principle of explicit designation of the Imam (*nass*) signified that the Imam's authority derived from divine appointment and not from human electors.[37] Al-Baqir's approach, says Lalani, underscores the separation of religious authority from political authority. Contrary to other opinions circulating at the time, al-Baqir— the fourth Imam in the modern Nizari chronology—argued that the Imam need not claim his right through force. Rather, the Imam is the Imam because he is the possessor of the special Knowledge (ʿ*ilm*), the salvific secrets of the Religion and the Book. This "Initiatory Knowledge," writes Mohammad Ali Amir-Moezzi, "is the constituent element of the imam's being."[38] Thus, knowledge is confirmed as a pivot of Shiʿi Islam.

In al-Baqir's conception, writes Lalani, the Imams are God's treasurers—not of gold and silver, but divine knowledge[39]—and thus *nass* (explicit designation) embodied ʿ*ilm* (special knowledge). The authoritative knowledge is inherited, passed from generation to generation, as "light upon light" (Q. 24:35), one to the next. "Thus," writes Lalani, "the doctrine of the imamate put forward by al-Baqir was based primarily on knowledge, not on political rule, although the imams were also entitled to the latter."[40] It was a significant point to make: al-Baqir was clarifying the nature and role of the Imamate in the face of multiple claims to the Imamate that viewed it as a bid for political power.

The genesis of Ismailism as an independent movement, says Daftary, can be traced to the dispute over the succession to al-Baqir's son, Imam Jafar al-Sadiq. The group we now refer to as Ismailis upheld the position that the Imamate had passed from al-Sadiq to his son, Ismail. The period after al-Sadiq's death in 765 was tumultuous, and the major Shi`i branches, still in their formative period, were for the most part severely persecuted and made to resort to underground existence.[41] This period—from the eighth century to the establishment of the Fatimid Caliphate in the tenth century—is obscured by a dearth of information about which even later Ismaili writers had little to say, since their focus was on philosophical rather than historical works.[42]

Nevertheless, there appeared in the tenth century a grand encyclopedic corpus dedicated to the exposition of available knowledge, ranging from geometry to music and logic to eschatology. This corpus of fifty-two epistles divided into four books, the *Rasa'il Ikhwan al-Safa* ("Epistles of the Brethren of Purity"), was produced secretly by a small group of scholars connected to the Ismaili movement.[43] While the work is not representative of official Fatimid Ismaili doctrines, it has been claimed by the Ismailis as part of the intellectual history of this obscure period.

According to el-Bizri, what is most emblematic of the Brethren's work is its pluralistic approach to knowledge. He writes that the *Epistles* seem to "embody a form of diversity in Islam that can accommodate miscellaneous ancient and monotheistic traditions," while promoting a "friendship of virtue" that "venerated the liberal spirit in Islam."[44] Ian Richard Netton writes, "Their quest for, and squirrel-like accumulation of, knowledge stands within the general framework of the Islamic tradition, and conformed to a paradigm which, from the earliest days, might be characterised as 'a thirst for global knowledge.'"[45]

Although grounded in the Qur'anic tradition, the *Epistles* readily incorporate Babylonian astrology, Indian mathematics, and Persian mysticism. But the Brethren's major influences, says Daftary, are the diverse schools of Hellenistic wisdom: "The *Epistles* are permeated throughout with Hermetic, Platonic, Aristotelian, Neopythagorean, and especially Neoplatonic ideas and doctrines."[46] According to the late Oxford University historian Hamid Enayat, the work of the Brethren expresses a palpable "spirit of tolerance towards other religions, and their abhorrence of prejudice as a reprehensible vice in doctrinal matters, which 'blinds men to the truth.'"[47]

There is in the *Epistles* a "logical nexus", says Enayat, between will, consciousness, and political action—since man possesses both knowledge and will, he is the best determinant of his life and the sociopolitical institutions that govern his relationships.[48] This, he argues, is the Brethren's foundation for their conception of governance in which "freedom of will is the *sine qua non* of responsible political activity."[49] On this view, they critiqued the perceived injustice of the Abbasids, making the point that calamity is the consequence of appointing a caliph from outside the Prophet's family, in defiance of the prophetic designation (*nass*).[50]

In articulating their conception of social justice, the Brethren employ fable and allegory, which, Enayat says, is a typically Ismaili method of clothing "truths in the guise of words, phrases and allusions."[51] For example, the parable of *The Case of the Animals versus Man* argues that human beings, through cruelty toward animals, have forfeited their moral dominion over them. It is an allegorical criticism of people's behavior toward each other, with a special concern for the sorry lot of the poor and destitute, whose security is the responsibility of a just society.

FATIMID

The tenth century has been called the Ismaili century of Islam. The most wide-ranging account of Ismaili history is Daftary's, who says that the Fatimid caliph-Imams (909–1094) administered over innovations in philosophical pursuits, educational institutions, art and architecture, and the longest sustained Shi`i experience in Islam. The most significant contemporaneous Ismaili accounts of the beginnings of the Fatimid caliphate and the exploits of the Ismaili mission are those of the scholar Ibn al-Haytham[52] and the famous *da`i* al-Qadi al-Nu`man,[53] who is regarded as the founder of Fatimid historiography.[54]

In the tenth century, the Ismaili Imam al-Mahdi (r. 909–934) revealed himself as Imam[55] and ended the Period of Concealment beginning with the death of Imam al-Sadiq in the eighth century. He established the Fatimid Caliphate in North Africa in 909 with the aim of gaining control of the entire Muslim Community, which was the culmination of the revolutionary philosophies and objectives of early Ismailism.[56] This new, public Ismailism faced both external and internal challenges. In Daftary's articulation, the Fatimids had (1) to struggle against the dominant Sunni groups in the region and (2) to balance the expectations of the *da`is* (missionary-scholars) who had helped bring the Fatimids to power on the one hand,[57] and the new needs of the state and responsibilities of sound government on the other.[58]

In 969 the fourth Fatimid caliph-Imam al-Muizz (932–975) entered Egypt victorious[59] after decade-long preparations and military victories by his general Jawhar, as well as the clandestine work of his *da`is* and secret agents who worked to advocate the Fatimids in Egypt and undermine the reigning, unpopular dynasty.[60] Michael Brett writes that the coming of al-Muizz represented for the Ismailis a "portentous history for the benefit of the Islamic world at large: the irresistible advance of the dynasty towards the goal of world dominion."[61]

Under al-Muizz's reign the Fatimid capital shifted to the new city they built, al-Qahira al-Mu`izziyya (Cairo), where the caliph-Imams founded what has been called the world's first university—al-Azhar. Contemporary historiography emphasizes the critical role of education in the Ismaili tradition. "Teaching and learning," says Halm, "are the very essence of the Ismaili mission."[62] For Halm, the *da`i*, the "summoner" to the mission, was the central figure of the community after the Imam.

Historically, the Imam's teaching was spread by the network of *da`is*, which operated secretly in many parts of the Islamic world. The *da`wa* had its greatest lasting successes outside Fatimid dominions, in areas with entrenched Shi`i histories, such as Yemen, Persia, and Central Asia.[63] The *da`wa* was organized into various "islands". The head of each island would have typically spent time at the Fatimid palace in Cairo under the tutelage of the chief *da`i* and perhaps even the Imam. The *da`is* had to be masters of rhetoric and philosophy, required to best all in debate and learning.[64] Individual instruction was their modus operandi.[65]

The relationship between teacher and pupil was central to Ismaili learning, mirroring the relationship between the individual believer and the Imam, and it forms the subject of one of the oldest works of Ismaili literature, *The Master and the Disciple*. Dating from the late ninth / early tenth century, the work is a fictitious account of a neophyte's initiation.[66] It outlines the philosophical and theological arguments used to justify the need for authoritative guidance and the Imam's role as the authoritative interpreter of the Qur'anic secret.

The fact that the Ismaili doctrine and initiation was kept so secret led to much speculation by its detractors, climaxing in the widespread accusation that the process wore down an individual's piously held beliefs until he became an unbeliever, a *kafir*.[67] On the one hand, the Ismailis had made a habit of secrecy as a result of their persistent persecution, but on the other hand, secrecy was an essential part of their doctrine. They emphasized the fundamental distinction between the exoteric (*zahir*) and the esoteric (*batin*) nature of revelation: while the outward form of religion changes, its hidden truths remain constant. These eternal truths hidden in the *batin* are made apparent through the *ta'wil* (esoteric exegesis) of the Imam,[68] the repository of undivulged knowledge and the possessor of the Qur'an's true interpretation, as referred to by the Qur'anic phrase "*al-rasikhun fi'l-`ilm*" or "those possessing firm knowledge" (Q. 3:7).[69]

This knowledge, while retaining its tint of secrecy, must be passed on. The author of *The Master and the Disciple* writes:

> I too used to be dead, and he gave me life; I was ignorant, and he gave me knowledge. I am not the first person to be ignorant ... nor am I the last one to be ignorant, so that the process of (spiritual) teaching will come to an end. Therefore it is only right for me, because of my gratitude for this blessing, to pass on this (divine) *trust* (4:58; 33:72, etc.) to those who come after me, just as those who preceded me have handed it down to me.[70]

Halm says: "these few words contain the entire Ismaili idea of knowledge, learning and teaching."[71]

It is a profound doctrine, he explains: "Knowledge means life; learning means resurrection from the death of ignorance; knowledge is a good entrusted by God to human beings (*amana*) who must not selfishly keep it to themselves, but instead pass it on."[72] This conception of knowledge—as a divine trust to be passed on—is at the core of Shi`ism and also a defining feature of the Imamate. Education, then, becomes a vital imperative, which, in the view of contemporary Ismaili historiography, the Fatimids exemplified in their establishment of various educational institutions.

The primary pedagogical institutions of the Fatimids were the sermons and learning sessions held by the chief *da`i* (missionary) and *qadi* (judge).[73] In keeping with the *zahir/batin* duality/unity, the posts of chief *da`i* and chief *qadi* were united in the same person. The first four caliph-Imams were served by the eminent al-Qadi al-Nu`man, who, in accordance with the needs of the new Ismaili state, founded the Ismaili school of law.[74] In keeping with his dual role, he penned the school's exoteric compendium, "The Pillars of Islam,"[75] as well as its esoteric counterpart, "The Interpretation of the Pillars of Islam."[76]

The chief *qadi* held public teaching sessions in the mosque after the Friday prayers, in order to educate the people about the new Ismaili school of jurisprudence, now the legal basis for daily life. Later, after the crowds dispersed, the Ismaili initiates would retire to a special room in the palace, where there was better control over admission and privacy. There, in these *majalis al-hikma* ("Sessions of Wisdom"), the chief *da`i* would administer to both men and women lessons in *batin*, which were typically proofread by the caliph-Imam himself, since, as Halm puts it, "the imam is the source of wisdom, the *da`i* is merely his mouthpiece."[77]

Accounts of medieval Ismaili history also emphasize the intellectually interactive and collaborative nature of Ismaili thought.[78] Ismaili philosophers and *da`is* tended toward Neoplatonic modes of expression,[79] with the exception of Hamid al-Din al-Kirmani (d. 1020),[80] who used the contemporary terminology of al-Farabi (d. 951) and Ibn Sina (d. 1037), those giants of Aristotelian articulation. The *da`is* Abu Ya`qub al-Sijistani (fl. 971),[81] al-Mu`ayyad fi'l-Din al-Shirazi (d. 1078),[82] and Nasir Khusraw (d. 1060)[83] describe the emanation of intellect from God's Command, through which existence is cast into being through the Universal Soul and the Universal Intellect.[84] They engaged and modified these Neoplatonic ideas to articulate the Shi`i conception of the soul's goal as a reorienting of itself toward its higher self, returning ultimately to its original state. This journey, they insist, requires the divinely inspired Guide to assist in the individual's reconnection with the Universal Soul and Universal Intellect.[85] That the *da`is*—like other Muslim philosophers—recognized in ancient philosophy the same truth embedded in Islam is viewed by contemporary Ismaili historiography as indicative of a pluralism of thought that showcases their intellectual liberalism and dexterity.

But, continues Halm, "an Ismaili *da`wa* without libraries is unimaginable." The Imams' fondness for books is noted by many contemporary sources, which relate al-Mahdi taking books with him on his travels, and the third caliph-Imam al-Mansur (d. 953), rejecting the advice of his son to move out of the sun because it would make him "lose the thread of his ideas." The palace in Cairo had a library that Halm says was "unmatched anywhere in the contemporary world."[86] Indeed, says Walker, the Fatimids were "justly famous" for their collections of books and interest in learning, which placed "no obvious limits" on the subjects of inquiry, a function of their understanding of religion as universalist. "For a religious mission built," he writes, "on the broad incorporation of a wide array of knowledge into a comprehensive understanding of the cosmos in all its aspects, the acquisition of books and treatises was essential, and as there were no obvious limits to the fields that Ismaili authorities studied, no subjects, authors, or works were excluded."[87]

Halm provides an account of the later Dar al-`Ilm ("House of Knowledge"), an institution where in 1005 "lectures were held there by the Qur'an readers, astronomers, grammarians and philologists, as well as physicians."[88] Servants were hired by the caliph to work there—a previously unheard of innovation—and ink and paper were provided to "people of all walks of life, whether they wanted to read books or dip into them."[89] Into this institution, states the firsthand account, was brought together "manuscripts in all the domains of science and culture, to an extent to which they had never been brought together for a prince."[90] To be sure, Walker concludes, "nothing like this new institution existed anywhere else at that time."[91]

From the beginning to the end of their rule in Egypt the Fatimids were a minority Shi`i power in a majority Sunni setting. Thus, says Daftary, their approach to governance was to adopt a model of inclusiveness and meritocracy.[92] This approach, he says, was the key to the successes of the Fatimids, which "were in large measure due to the remarkable ethnic and religious tolerance of the dynasty and the administrative stability of the Fatimid state."[93] According to Jiwa, however, this approach was not solely utilitarian. She argues that the Fatimid caliph-Imams recalled the ethic of both the Qur'an and the Prophet's Medinan Constitution in their appeal to equity and social justice as the basis for good governance.

This is evidenced, she says, by al-Muizz's *Aman* document[94]—read by his general Jawhar to the grateful Egyptians upon taking control in 969—which ensured the restoration of security and the promotion of justice where previously the people had suffered economic instability as well as violence at the hands of raiders on the pilgrimage routes.[95] Jiwa argues that the *Aman* document echoes both the Medinan Constitution and Imam 'Ali's Letter to his Egyptian governor, which, she says, appears in al-Nu'man's *Da'a'im*, thereby giving credence to the notion that it was foundational for al-Muizz's political program and his conception of the state.

In Jiwa's contention, the insistence in the *Aman* document on justice and pluralism derived from the Fatimid caliph-Imam's conception of himself as the legitimate protector and caretaker of the Community, which included both Muslims and the People of the Book. In their self-view as the divinely designated (*nass*) spiritual and temporal rulers, writes Jiwa, the caliph-Imams were the sole legitimate interpreters of the Qur'an and their directives were thus law. In this sense, religious and secular authority were combined in the Fatimid state in the person of the Imam—with the *da'is* acting as propagators of law and the Imam its guardian—unlike in Sunni lands, where the 'ulema were the safeguards of the law and watchdogs of the monarch.[96]

But Jiwa concludes that the caliph-Imams' self-promoted "exalted rank"[97] freed them from the constraints faced by Sunni rulers, to positive effect. Al-Muizz, she writes, affirmed the internal pluralism of the various theological and legal proclivities within Islam and promised in the *Aman* to "undertake the repair of your mosques and adorn them with carpets and lighting," as well as to give allowance to the mosque administrators from the treasury, not from the taxes.[98] As caretaker and protector, al-Muizz took an inclusive stance toward the People of the Book that he declared to be "in accord with custom." According to Jiwa, the caliph-Imam purposefully connected himself with the Prophetic example of pluralism, negating any examples of exclusivism that occurred over the centuries in other Muslim societies. In her view, "the interpretation of custom here is Fatimid Shii and harkens to the Prophetic example, self-consciously bypassing its various other political and theological expressions over the course of centuries, some of which were less favourable to these communities."[99]

Continuing in this very liberal vein was Al-Aziz (r. 975–996), the fifth Fatimid caliph-Imam, whom Daftary praises as being an administrator that utilized capable men, regardless of their religious beliefs. His first vizier was the expert politician and jurist Ibn Killis, a Jewish convert, and his last vizier was a Coptic Christian named Isa b. Nasturus, the first of several Christians to occupy that high position under the Fatimids. Daftary writes that such a policy of tolerance was typical for the Fatimids: "The unusual policy of assigning numerous high administrative posts to Christians and Jews in a Shi`i Muslim state was basically in line with the religious toleration practised by the Fatimids."[100] He continues to say that al-Aziz, perhaps influenced by his Christian wife, went further than his predecessors: "the Christians in particular enjoyed a large degree of religious freedom and participation in government under al-Aziz,"[101] despite violent Sunni opposition to important posts being occupied by non-Muslims.

This growing and virulent opposition came to a head in the reign of al-Aziz's successor, al-Hakim (r. 996–1021), the most controversial member of this dynasty. Al-Hakim faced numerous disturbances and revolts during his caliphate, and he was forced to subdue agitation by imposing restrictions on the Jews and Christians. A large number of churches and monasteries were demolished or converted into mosques, with their properties and revenues confiscated, causing the Byzantine emperor Basil II to issue an edict in 1015–1016 forbidding commercial relations with the Fatimid Caliphate, thereby bringing to an end the Fatimid-Byzantine truce.[102]

Halm argues that al-Hakim's image has been distorted by hostile historiographers and that, in spite of reports of inconsistency,[103] al-Hakim's religious policy was consistent in that he sought always to enforce the *shari`a* and to mete out severe punishment.[104] His reign is remembered as one of both eccentricity and executions[105] as well as of political tact[106] and immense intellectual patronage, typified by his establishment of the Dar al-`Ilm mentioned earlier. Halm paints a picture of al-Hakim as extremely popular with the people of Cairo, among whom he used to mix on Christian and Muslim holidays, showing himself at night in the city's narrow lanes with orders that all petitioners be allowed to approach. He wore simple garments and eschewed his retinue and bodyguards for a donkey and two grooms, evidently having nothing to fear from his subjects.[107]

Recalling al-Muizz's *Aman*, al-Hakim issued in 1009 an edict of tolerance, legally putting Sunni rites on par with Shi`i rites, allowing the celebration of the feast of breaking the fast of Ramadan on different days, according to different interpretations of the Law. Basing himself on the Qur'anic injunction that "no compulsion is there in religion" (Q. 2:256), he ended his edict with what Halm calls the "liberal principle" that "Each Muslim may try to find his own solution within his religion."[108]

While al-Hakim left "bitter memories" among the Christians for ordering the destruction of churches, including the Church of the Holy Sepulchre in Jerusalem, Halm argues that there was no edict forcing Christians to convert to Islam; nor was there any general persecution of the Christians, "as has been falsely maintained time and again."[109] He asserts that al-Hakim's measures were "an attempt to contain the rise of anti-Christian sentiment" and not part of a concerted policy.[110] Indeed, writes W. Ivanow, al-Hakim's exploits "were nothing but the materialisation of the similar dreams of the masses, carried out with maniacal ruthlessness."[111] Canard agrees on this last point, stating that al-Hakim's actions had not only been mirrored by the `Abbasid caliphs, but also had the approval of the Muslims, "who hated the Christians because of acts of misappropriation and of favouritism by the Christian financial officials."[112] Considering this, the measures taken during al-Hakim's reign were likely a reaction to civic discontent regarding the tolerant policies of the Fatimids and had been percolating over the course of the dynasty's rule in Egypt, coming finally to a head in the eleventh century.

Halm concludes by stating that al-Hakim eventually returned to the Christians their land and allowed them to rebuild the demolished buildings, a fact often overlooked by historians, as is al-Hakim's seemingly charismatic and popular persona.[113] Despite everything, writes Canard, all the historians agree that al-Hakim was generous, that he tried to curb famine by making gifts and adjusting public policy, and that his great concern for social justice was exemplified by his presence at financial litigations and among the people, where he endeavored to satisfy their requests.[114]

Modern Ismaili scholarship contends that the Fatimid caliph-Imams upheld a policy of what has been called "remarkable" inclusiveness and tolerance. Even Ahmad Moussalli agrees that the Islamic world in general had high levels of religious toleration, which was envied by the Jews of Europe, and Egypt was a prime example. He writes: "during medieval times, the Jews of Europe looked to the Jews of the Islamic world for inspiration. For instance, the Jews of Egypt lived side by side with Muslims and Christians, not in ghettos. They lived like other members of Egyptian society and participated in its affairs."[115]

This pluralist attitude spilled over into other aspects of life, argues Sajoo, who paints an expansive picture of a society that embraced a creative pluralism: "from Roman architectural elements and Spanish mosaic decoration, to Chinese ceramics and Iraqi calligraphic styles, a freewheeling approach in the late 10th to 12th centuries produced in Egypt what experts today regard as among the most creatively brilliant epochs in Islamic cultural history."[116] Thus, the Fatimid "spirit of pluralism," as it may be called, seems to have encompassed politics and religion, and also to have given life to creative forms of expression, reflecting the dynasty's repeated and self-articulated emphasis on the infiniteness of creation.

ALAMUT

The death of the eighth Fatimid caliph-Imam al-Mustansir in 1094 led to a major dispute over succession. The Persian Ismailis—led by the capable Persian *da`i* Hasan-i Sabbah (d. 1124)—supported the Imamate of al-Mustansir's son Nizar and thus came to be called Nizaris. Nizar's brother Musta`ili was made caliph by the regent al-Afdal, and Nizar was eventually imprisoned; Musta`ili's supporters came to form the other major branch of the Ismaili movement. The Nizari movement, however, grew and became centered in Persia through Hasan's efforts, where he seized the mountain fortress of Alamut in 1090, marking the foundation of what is now referred to as the Nizari state.

Though centered at Alamut, the Nizari state was spread over a scattered territory from Syria to eastern Persia and controlled numerous fortresses and their surrounding villages, as well as a few towns.[117] Making a connection to the contemporary globalized form of Ismailism, Steinberg argues that it was in the Alamut period that the "possibility of an Isma`ili polity with little territorial contiguity began to emerge."[118]

The seizure of Alamut marked the initiation of the Persian Ismailis' revolt against the Saljuq Turks, ushering in a new and public revolutionary phase—a recurring theme in Ismaili history—for the hitherto clandestine Persian Ismailis.[119] Operating in a hostile Sunni environment controlled mainly by the Saljuqs, Hasan used the strong *da`wa* network to gain allies, often through the conversion of local governors and princes who would offer protection to local Ismaili communities, who were often attacked and massacred by the Saljuqs. The charismatic Hasan, realizing that he would not get support from Cairo, acted independently and infiltrated Alamut disguised as a teacher. Through the clandestine work of his *da`is* he was able to convert most of its soldiers and initiate a bloodless coup in which he even provided the astonished lord of the castle with a draft for three thousand dinars. According to Daftary, the employment of the *da`wa* network had political ramifications, just as it did when employed by the early Fatimid caliph-Imams in their efforts to control Egypt as part of their larger struggle for headship of the entire Muslim community.

Although the Imam's headship persisted as the Nizaris' ultimate goal, they now had to adapt their strategy to prevailing conditions. The Saljuq Empire had become increasingly localized, with power concentrated in the hands of loyal but independent military and religious leaders. Under these circumstances, says Daftary, decentralization was the best strategy for the rebellious movement, who would seize strongholds from where they would launch multiple simultaneous risings in order to destabilize the existing sociopolitical structure from within.[120]

In this environment of atomized power, the Nizaris developed an auxiliary technique to achieve their political and military ends, namely the technique of assassination, with which they have come to be associated and from whom the word ultimately derives.[121] Unable to launch full-scale attacks against the Saljuqs, because of their small size and geographic dispersal, the Ismailis of Alamut employed the defensive tactic of assassinating key figures who led or incited massacres against their communities. Although assassination was a commonly used political tool at the time of the Nizari revolt, they assigned it a major role in their methods of struggle such that almost all assassinations and attempts were attributed to them.[122] Virani speaks admiringly, arguing that the Nizaris' skillful combination of propagation and assassination "yielded some astonishing results," inspiring both legend and fear to the extent that "so many of the Saljuq Sultan Barkiyaruq's (d. 498 AH / 1105 CE) courtiers and soldiers had become Ismailis that some of his officers requested his permission to appear before him in armour lest they be attacked, even in his very presence."[123]

But the Nizaris' motives, says Marshall Hodgson, were usually defensive or retaliatory, as part of a complementary pattern of massacre and assassination.[124] The assassinations were carried out by young male volunteers (*fida'is*) in public settings, in order to intimidate other actual or potential enemies.[125] Daftary explains that the technique held deeper relevance for the Nizaris as a more "humane" tactic because it served to limit the death of multiple soldiers on the battlefield. In this view, the Nizari strategy of assassination derives from the humane principles of just conflict. Daftary writes, "The assassination of single prominent individuals who caused the Nizaris special damage, often served to eliminate bloodshed among many ordinary men on battlefield. Consequently, the Nizaris presumably saw even a humane justification for their assassinations."[126]

In a sense, both Daftary's and Virani's laudatory reading of this Nizari practice may suggest a contemporary view of Ismaili tradition and identity as one that is not mainstream, yet is effective and is validated in time. Indeed, the conception of targeted criminal justice seems acutely contemporary, reflective of the modern practice of targeting high-ranking elements as the focus of military and legal action, such as those initiated against Saddam Hussein or Augusto Pinochet. The arrest of the former Chilean president in 1998 was the first time a former government head was arrested under public international law, going against not only convention but also the post-Westphalian moral absolute of respect for the sovereign. Nevertheless, it seems to be the current policy of many Western states to resolve military situations with minimal damage—either through drone attacks or targeted killing—taking Just War Theory beyond itself, as it reflects a concern not only for civilian lives but also for the lives of soldiers involved in military action.

If this was the motivation for the Nizaris, it was also practical, as the Nizari state was dispersed and its territories separated by long distances. Yet, says Daftary, it was able to maintain a cohesive unity and a successful system of centralized authority, which he contends was due largely to their common vision of the community and its mission, which was to prepare the way for the general rule of the Imam. While each territory conducted its local affairs with independence, the Nizari state as a whole exhibited a rare stability relative to other small Muslim principalities, and the most drastic policy changes at Alamut were accepted throughout the Nizari community.[127] Scholars identify the community's sense of unity and solidarity, complete dedication, and innovative initiative, as well as the movement's appeal to outstanding individuals in the Muslim community, as having played a part. "For a century and a half," writes Hodgson, "the Nizari state kept its hold on a remotely scattered territory with few losses or humiliations, and with little internal disruption: this should be a sign of moral strength."[128]

Despite the tumultuous times, the Nizaris seemed to have retained the typically Ismaili concern for learning, which, Hodgson writes, is characteristic: "In all the chief Ismaili areas we find that community cultivating the learned disciplines."[129] According to contemporary accounts, the libraries the Nizaris established at their fortresses were renowned and were visited by leading thinkers from around the Muslim world, which Daftary says gave renewed vitality to the community. Indeed, when Hulagu Khan attacked Alamut in 1256 with orders to put to death all Ismailis, he was attended by Juwayni, who requested permission to visit the library, "the fame of which had spread throughout the world."[130] There, Juwayni condemned to destruction the multitudes of books on the Ismaili religion, saving only a selection of treatises and copies of the Qur'an. Virani uses this narrative to accent the intimate relationship between education and Ismaili identity, drawing a parallel between the extermination of their books and the Ismailis in general. "Consigned to a fate similar to that of their religious books," he writes, "the Ismailis themselves were hunted down and slaughtered indiscriminately."[131]

As a result of this precarious situation, writes Daftary,[132] the Nizaris of Alamut focused less on works of cosmology and esotericism—unlike their Fatimid predecessors—and gave priority to elaborating the the doctrine of Imamate. Hasan-i Sabbah himself wrote an important treatise on the doctrine of *ta'lim*, the authoritative guidance of the Imam. His ideas survive in the work of the renowned thinker al-Shahrastani (d. 1153), who is believed to have been a secret Ismaili employing the Shi'i political technique of *taqiyya*, the dissimulation of one's beliefs in times of persecution. Building on an old Shi'i conception, Hasan perceived knowledge as dialectical: the individual's own reasoning causes him to realize his need for an authoritative teacher, the Imam, who, in turn, presents himself as satisfying this need.[133]

Thus, education and learning are once again iterated as the core of Ismaili doctrine. Hasan's articulation of *ta'lim* reformulated into a powerful intellectual tool the doctrine articulated by the *Ikhwan al-Safa*, al-Sijistani, al-Kirmani, al-Shirazi, Nasir Khusraw and others. The sophistication of his articulation posed a serious intellectual challenge to the Saljuqs, and provoked a refutation by the famous Sunni theologian al-Ghazali (d. 1111).[134] A century after Hasan's work, the doctrine of *ta'lim* came into the fullness of its maturity in the hands of the famous ethicist and astrologer Nasir al-Din al-Tusi (d. 1274)—the foremost Muslim philosopher of his time—who wrote about the limits of speculative reason in his autobiographical treatise.[135]

Hasan-i Sabbah died in 1124 and was succeeded as lord of Alamut by a companion and, later, the latter's progeny. On August 8, 1164, the reigning lord of Alamut, Hasan 'ala dhikiri'l-salaam declared the *qiyama*, the Great Resurrection, in which the Nizari community was to have entered a completely spiritual phase of existence and thus were no longer bound by the Shari'a.[136] Daftary explains: "according to this interpretation of the Resurrection, all believers could come to know God and the mysteries and realities of creation through the Nizari Imam, as was appropriate in paradise."[137] Hasan 'ala dhikiri'l-salaam's successor, Nur al-Din Muhammad, declared openly his Imamate as well as that of his father, claiming that he was smuggled into Alamut as a baby. Thus began the reign of the Nizari Imams at Alamut.

In 1256, when the Mongols swept across the Muslim world—eventually setting fire to the city of Baghdad—the eighth lord of Alamut, Imamimam Rukn al-Din Khurshah, surrendered after months of siege. Despite the historical impregnability and self-sufficiency of the Nizari fortresses, as well as their previous decade-long experiences holding off the Saljuqs, Khurshah capitulated to the Mongol armies. Daftary speculates that the Imam's reason for capitulation was to put an end to the Mongol genocide of Ismailis outside the fortresses. In any case, the Nizari fortresses were eventually dismantled, and Alamut was destroyed and its library plundered. The Mongols had massacred over ten thousand Nizaris in villages and towns and attempted to wipe out their history by destroying their libraries, in accordance with Genghis Khan's aforementioned edict that "None of that people should be spared, not even the babe in its cradle."[138] Thus, it came as a shock to Western scholars in the nineteenth century that the Nizaris had not only survived but were also flourishing.

Although Virani is able to dredge up references and allusions to the existence of Ismailis in post-Alamut history—a mislabeled Persian manuscript here, a single sentence by a Damascene geographer there, a mention in the Latin tome of a Dominican traveler, etc.[139]—it was accepted as fact that the Ismailis had been exterminated. After all, Juwayni had declared: "He [the Imam Rukn al-Din Khwurshah] and his followers were kicked to a pulp and then put to the sword; and of him and his stock no trace was left, and he and his kindred became but a tale on men's lips and a tradition in the world."[140] In light of such declarations, combined with the community's retreat to secrecy, it is little wonder that the extermination of the Ismailis was accepted as fact by Western scholarship for centuries. It was the pioneering efforts of the twentieth-century Russian scholar Wladimir Ivanow, says Virani, that brought the continued existence of the Ismaili community to the attention of Western scholarship.

Virani recounts Ivanow's letter to his learned friends in Europe, who "plainly disbelieved" the Russian scholar when he wrote to them about his discovery in February 1912 that the Ismaili community persisted despite the most brutal persecution and wholesale slaughter. It was only later on, Ivanow wrote, when he grew more intimate with the community, that he began to see the reasons for what he calls "such surprising vitality." It was their "extraordinary devotion and faithfulness to the tradition of their ancestors," he writes, as well as their "ungrudging patience with which they suffered all the calamities and misfortunes." Virani quotes the full text of Ivanow's article, in which the Russian scholar writes:

> They with amazing care and devotion kept through ages
> burning that Light, mentioned in the Koran, which God
> always protects against all attempts of His enemies to
> extinguish It. I rarely saw anything so extraordinary
> and impressive as this ancient tradition being devoutly
> preserved in the poor muddy huts of mountain hamlets
> or poor villages in the desert.[141]

For his own part, Virani contends that the Ismailis' religious doctrines and worldview helped them to survive "the intervening centuries between what appeared to have been their total annihilation in 654/1256, and their modern, seemingly phoenix-like renaissance."[142] He defines three aspects of Ismaili thought as being crucial to the community's survival: *taqiyya*, precautionary dissimulation of one's beliefs under duress; the Ismaili *da'wa*, its "mission" or propaganda machine; and the emphasis on the soteriological role of the Imamate, especially the role of the Imam of the time in leading the believer to the mystical recognition of God.[143]

To survive those centuries of living in secrecy—marked by the constant fear of persecution as well as the lack of direct physical guidance from the Imam—the community viewed its survival as linked to faithfulness to its tradition and thus built upon doctrinal tools that helped them maintain that link. Apart from precautionary dissimulation and secret propagation, the most significant development to arise was the shift to a more spiritualized conception of the role of the Imam. While in previous centuries—when the community ruled Egypt and administered a state from Alamut—there was a prevalence of historical and philosophical works by Ismaili authors, the works of the post-Alamut period emphasize the Imam's esoteric reality and the importance of not focusing one's mind on his physical person.[144]

The practical result seems to have been an understanding of Imamate as almost entirely spiritual, with a conception of its political aspect as more remote. In a sense, this is a culmination of a spiritual teaching that began with Imam 'Ali but whose edification progressed incrementally over the centuries and includes, for example, the eighth-century principle of *nass* (designation of the Imam based on special religious knowledge); the eleventh-century principle of *ta'lim* (spiritual guidance of the Imam); and the *qiyama* (Great Resurrection) of the twelfth century, when the Imam declared that the community would henceforth live in a state of spirituality and would no longer be tied to the physical Shari'a (Law). Thus, after 1256, when the community was forced to be physically separated from its now incognito Imam, it had been prepared over centuries of doctrinal development to accept the idea of the Imam as a religious authority that needs no political entity to lead the believer's soul to salvation. In a sense, however, it was the near-death experience of the Mongol invasion that cemented the idea and which, ultimately, allowed the community to become adapted to the present modernity.

MODERN

Ivanow divides postmedieval Ismailism into three phases. The first period, lasting roughly two centuries, is relatively obscure, as the Nizari Imams were in hiding.[145] The Persian Nizaris operated clandestinely, following the principle of *taqiyya* and blending in with various Sufi groups while trying to regain control over their surroundings. It was also a period of schism, leading to multiple Nizari groups—the Imam-Shahis, the Muhammad-Shahis, and the Qasim-Shahis. The Imams of the latter group came to be acknowledged by the majoritarian and emerged in a village in Persia called Anjudan in the fifteenth century. This marks Ivanow's second period, which he termed the Anjudan revival, a period of renaissance in Nizari thought and *da'wa* activity that also saw a flourishing of the community in Central Asia built on the efforts of the famous eleventh-century *da'i* Nasir Khusraw. The third period is characterized by the Aga Khans, the Nizari Imams who emerged on the world scene in the nineteenth century and who moved the seat of the Nizari Imamate to India in an effort to consolidate their leadership of the growing community in that region as well as to improve its socioeconomic conditions.[146] This phase is the critical period for contemporary Ismaili social and political thought.

To be sure, the shape of contemporary Ismailism owes much to this period, which is one of the longest continuous phases of Ismaili history. Although the Nizari Imams arrived in the Indian subcontinent relatively recently—Aga Khan I (d. 1881) was the first to set foot in India—Ismaili *da'wa* activities had been ongoing there since the thirteenth century and had developed into what was termed the Satpanth ("True Path") tradition, whose members Daftary says "comprised the most important section of the Nizari community."[147] The abiding relevance of this tradition for contemporary Ismailism is that today's most prosperous, educated, and Westernized Ismailis are the diasporic Khojas, the South Asian Ismailis whose socioreligious origins are in the Satpanth tradition and who now inhabit the top tiers of Ismaili religious and institutional leadership—including the IIS—and whose practices and views thus form an implicit Ismaili cultural normative. All of this is due to the leadership of the Aga Khans, who, operating in the milieu of the Indian subcontinent, defined explicitly for the first time the Shi`i Ismaili identity of a modern Ismaili community, and then brought that community into the fold of modernity by encouraging its formal education as well as its education in the habits of the West.

According to IIS collaborator Tazim Kassam, the *ginan*s—devotional literature of the Satpanth tradition—played a crucial role in defining the Ismaili religious identity of the Khojas, who until the arrival of the Aga Khans labored under an ambiguous religious identity that was an admixture of Sunnism, Shi`ism, and Vaishnavism.[148] The need to adapt to hostile circumstances,[149] she says, had created a sense of multiple identities among the Khojas, but Aga Khan I realized that, with the changed circumstances of his community under the British, such ambiguity would be a serious liability for his followers.[150] Ismaili identity was finally defined in the decisive 1866 Bombay court case, says Kassam, because of Justice Arnould's ruling that, "based on the authority of the *ginan* literature, the Agha Khan was the true spiritual head and hereditary *imam* of the Satpanth Khojas, who were, at root, a Shi`iah Isma`ili Muslim sect of converted Hindus."[151] Thus, she argues that the Satpanth tradition helped define the legal identity of modern Ismailism and that, because the Indian Ismaili tradition was the first to enter modernity—ahead of the Middle Eastern and Central Asian Ismaili traditions—the Satpanth tradition "forms the bedrock of the modern Ismaili community."[152]

Steinberg goes further and argues that the modern Ismaili community owes its genesis to the role of the British courts in defining its identity. Taking his cue from Amrita Shodhan's study on colonial law,[153] he argues that the contemporary shape of the global Ismaili movement is a result of colonial discourse on community and the imperialist tendency to legally classify social groups.[154] Steinberg's core argument about the origins of global Ismailism is that it is a "product of empire": the British (1) used colonial courts to define previously nonsectarian groups like the Ismailis and (2) acted as "a channel for Ismaili globalization" by allowing for intensified migration to its African colonies. This is not to say, he writes, that the British invented the Ismailis. Rather, "the British in some ways created the boundaries that delineated the Khojas as a distinct, separate, and internally cohesive 'community,' and that they came to see themselves as Isma`ili through the lens of the British construction of legal community."[155]

The 1866 Aga Khan case in Bombay, he argues, played the key role in institutionalizing the office of the Aga Khan and crystallizing the community's disparate elements into a community. As the governor of the Persian province of Kirman, Aga Khan I was a member of the Persian elite and was given by the Shah both his daughter in marriage and the hereditary title of Aga Khan (loosely translated as "Chief of Chiefs" or "Lord and Master"). After the death of the Shah, Aga Khan I became involved in a dispute with the new prime minister and, after a conflict, left for India via Afghanistan,[156] where his military and diplomatic influence was of essential aid to the British, who repaid him with a large yearly stipend and the title of "His Highness". He eventually settled in Bombay, which Aga Khan III says in his memoirs was a "happy and wise personal decision" that had "an admirable effect on the religious and communal life of the whole Ismaili world."[157] In Bombay, Aga Khan I established a large residence, held weekly audiences for his followers at his new *Durkhana* (reception hall), and began associating the Imamate with European royalty,[158] such as King Edward VII, who visited him.

The Aga Khan's move to Bombay was what Ernest Gellner called "the crucial event in modern Ismaili history,"[159] and what Steinberg asserts was the "fundamental turning point" that 'radically altered the very nature of Isma`ilism."[160] The colonial courts "actively defined religion,"[161] writes Shodhan, who argues that this process led to an unrefined definition of the Khojas due to their seemingly anomalous doctrines and practices. The anomaly appeared to be a function of their overlapping and multivalent traditions, which led to the community being perceived as a Hindu-Muslim amalgam, though they themselves claimed membership in Islam. In any case, says Steinberg, their anomalous status was at the heart of the case, whose ultimate and critical result was the classification of Ismailism and the Khoja community into a palatable category for the colonial administration.[162]

The case was brought against the Aga Khan by a set of Bombay Khojas who—used to independence before the arrival of the Aga Khan and now apparently resentful over the scale of the Aga Khan's tithe collection—asked that the Aga Khan distance himself from the community's affairs. In the wake of the Aga Khan's religious reforms, they questioned his status as their rightful leader, his right to the tithe funds, and the claims on the house of prayer (*jamatkhana*), and ultimately they argued that his followers were not entirely Muslim. The court, under Justice Arnould, found that the Aga Khan was the rightful leader of the Khojas and that claims to the contrary were a perversion of proper Ismailism. Thus, writes Steinberg, the colonial courts decided what constituted "proper Isma`ilism" and defined the "Isma`ili Khojas as a *sect* of the Isma`ili *community*."[163]

For Steinberg, the Aga Khan case is the birthdate of modern Ismailism, but for Asani it is simply an evolution of the tradition's definition and position in the world. He is less stringent than Steinberg on this score, and says that "while the British courts may have contributed to defining the Ismaili identity of the Khojas legally," for the resolution of their doctrines and practices the community would rely on "the various reform initiatives instituted by the Aga Khans."[164] Thus, for Asani, the substance of the tradition is defined firmly by the religion, not by the courts.

Nevertheless, the 1866 case is a watershed moment in the community's modern history. After Aga Khan I's death in 1881, the Imamate passed to his son, Aga Khan II, who had a short reign of four years, after whom his son Sultan Muhammad Shah al-Husayni took up the mantle of the Qasim-Shahi Nizari Imamate in 1885 at the age of eight, becoming the forty-eighth Imam and the third Aga Khan.

Aga Khan III became deeply involved in both Indian affairs and global politics. He was the first president of the All-India Muslim League, a founder of the Muslim university of Aligarh, and a president of the League of Nations from 1937 to 1938, and he led both the Muslim Delegation and the British Indian Delegation to the Round Table Conferences in London from 1930 to 1933. Pakistani historian K. K. Aziz wrote that no other leader in the history of Indian politics loomed so large over so many years: "For half a century he strode the scene like a colossus."[165]

Aga Khan III expressed strong opinions throughout his life on a variety of subjects—in newspapers like *The Times of London*, as well as personal essays and books, such as *India in Transition: A Study of Political Evolution* (London, 1918). But, asserts Aziz, "education was the ruling passion of the Aga Khan's public life."[166] In a life full of achievements that would have satisfied any man of high ambition, he says, Aga Khan III "was content to say that in his own opinion one single achievement which gladdened his heart and that his single greatest success was the creation of the Muslim University of Aligarh,"[167] which was "his lasting joy and pleasure which he called his greatest service to Islam."[168]

Another of his most abiding concerns was social reform for women. He pioneered instruction in midwifery and nursing, as well as the abolition of the veil. He was deeply concerned with the advancement of women, especially regarding their education, and told the Transvaal Muslim League in Johannesburg on August 12, 1945 that "if I had two children, and one was a boy and the other a girl, and if I could afford to educate only one, I would have no hesitation in giving the higher education to the girl." He states in his memoirs:

> I have always sought to encourage the emancipation and education of women. In my grandfather's and my father's time the Ismailis were far ahead of any other Muslim sect in the matter of the abolition of the strict veil, even in extremely conservative countries. I have absolutely abolished it; nowadays you will never find an Ismaili woman wearing the veil. Everywhere I have always encouraged girls' schools, even in regions where otherwise they were completely unknown. I say with pride that my Ismaili followers are, in this matter of social welfare, far in advance of any other Muslim sect.[169]

In his conception of the Ismaili faith and the authority of the Imam he was resolute, arguing firmly that they have remained unchanged since the genesis of the faith:

There has never been any question of changing the Ismaili faith; that faith has remained the same and must remain the same. Those who have not believed in it have rightly left it; we bear them no ill-will and respect them for their sincerity.[170]

In his political guidance to his Ismaili followers, he advocated the authority of the state in which they resided, and, interestingly, turned to the Christian scriptures to help validate this principle:[171]

It has been the practice of my ancestors, to which I have strictly adhered, always to advise Ismailis to be absolutely loyal and devoted subjects of the State—whatever its constitution, monarchical or republican—of which they are citizens. Neither my ancestors nor I have ever tried to influence our followers one way or another, but we have told them that the constituted legal authority of any country in which they abide must have their full and absolute loyalty. [...] All my teaching and my guidance for my followers has been in fulfilment of this principle: render unto God the things which are God's and to Caesar those which are Caesar's.[172]

His political ideals were decidedly democratic, expressed, for example, in his Presidential Address to the All-India Muslim Conference in Delhi on December 31, 1928, in which he declared:

You are part of [the people]. It is your duty to interpret as far as you can their wishes, their aspirations and their ideals ... The policy to be pursued during the immediate years, I would once more emphasize, must not be based on our personal views and predilections, but on what you know to be the general desires of the people to whom you belong.

Aga Khan III died in 1957, passing the Imamate to his twenty-one-year-old grandson, writing in his will that the young man would be able to manage the expectations and tribulations of the Atomic Age. Karim al-Husayni thus became the forty-ninth Imam and the fourth Aga Khan; he promptly took a year off from Harvard University to visit the Ismaili populations of the world. Recalling the socio-economic and educational concerns of previous Ismaili Imams, he founded the Aga Khan University, an international university based in Karachi, as well as the Aga Khan Development Network, one of the world's largest private development networks, which aims to improve living conditions and opportunities for the poor through localized and sustainable development.

The essence of the AKDN's development strategy, says Aga Khan IV, is to create or strengthen civil society in developing areas: "this single goal, when it is achieved, is in fact necessary and sufficient to ensure peaceful and stable development over the long term, even when governance is problematic."[173] But, he concludes, civil society cannot exist without apolitical and secular social, cultural, and economic institutions, the creation and sustenance of which are part of the challenge of international development.

He identifies four key areas of concern to meet this challenge, outlined in his speech at the graduation ceremony of the University of Alberta in June 2009.[174] His comments represent the contemporary attitude of the Ismaili movement. First, he identifies the faltering instruments of government in many Asian and African countries. These governments, he says, are "plagued by dysfunctional constitutional frameworks which ignore inherited traditions, poorly apportion responsibilities among central versus provincial authorities, fail to ensure equity and liberty for minority and tribal communities, and are unresponsive to their vast rural populations." Students of government can help correct this inequity, he says, and educational institutions should give more attention to disciplines of comparative government.

The second topic he raises is the enormous impact of civil society in the development process:

> Even when governments are fragile, or even nearly paralyzed in their functioning, strong civil society organizations can advance the social and economic order as they have done in Kenya and Bangladesh. Civil society

is a complex matrix of influences, but its impact can be enormous, especially in rural environments, where, for example, the need for stronger secondary as well as primary schools is dramatically evident.

His third theme is ethics:

> When we talk about the ethical realm, when we attack corruption, we are inclined to think primarily about government and politics. I am one, however, who believes that corruption is just as acute, and perhaps even more damaging, when the ethics of the civil and private sectors deteriorate. [...] When a construction company cheats on the quality of materials for a school or a bridge, when a teacher skimps on class work in order to sell his time privately, when a doctor recommends a drug because of incentives from a pharmaceutical company, when a bank loan is skewed by kickbacks, or a student paper is plagiarized from the internet - when the norms of fairness and decency are violated in any way, then the foundations of society are undermined. And the damage is felt most immediately in the most vulnerable societies, where fraud is often neither reported nor corrected, but simply accepted as an inevitable condition of life.

He singles out universities as among the institutions that can respond most effectively to such threats:

> It seems to me to be the responsibility of educators everywhere to help develop "ethically literate" people who can reason morally whenever they analyse and resolve problems, who see the world through the lens of ethics, who can articulate their moral reasoning clearly - even in a world of cultural and religious diversity - and have the courage to make tough choices.

The fourth theme he highlights is "the centrality of pluralism as a way of thinking in a world which is simultaneously becoming more diversified and more interactive." Pluralism, in his conception, goes beyond the acceptance of difference; it embraces human difference and regards encounters with others as opportunities rather than threats. It does not mean homogenization; rather, it means recognizing the role of individual identity in the goal of cooperative collaboration. The failure of pluralism, he argues, has had dramatic consequences, and he lists affected areas like Pakistan, Afghanistan, India, Sri Lanka, Kenya, Rwanda, Iraq, Congo, the Balkans, and Northern Ireland. "[N]o continent," he declares, "has been spared."

The role of education here is paramount, he insists:

> A pluralistic attitude is not something with which people are born. An instinctive fear of what is different is perhaps a more common human trait. But such fear is a condition which can be transcended - and that is why teaching about pluralism is such an important objective - at every educational level. In the final analysis, no nation, no race, no individual has a monopoly of intelligence or virtue. If we are to pursue the ideal of meritocracy in human endeavour, then its most perfect form will grow out of a respect for human pluralism, so that we can harness the very best contributions from whomever and wherever they may come.

This matrix of themes explains and undergirds the work of the AKDN, which the Aga Khan articulates as being a function of his office as Imam, following in the tradition of previous Imams to employ the institutions of the day to further the ends of just governance, pluralism, and education.

According to Asani, the institutionalizing work of the Aga Khans is a crucial element in the effort to forge the modern pan-Ismaili identity. In his articulation, the Aga Khans, through various institutions, "modernized the structure and ethos of the Ismaili Khoja communities," thereby "formulating doctrines, religious practices and forms of devotional literature so that they would be aligned with universally accepted idioms of the Islamic tradition, while at the same time reinforcing the core of the Shi`i Ismaili principles of the faith."[175] These principles were solidified in the 1986 Ismaili constitution, which "expresses Ismaili identity in pan-Islamic and pan-Ismaili terms" and reiterates Ismaili ideas within an Islamic framework.[176]

The constitution provided legal recognition for the new international and cosmopolitan Ismaili community and is thus a pivotal moment in Ismaili history because, says Asani, it symbolizes the transnationalization process.[177] For Asani, the Khoja community's movement from a culturally specific faith into a global Muslim community sharing a distinctive interpretation of Islam is a process that was led solely by the Islamic institution of the Ismaili Imamate. That institution and its defining doctrine of the ultimate authority of a living Imam, he says, is the bedrock of Shi`i identity and gives the Ismailis of the world their unique identity among Muslims today.[178] And the role of Aga Khan IV, he asserts, has been pivotal in negotiating the balance between tradition and modernity, and in navigating the cross-cultural encounters between Ismailis from India, Central Asia, Africa, the Middle East, North America, and Europe.

Coda

The evolving body of contemporary historiography on the critical phases in the development of the Ismaili tradition advances a distinct narrative account that contains a number of normative hermeneutical positions. They could be summarized as follows.

The Qur'an articulates no best model of governance. Rather, it emphasizes the importance of *ethical* governance and any system that ensures social justice. The history of the Ismaili community reflects this typically Qur'anic model of applying ethical ideals in different forms in different times, according to the needs of the day. At times they ruled over states, and at other times they were in hiding, but the ethical teachings of the Imams seem to have remained consistent over time, always emphasizing the important roles of education and pluralism in the inculcation and maintenance of justice. Indeed, when they controlled the Fatimid state, they employed meritocratic pluralism to rule over a populace in which they were the minority.

For the Imams, headship of the Muslim community was both a birthright and a duty, as they perceived the creation of justice as essential to their function. And, certainly, when they entered Egypt victorious and when their revolutionary movement continued in Persia, they were hailed by the people as an appealing substitute to previously unjust rulers. To be sure, their political successes owed much to the effectiveness of their *da`wa* network, a highly skilled propaganda machine whose primary function was to cultivate and disseminate knowledge of the Ismaili faith. Knowledge and learning were central to Ismailism from the beginning, since the conception of the Imam as the font of divine knowledge is their core doctrine.

The *da`wa* network can be said to represent the interaction between faith and world that typifies Ismailism. It was an institution that existed because of the doctrinal necessity to learn from and propagate the Imam's divine knowledge, but it was also a political enterprise because of its belief in the Imam's divinely legislated right and duty to rule and protect. In a sense, the Ismailis have always been a revolutionary movement, as they sought to replace the injustice of pretenders with the justice of the Imam— an ideal they propagated through a network of learning characterized by a pluralism of both thought and culture.

The intermingling of thought and culture is a natural consequence of human interaction, but *active* intermingling—pluralism—is taken up by contemporary Ismailism as a defining ethic. The subtlety of that activity can be seen in the noticeable tinge of Shi`i, and specifically Ismaili, ideas in Rumi's poems—ideas which are typically attributed to the influence of his spiritual preceptor, Shams-i Tabrizi, who Virani indicates was a descendent of the Ismaili Imams.[179]

That America's best-selling poet is an eighth-century Central Asian Muslim mystic is remarkable in a post-9/11 society.[180] In some ways, that Rumi reaches out to an audience separated by time and prejudice with words suffused with Ismaili ideas is an indicator, for Ismailis, of the tradition's esoteric power and enduring relevance. Perhaps, too, it is viewed as an indicator of its universalism, for Rumi can be eternally relevant only if he plumbs a universal gnosis and, as Halm writes, Ismailism is "a gnostic tradition on a par with the well-known creators of earlier Gnostic systems such as Simon Magus, Valentinian, or Mani."[181] Indeed, Rumi's contemporary relevance is apparent in the "Song of the Reed," quoted in this chapter's final epigraph, which speaks of the pain of separation—a metaphor applicable to the modern man's quest to be no longer enclosed in his own heart, to paraphrase Alexis de Tocqueville, and to reconnect with "a sense of a higher purpose, of something worth dying for,"[182] as Charles Taylor words it.

The reed, plucked from its bed, harks back for the time when he was one with his source. That, too, is true of contemporary Ismailism, which views itself as a tradition spread across history and geography like a reed carried on the wind, and which seeks in its contemporary self-narrative to return to its source by presenting the tradition as grounded in an eternal ethic, unbounded by time, yet ever present in history.

4

ISMAILI APPROACHES TO THE QUR'AN

I

Elucidating the esoteric nature of the Qur'an is the defining feature of Ismaili hermeneutics. Building on their essential conception of the dual and complementary nature of all things, the Ismailis used the foundational doctrine of *ta'wil* (esoteric exegesis) to interpret Qur'anic concepts. *Ta'wil*—allegorical or symbolical interpretation—came to be the "hallmark" of Ismailism, says Daftary.[1] Even when the Ismailis lived in difficult times, writes Steigerwald, "they were still the champions of *batin* (the 'inner meaning' of revelation)."[2] This commitment, she argues, is due to the Nizari belief in the necessity of the Imam, the "speaking Qur'an" who must be accessible in the physical world and whose function it is to interpret the Qur'an for the present time.[3]

The immediate origins of the Ismaili *ta'wil* are Islamic, says Daftary, and can be traced to the Shi`i circles of the eighth century CE.[4] The purpose of the *ta'wil* was to unveil the true spiritual reality by making what was hidden manifest. The truths behind the revealed scriptures and laws could be made apparent by this method, the Ismailis argued. The *ta'wil*, writes Daftary, "supplemented the Qur'anic worldview with a more elaborate view which rapidly developed into an intellectual system."[5] Indeed, writes Steigerwald, the Ismaili method of approaching the Qur'an is intellectual: "the Ismailis seek to understand the Qur'an by penetrating to the roots, and then retrieving and disclosing that which is interior or hidden."[6]

II

During the early phase of Ismailism, the Ismailis were in a "Period of Concealment" (*dawr al-satr*). Due to this, the early exegetes of *ta'wil* are confined to the tenth-century Ikhwan al-Safa ("Brethren of Purity"), though their work presents no systematic exposition of *ta'wil*.

The Fatimid period (909–1094), however, was a time of great intellectual output for the Ismaili *da'is* (missionary-scholars). In her article on Ismaili *ta'wil*, Steigerwald outlines a history of Ismaili thinkers, all of whose works are exemplars of *ta'wil*. The Ismaili theosophy was initially structured by the *da'is* al-Nasafi (d. 942); Abu Hatim al-Razi (d. 933–4), who wrote *Kitab a'lam al-nubuwwa* ("The Book of Signs of Prophecy"); Abu Ya'qub al-Sijistani (d. tenth century), whose works include *Kashf al-mahjub* ("Unveiling of the Hidden") and *Kitab al-yanabi* ("The Book of Sources"); and al-Qadi al-Nu'man (d. 974), well-known for his *Ta'wil al-da'a'im* ("The Spiritual Exegesis of the Pillars of Islam") and *Asas al-ta'wil* ("The Foundation of Spiritual Exegesis").[7]

Later Fatimid theosophy was cemented by Hamid al-Din al-Kirmani (d. 1024), who wrote *Rahat al-'aql* ("The Tranquility of Intellect"); Nasir Khusraw's (d. 1072) works, such as *Gushayish wa Rahayish* ("Knowledge and Liberation"); and "The Assemblies" (*Al-Majalis*) of al-Mu'yyad fi'l-Din al-Shirazi (d. 1078).[8]

Due to the scattered nature of the Alamut period (1124–1256), there are fewer but nevertheless important exegetes. These thinkers, like their Fatimid predecessors, wrote large volumes on all aspects of Ismaili theosophy, framing their arguments through esoteric exegeses of the Qur'an. Al-Shahrastani (d. 1153) was an influential historian who adhered to Nizari Ismailism secretly, but wrote an esoteric commentary on the Qur'an entitled *Mafatih al-asrar* ("Keys to the Arcana"). Nasir al-Din al-Tusi (d. 1274), the most well-known Alamut-period writer, was also one of the most influential Islamic polymaths. He converted to Ismailism (and, some argue, later recanted because of persecution), but left behind an in-depth exposition of Ismaili thought called *Rawdat al-Taslim* ("Paradise of Submission"). After the fall of Alamut in 1256, the Ismailis entered their second Period of Concealment, a period with a dearth of both information and output. Two notable post-Alamut thinkers, however, are the *da'i* Abu Ishaq-i Quhistani (d. 1480) and the Imam Mustansir bi'llah II (d. 1480), the latter of whom provided instruction to his followers in his *Pandiyat-i Jawanmardi* ("Advices of Manliness").

The next phase of Ismaili history, called by some scholars the Anjudan period (1320–1818) is characterized by Pirs (*hujja*), the second-most-important dignitary after the Imam in the spiritual hierarchy.[9] The most important Pirs were Pir Shams (d. mid fourteenth century), Pir Sadr al-Din (d. end fourteenth century), and Pir Hasan Kabir al-Din (d. end fifteenth century). "The Pirs composed *Ginan*s (mystical odes) which give an esoteric interpretation of the Qur'an and contain moral and religious instructions leading to the *sat panth* ('true path' or *al-sirat al-mustaqim*)."[10] In their attempt to convert Hindus, the Nizari Pirs presented the spirit and philosophies of Islam using vernacular religious terms and scriptures, such as the *Ginan*s, which were an already popular form of religious literature. Giving the *ta'wil* of the Qur'an in their *Ginan*s, the Pirs presented Islam as the final Veda and thus the final phase of Hinduism.[11]

Steigerwald defines the exegetes of the modern period as Pir Shihab al-Din Shah (d. 1885), the son of Aga Khan II; Aga Khan III (d. 1957); and Aga Khan IV. The current Imam, she says, provides a spiritual exegesis suited for modern times because it promotes an intellectual approach to the Qur'an and the use of `aql (intellect) to acquire knowledge.[12]

Contemporary Ismaili scholars reinforce the importance of intellect as the means to understanding the spiritual realities of the Qur'an. While no new works of *ta'wil* are published by Institute of Ismaili Studies (IIS) scholars, there are Ismaili thinkers such as Allamah Nasir Hunzai in Pakistan who, building on the work of past Ismaili thinkers as well as their own spiritual experiences, do produce works of *ta'wil* for their own audiences. The IIS, being a Western academic institution, publishes edited and translated editions of works of Ismaili *ta'wil* from the past. Scholars connected to the IIS like Bulbul Shah, Azim Nanji, and Faquir M. Hunzai, as well as Paul E. Walker, Toby Mayer, and S. J. Badakhchani, all work to explicate the ideas of the thinkers mentioned above.

III

At the core of both historical and contemporary Ismaili thought is the notion that there are multiple levels of meaning in the Qur'an, the understanding of which are predicated on the use of *ta'wil* to arrive at the root of the original meaning.[13] It views this principle as embedded in the internal logic of the Qur'an as well as the history of Ismaili Qur'anic interpretation. Citing verse 51:49 ("And of everything have We created in pairs [*zawjayn*], that you may reflect"), the *da'i* al-Nu'man expresses the typically Ismaili idea that everything has two aspects: the exoteric (*zahir*) and the esoteric (*batin*). To exemplify this complementary duality, he says that the human body has two entities—the body and the soul—of which one is evident and the other is hidden. According to IIS scholar Bulbul Shah: "He defines the exoteric aspect (*zahir*) as perceptible through the senses and the esoteric aspect (*batin*) as comprehended by knowledge."[14] While *batin* is the true object of knowledge, it does not invalidate the *zahir*. Nanji explains: "[The *batin*] represented a dimension which went beyond the *zahir* by elaborating its meaning rather than contradicting it. Thus Ismaili thought did not deny a literal interpretation, it merely pointed out that such an interpretation was incomplete."[15]

In Shi'i Islam, says Hunzai, *ta'wil* is necessary to fulfill the purpose of religion, since the Qur'an informs about the next world, which is imperceptible to human senses. *Ta'wil* is a hermeneutical approach used to understand the inner meaning (*batin*) of revelation. The complement to *ta'wil* is *tanzil*, the part of revelation that defines life's formal aspects, what Nanji calls "the vessels within which the truths are contained."[16] The *da'i* al-Sijistani explains: "*tanzil* is similar to the raw materials, while the *ta'wil* resembles the manufactured goods."[17]

Ta'wil, says the *da'i* Nasir, "is to take the perceptible things back to their original state."[18] This is, in fact, its lexical root, namely "to cause a thing to return to its beginning or origin." "In Ismaili terminology," writes Hunzai, "it means to cause spiritual realities that are revealed in the form of parables (*amthal*) to return to their origin, the spiritual world."

The *da'i* al-Kirmani, like other *da'i*s, argues that human intellects cannot recognize the imperceptible realities of the Qur'an except through the perceptible examples and practices taught by the prophets. Importantly, however, since God commanded the Prophet to invite people on the basis of wisdom (Q. 16:125), these examples have to be based on the foundation of intellect and logic.[19] "But," according to al-Kirmani, "the *zahir* or exoteric aspect of the Qur'an and the *shari'a*, which the Prophet brought, conflicts with the rules of intellect."[20]

By way of example, the *da`i* discusses the apparent difficulty of God taking covenant from the children of Adam, while at the same time, God has elsewhere commanded that one cannot accept the testimony of children:

> [...] such as the verse "And when your Lord brought forth from the children of Adam, from their reins, their seed, and made them testify of themselves, (saying): Am I not your Lord? They said: Yes verily" (Qur'an 71:72). The impossibility of bringing forth the children of Adam as particles and to take covenant of His Lordship from them, has created difficulties explaining this for the people of the *zahir* for elsewhere He commands that one cannot accept the testimony of children, let alone babies or seed, because they are not yet of an age where they are obliged to observe the requirements of religion. [...] But, as the Prophet is a sage and free from ignorance, it becomes necessary to look beyond the exoteric aspect of what the Prophet has brought so that it is not devoid of meanings with which the intellect can agree and the revelation can be established as true and full of wisdom.[21]

"These meanings," al-Kirmani concludes, "are called *ta'wil*."[22]

IV

"As the *ta'wil* unfolds," writes Nanji, "it moves always from the level of the specific and temporal to that of the cosmic and eternal." It is rooted in the community and in tradition, but "it builds and shapes itself until the individual experiences it as part of his intellectual and spiritual growth."[23]

He gives the example of the *da`i* al-Shirazi's interpretation of verse 7:54, "God created the heavens and the earth in six days." Al-Shirazi argues that "day" here does not refer to the conception of days as measured by the rising and setting of the sun, since there was no sun before creation. It would be absurd, the *da`i* asserts, to suppose such a measurement of time over God's creative power, which, as other Qur'anic verses attest, He employs at will, creating things faster than the twinkling of the eye.

Al-Shirazi thus concludes that the reference to heaven, earth, and the days has nothing to do with how they are typically conceived.

The *ta'wil* of the verse, according to him, is that the reference to six days connotes the six cycles of Prophecy—referring to the six Speaking-prophets (*natiqs*) of the Qur'an: Adam, Noah, Abraham, Moses, Jesus, and Muhammad—each of which represents a time-cycle. Each of the days, says al-Shirazi, represents the fulfillment of the creative process embodied in the mission of the six prophets. Nanji clarifies: "Each Prophetic mission is to provide a *shari'a*, a pattern of life revealed to ensure that society will conform to the Divine Command. Each action contained in the *shari'a*, according to Ismaili thought, reflects a passage in one's inner growth and must be accompanied by a deeper spiritual understanding to guide the act."[24]

Reflecting this idea is the *da'i* Tusi's explanation of the seven pillars of religious law, each of which he says has been assigned a spiritual meaning and truth. The Prophet's mission, he says, was "expressed in the form of creaturely realities consisting of divine mandates, physical substances made from spiritual substances, practical activities based on intellectual realities [etc.],"[25] and there is thus an esoteric exegesis to all the Prophet's teachings.

He goes on to explain the inner realities of the seven pillars: ritual ablutions (*tahara*) means to "disassociate oneself from previous religious customs and traditions"; the profession of faith (*shahada*) means to "know God through Himself"; ritual prayer (*namaz*) means to have perpetually the knowledge of God in mind; fasting (*ruza*) means to practice precautionary dissimulation (*taqiyya*) by not revealing the esoteric meanings of the Qur'an to all and sundry; alms-giving (*zakat*) means to impart to one's brothers in religion what has been imparted unto one; pilgrimage (*hajj*) means to "abandon this temporal world and seek the eternal abode"; holy war (*jihad*) means "to annihilate oneself in the Essence of God Almighty."[26]

V

One may ask now, what is the source of the *ta'wil*, of the esoteric exegesis that informs the opinions and writings of the Ismaili *da'is*? The designated Imam, says al-Nu'man, is the source of the knowledge of the *batin*. The *zahir* (exoteric), he writes, is the miracle of the prophets while the *batin* (esoteric) is the miracle of the Imams.[27] According to al-Sijistani, the prophet's role is to bring *tanzil* (Revelation) and the *shari`a* (Law) to the people while the function of the successor is to reveal gradually the hidden meanings through *ta'wil*.[28] "It is the practitioner of the *ta'wil*," he writes, "who extracts the intended meaning from each word and puts everything in its proper place."[29]

Ismaili thinkers typically argue that the Qur'an makes reference to the necessity for *ta'wil* and its practitioners in verse 3:7: "He it is Who has revealed unto you (Muhammad) the Book wherein are clear verses. They are the mother of the Book and others are allegorical. But those in whose heart is perversity, pursue the part thereof that is allegorical, seeking discord, and searching for its *ta'wil*, but no one knows its *ta'wil* except Allah and those who are firmly grounded in knowledge (*al-rasikhun fi'l-`ilm*) saying: 'We believe in it (Book); the whole is from our Lord; but only men of understanding really heed.'"

This is a typically Shi`i reading of this verse, which does not put a full stop after the word "Allah," thereby maintaining that the *ta'wil* of the allegorical verses is known to Allah as well as "those who are firmly grounded in knowledge" (*rasikhun fi'l-`ilm*), who they argue are the Imams following `Ali ibn Abi Talib. On the other hand, some commentators maintain that the *ta'wil* of the Qur'an is not possible and thus place a full stop after "Allah," thereby confining the knowledge of the *ta'wil* to Allah only and considering *rasikhun fi'l-`ilm* a new subject.[30] Such commentators, says Hunzai, are the Literalists—those who do not seek deeper allegorical meanings beyond the apparent wording of the Qur'an.

Hunzai recounts the commentary of Ibn Qutayba, a prominent ninth-century Sunni scholar, who argues that according to Arabic grammar there should be no full stop.[31] Ibn Qutayba contends that it is logically fallacious to suggest that no one but Allah should have knowledge of the *ta'wil* because (1) that would mean that the Prophet did not know the *ta'wil* of the allegorical verses, and (2) "those who are firmly grounded in knowledge" would have no special knowledge to distinguish themselves from the ignorant Muslims, thereby invalidating any supposed special rank.

Hunzai further explains that those who maintain that the *rasikhun fi'l-`ilm* know the *ta'wil* are divided into two groups. For those who argue that truth can be arrived at through logic and speculation, anyone who attains enough knowledge of the Qur'an, the Prophetic tradition, and classical Arabic literature can claim to be among the *rasikhun fi'l-`ilm*. For those who claim to attain truth or *ta'wil* from the infallible Imam, the *rasikhun fi'l-`ilm* are the Imams from the house of the Prophet, namely `Ali and his designated descendents.[32]

In the Ismaili sources, writes Hunzai, it appears that the *ta'wil* in the case of the prophets and the Imams is not something acquired, but is given or taught directly by God. Thus, it is perfect and complete knowledge of who and what has passed and who and what is to come. However, since people do not have the capacity to grasp all this knowledge at once, it is revealed gradually and continuously through the chain of Imams. "It is because of this perfect and firm knowledge," concludes Hunzai, "that the Prophet and the Imams are called the *rasikhun fi'l-`ilm*."[33]

VI

In his memoirs, Aga Khan III explains the role of the Imam as:

> [...] the successor of the Prophet in his religious capacity; he is the man who must be obeyed and who dwells among those from whom he commands spiritual obedience ... The Shias say that this authority is all-pervading and is concerned with spiritual matters also, that it is transferred by inherited right to the Prophet's successors of his blood.[34]

He warns readers of the Qur'an "not to allow their material critical outlook to break in with literal, verbal explanations of something that is symbolic and allegorical."[35] He expounds further on his approach to the Qur'an:

> Fortunately the Koran has itself made this task easy, for it contains a number of verses which declare that Allah speaks to man in allegory and parable. Thus the Koran leaves the door open for all kinds of possibilities of interpretation so that no one interpreter can accuse another of being non-Muslim. A felicitous effect of this fundamental principle of Islam that the Koran is constantly open to allegorical interpretation has been that our Holy Book has been

able to guide and illuminate the thought of believers, century after century, in accordance with the conditions and limitations of intellectual appreciation imposed by external influences in the world. It leads also to a greater charity among Muslims, for since there can be no cut-and-dried interpretation, all schools of thought can unite in the prayer that the Almighty in His infinite mercy may forgive any mistaken interpretation of the Faith whose cause is ignorance or misunderstanding.[36]

At the "Word of God, Art of Man: The Qur'an and its Creative Expressions" Colloquium in London on October 19, 2003, Aga Khan IV expressed a similar understanding of the Qur'an as deeper than textual:

Scientific pursuits, philosophic inquiry and artistic endeavour are all seen as the response of the faithful to the recurring call of the Qur'an to ponder the creation as a way to understand Allah's benevolent majesty. As Sura al-Baqara proclaims: "Wherever you turn, there is the face of Allah." Does not the Qur'an challenge the artist, as much as the mystic, to go beyond the physical - the outward - so as to seek to unveil that which lies at the centre but gives life to the periphery?[37]

He concludes, alluding that the Qur'an's infinity of interpretation reflects the pluralism of humankind:

The Qur'an's is an inclusive vision of society that gives primacy to nobility of conduct. It speaks of differences of language and colour as a divine sign of mercy and a portent for people of knowledge to reflect upon. Ours is a time when knowledge and information are expanding at an accelerating and, perhaps, unsettling pace. There exists, therefore, an unprecedented capacity for improving the human condition. And yet, ills such as abject poverty and ignorance, and the conflicts these breed, continue to afflict the world. The Qur'an addresses this challenge eloquently. The power of its message is reflected in its gracious disposition to differences of interpretation; its respect for other faiths and societies; its affirmation of the primacy of the intellect; its insistence that knowledge is worthy when it is used to serve Allah's creation; and, above all, its emphasis on our common humanity.[38]

VII

"The Ismailis," writes Steigerwald, "attempted to raise human consciousness to a higher plane."[39] Ismailism, she says, is not a philosophy or a theology, but a theosophy (divine wisdom), and by interweaving elements of the Qur'an, the science of the cosmos, and neo-Platonism, the Ismailis built a remarkable speculative system that provides a rich and coherent worldview.[40] By penetrating to the roots of the Qur'an and disclosing what is hidden, "they engage both the intellect and the spirit in order to discover the truths"[41] that are at the essence of the Revelation.

Ta'wil thus opened the door to an infinity of possibilities about how to implement the Qur'anic ethic in different times and spaces, allowing it to adapt to the norms of the day. In the contemporary context, the hermeneutical principle of allegory leads to an emphasis on the value of diverse and evolving interpretations open to new cultural and intellectual developments. One could argue that historical Ismaili allegorical interpretation did not accent themes like diversity, tolerance, or reform, but the Ismailis nevertheless conceive of an interpretative outlook that fits well in the modern world, where the liberal values of pluralism and openness are prized. Indeed, contemporary Ismaili allegorical interpretations—as evinced by the quote from Aga Khan IV above—seek to articulate Qur'anic ethics in the language of contemporary liberal ethics like pluralism, which is at the center of contemporary Ismailism.

5

The AKDN in Afghanistan:
Ethos and Praxis

*I have never met anybody who not only has the vision but has
the personal management capacity to be able to take these visions
and realize them ... [The Aga Khan] has a wonderful way of
doing it, which perhaps gives him an advantage over most of the
rest of us, in that he draws on remarkable experts, but he makes
the decisions ... [He] is one person who stands out in my mind
as an icon of not only thought and philosophy but of action.*
— James Wolfensohn, former president of the
World Bank Group

In his keynote address at the Governor General's Canadian Leadership
Conference in Quebec on May 19, 2004, the Aga Khan stated that his
involvement in development is motivated by his interpretation of Islamic
ethics. The Aga Khan Development Network (AKDN), he says, is an
institutional embodiment of Islamic ethics:

> The engagement of the Imamat in development is guided
> by Islamic ethics, which bridge faith and society. It is on
> this premise that I established the Aga Khan Development
> Network. This Network of agencies, known as the AKDN,
> has long been active in many areas of Asia and Africa to
> improve the quality of life of all who live there. These
> areas are home to some of the poorest and most diverse
> populations in the world.[1]

He further articulated that the Network's concrete experience on the ground has taught that democracy cannot function without two preconditions: civil society and pluralism. Civil society, he says, provides citizens with channels through which to exercise both the rights and duties of citizenship. And, more importantly, only a strong civil society—even at a very basic level—can assure equity and personal security for isolated rural populations and the marginalized urban poor. The erosion of social pluralism, he says, plays a significant role in breeding destructive conflict. Thus, the development of robust civil society associations and the cooperation of peoples and organizations of diverse backgrounds and interests "is no less important than human rights for ensuring peace, successful democracy and a better quality of life."

In the Address, the Aga Khan points to the network's work in Northern Pakistan over the last twenty years as an example of how isolated and poor rural communities living in a harsh mountain desert ecosystem have been able, over time, "to create sustainable, inclusive processes of development in which diverse communities could participate together and seek joint solutions to common problems." He continues to say that such endeavors—which in this case benefited from the partnership of the Canadian International Development Agency (CIDA)—demonstrate that "the careful, patient development of institutions of civil society helped to create the capacity to manage and legitimise pluralism."

Part I: The AKDN
The Network
The Aga Khan Development Network describes itself on its website as a group of development agencies that focus on economic, social, and cultural development. The various agencies of the network have mandates that include the environment, health, education, architecture, culture, microfinance, rural development, disaster reduction, the promotion of private-sector enterprise, and the revitalization of historic cities.[2] AKDN agencies such as Aga Khan Health Services (AKHS), Aga Khan Agency for Microfinance (AKAM), Aga Khan Fund for Economic Development (AKFED), and Aga Khan Trust for Culture (AKTC), to name a few, are

expected to conduct their programs without regard to faith, ethnic origin, or gender.[3]

Malise Ruthven argues in the 2011 IIS volume on Ismaili history that the AKDN "eludes familiar definitions" because of the range and complexity of its organization and activities.[4] In his words, the AKDN "is neither a non-governmental organization (NGO) concerned with international development nor a faith-based charity (although it has some characteristics of both)." And, "in several countries its representatives enjoy diplomatic statues and have close relationship with governments, allowing them to engage in policy discussions at the highest levels. However, they are not state actors and operate within a tradition of strict political neutrality."[5]

According to the AKDN website, the network's agencies are "private, international, non-denominational development organizations" that work to improve the welfare of people in the developing world, particularly in Asia and Africa.[6] Each agency—registered in Switzerland as nonprofit institutions—has its own mandate, but they work together within the network's overarching framework "so that their different pursuits interact and reinforce one another."[7] An interesting aspect of the network is that in addition to its not-for-profit activities, it views for-profit enterprises as essential to its development strategies. According to Ruthven, these enterprises—clustered under the Aga Khan Fund for Economic Development (AKFED)—"are not conventional capitalist entities aimed at maximizing profits but rather companies whose primary aim is to foster economic development," and thus the network "does not fit the model of the business conglomerate that claims to be committed to 'good corporate citizenship.'"[8] Rather, says Ruthven, the Aga Khan "takes a long-term view, aiming to ensure that the businesses become self-sustaining by achieving 'operational break-even,' within a 'logical time frame.'"[9]

The network operates in thirty countries and employs approximately 80,000 people. Most of the work is based in developing countries, though notable programs in education and culture operate in Europe and North America as well. Its annual budget for nonprofit development in 2010 was approximately US$625 million.[10] At the same time, the project companies of AKFED—the only for-profit agency in the AKDN, which cofinances major infrastructure projects such as the Roshan mobile phone network in Afghanistan and the Bujagali hydroelectric project in Uganda—generated revenues of US$2.3 billion, the surpluses of which are reinvested in further development activities.

A significant portion of the funding for development activities comes from national governments, multilateral institutions, and private sector partners;[11] the Aga Khan regularly signs memorandums of agreement with various governments and multinational organizations across the world. As well, the Aga Khan provides funding for administration and new initiatives, while the Ismaili community contributes volunteer time, professional services, and "substantial" financial resources.[12] Another significant source is the fundraising activities of the Partnership Walks and Partnership Golf tournaments held in Canada, the US, and the UK, all of which are organized by Aga Khan Foundation (AKF) affiliates, which are registered as nonprofit organizations in their respective countries.

While several AKDN agencies were established initially to meet the needs of the Ismaili community in South Asia and East Africa, the network has grown under the leadership of the Aga Khan to encompass projects in areas where there are many faiths and ethnicities, and where Ismailis are not living, such as Egypt, the Kyrgyz Republic, and Mali. In fact, Ismaili communities are now explicitly excluded as a specific focus of AKDN work: "Ismaili communities in poor and remote areas do benefit from AKDN projects, but the programmes, when at full scale, typically benefit a wide cross-section of the population."[13] As well, it puts an emphasis on the role of Ismaili volunteers, which it says are working within a historic tradition of voluntary service to assist in the implementation and maintenance of projects.

The Ethic

The Institute of Ismaili Studies in 2000 prepared an important document for the AKDN called "Aga Khan Development Network (AKDN): An Ethical Framework," which argues that the work of the AKDN is motivated by certain key Islamic ethical perspectives, such as inclusiveness, inquiry, good governance, compassion, self-reliance, respect for life, and sustainable environmental development.[14] According to the document, the AKDN is a "contemporary endeavour of the Ismaili Imamat to realise the social conscience of Islam through institutional action," and its "combined mandate is to help relieve society of ignorance, disease and deprivation," without regard to faith or ethnicity. The driving impetus of the network, says the document, is the bridging in Islam of the two realms of faith—*din* (faith) and *dunya* (world), the spiritual and the material.

In this conception of Islam, the material life must be dignified, as it is the receptacle of the soul, and so it is one's responsibility to help one's fellow man become self-reliant and become able to help those weaker than themselves. The "Ethical Framework" document, alluding to key Qur'anic verses, offers a theological grounding for this ethical perspective: "The central emphasis of Islam's ethical ideal is enablement of each person to live up to his exalted status as vicegerent of God on earth, in whom God has breathed His own spirit and to whom He has made whatever is in the heavens and the earth an object of trust and quest." It contends that worship is not only service of God but also service to humanity, because righteousness, says the Qur'an, is not only fulfilling one's religious obligations; "without social responsibility," it says, "religiosity is a show of conceit."

By making societal values a principle of human moral responsibility to the Divine, Islam makes the sense of public and social order transcendent. The document argues that while personal moral responsibility is a central demand of the faith, Islam's vision for social order is buttressed on the expectation of each individual's morally just conduct toward others. "The function of ethics," it concludes, "is to foster self-realisation through giving of one's self, for the common good, in response to God's benevolent majesty."

This is part of the Prophetic example, it says, whose lasting legacy for Muslims everywhere is the suffusion of daily life with the sense of the spiritual. Within Shi`a Islam, the responsibility to continue this legacy is inherited by each hereditary Imam from the Prophet's progeny, whose mandate—as the legatee of Prophetic authority—is to seek to realize that paradigm through an institutional order that suits the exigencies of the time and place. "In a world of flux," says the document, "the Imam gives leadership in the maintenance of balance between the spiritual and the material in the harmonious context of the ethics of the faith, of which he is the guardian." In this context, the AKDN, as an Imamate endeavor, seeks to realize the social vision of Islam through a communitarian strategy of social action. Thus, says the document, "although the outcome of its action is pragmatic, the motivation for it is spiritual."

One of the abiding traits of Islam's ethical ideal that informs the AKDN mandate is the ethic of inclusiveness. The document contends that Islam's is an inclusive vision of society that that invites people of all faiths to a common platform to "vie for goodness." Again alluding to key Qur'anic verses about pluralism, the document argues that the divine spark in each individual also bonds one to another in a common humanity, since the Qur'an says that humankind was created from a single soul so that people may come to know one another. The document then references the Prophetic example on this issue: "The Prophet sought to harness individual and group differences and talents to serve common needs of different religious groups, among whom he encouraged a spirit of harmony and toleration as constituents of a larger community of his time."

Another key ethic that informs the work of the AKDN is the ethic of education and research. "The key to the nature of society that Islam espouses," says the document, "is an enlightened mind, symbolized in the Qur'an's metaphor of creation, including one's self, as an object of rational quest." Further, it contends that the person of knowledge has the obligation to share it. To support the ethic of acquiring knowledge, the document quotes the Qur'an, the Prophet, the *da`i* (missionary-scholar) Nasir Khusraw, and Imam 'Ali, who said that "the most self-sustaining wealth is the intellect," which "gives one mastery over one's destiny."

The document asserts that, for the Muslims of history, the spirit of inquiry was an ethical duty, since the intellect is a divine gift to be cherished and cultivated. Further, it says that scientific research was considered a meritorious duty throughout Muslim history, and it was recognized as a way of intellectual growth. This is exemplified by the powerful intellectual institutions that cropped up all over the Muslim world, like Cairo, Baghdad, Cordova, Bukhara, and Samarqand. In this view, research "was the response of the faithful to the persistent call of the Quran to ponder creation in order to understand God's greatness."

The document contends that this spirit of inquiry was typified by a pluralism of thought, following the Prophetic tradition to "accept whatever adds to your wisdom, regardless of the nature of its source," leading ultimately to an attitude that cultivated an open and inquiring mind among Muslim thinkers. To further showcase the pluralism of thought evinced in Muslim history, the document quotes the ninth-century philosopher al-Kindi, who wrote that truth, whatever its source, never abases. It also provides the example of the medical philosopher Al-Razi (d. 925), who critically examined the work of Galen, as well as that of Ibn Haytham, whose examination of Euclid and Ptolemy laid the foundations for modern optics.

The document also highlights the important ethic of compassion and sharing, saying that the mark of an enlightened society is that it urges the care of the weak by the powerful. It makes a powerful argument that the pious are those who recognize that the indigent have a right to their wealth: "The pious are the socially conscious who recognise in their wealth a right for the indigent and the deprived whom they help for the sake of God alone." But charity is not just sharing one's material wealth. Rather, generosity extends to intellectual, spiritual, and physical gifts as well, and when withheld, "such gifts are a futile burden, 'a twisted collar tied to the miser's neck.'" The ethic of voluntary service is thus highlighted as an important trait of Muslim tradition, which the document links to the example of the *Ansar*, the citizens of Medina who helped the Prophet and his fellow fugitives from Mecca.

Tied to the ethic of compassion, however, is the ethic of self-reliance, which the document says appears frequently in Muslim tradition. It states: "Muslim ethic discourages a culture of dependency since it undermines one's dignity, preservation of which is emphatically urged in Muslim scripture. 'Man shall have only that for which he labours,' says the Quran." Thus, says the document, the emphasis of charitable effort has been, from the time of the Prophet, to help the needy become self-reliant.

Finally, an important ethic that the document says undergirds the AKDN is that of ethical governance. Muslim law, it says, is emphatic that the ethic of governance lies in the principles of "trust, probity, equity, and accountability." The scripture warns sternly against corruption and warns guardians of orphans and the weak not to compromise their fiduciary obligations. The document makes the point that the tradition "obliges administrators of a charitable foundation not only to maintain, but to seek to enhance, the value of its corpus and maximise its yield in order to sustain its charitable commitments." Above all, the document emphasizes the importance of the duty of trusteeship, saying that those who control and administer resources for others are bound by that duty. "In Shia Islam," it concludes, "this duty is owed to the Imam."

Ultimately, this is the network's foundational ethic—the Qur'anic dictum that humankind is the custodian of Earth and vicegerent of its creatures. It is the duty of the individual Muslim to work for the betterment of humankind, fulfilling the aforementioned Qur'anic dictum as well as the complementary tradition of voluntary service in Islam. For the Ismailis, the Imam is the ultimate authority and the duty of trusteeship thus falls to him, while the individual Ismaili works to achieve the goal outlined by the Imam according to the best of his or her capacity. In contemporary times, the Ismaili Imam seems to view the institutionalization of social action as the best means to fulfill the ethics mentioned above, which the AKDN says are the motivation for its existence and its work.

A Constructed Ethic?

In his anthropological study of the AKDN, Steinberg argues that Ismailis are made Ismaili through the global institutions. For example, he observes that the network's rural development programs instill liberal values into the communities in which it operates, as they "provide a forum for local participation in a global network and socialize the villagers to basic ideological tenets of liberal modernity, entrepreneurial capital, rational humanism, and civil society."[15]

He concedes that the institutions are not the sole element in determining Ismaili identity; but they are paramount, he believes, since "no instrument has been more significant for the unification and consolidation of disparate communities under a single Isma'ili banner than the construction of common institutions."[16] The institutions are the spaces "constitutive of the Isma'ili nonterritorial assemblage," as they are the spaces where global Ismailis move and thus where Ismaili transnationalism is created. These spaces are where modern Ismaili values are instilled and how modern Ismailis are unified. In his view, "the institutions provide a vehicle to bring those distant communities into the fold of the imamate (and the sphere of the Khojas); to socialize them to ideologies of modernity and capitalism; to teach them how to be Isma'ili in a modern way, or modern in an Isma'ili way; to ensure their active, loyal, and enthusiastic participation; and to produce from a fragmentary constellation a unitary ecumene or polity. In these global institutions in part Isma`ili subjects (local and transnational alike) are made Isma`ili."[17]

Additionally, he views the religious institutions of the Imamate as forming a prescriptive and centralized "formal, institutionalized religious structure of Isma`ilism."[18] The Isma`ili Tariqah and Religious Education Board (ITREB) (or Committee [ITREC] in Tajikistan) and the Institute of Ismaili Studies are *jama`ati* (religious) institutions that encourage uniformity in global Ismaili practice because they prescribe the current proper forms of worship and practice, acting as emissaries of the Imam in local and remote areas, where they carry out and enact the interpretation of his religious directives.[19] Here, the IIS—which is an umbrella institution for the local ITREBs in each region—is a particularly "important node in the Isma`ili transnational institutional structure, a key hub from which many connections radiate like spokes."[20]

The religious institutions, he says, play a central role in unifying the global Ismaili community by creating a "pan-Ismaili sense of connection"[21] through the "*creation* of Isma`ili images and discourses of the past, and the selective emphasis on certain elements of the past."[22] He argues that "the *jama`ati* institutions are central in the creation, negotiation, and refinement of Isma`ili images and imaginings of self. They are interested in and focused on the Isma`ili past, particularly as it relates to themes of `Alid descent and the Fatimid Empire. As is the case with many communities, for Isma`ilis history has become a central motif or emblem of contemporary identity."[23]

Importantly, Steinberg views this sort of identity construction as deliberately constructed and argues that modern Ismailism is a product of global politicoeconomic realities as well as the postcolonial discourse of empire and the resulting transformation of markets. He declares that "contemporary Isma`ilism is much less a product of the distant past its institutions focus on than of more recent developments."[24] In his view, then, the articulation of the "Ethical Framework" document outlined above would likely be seen as an attempt to construct a link between the work of the AKDN to a wider ethical framework.

An important institution in the "global semiotic process of the Isma`ili network," he asserts, is the Aga Khan Trust for Culture, which he says creates a "specifically imamate-driven" vision of Islam and its history.[25] This is most visible in the AKTC's Aga Khan Award for Architecture, which, by honoring architectural initiatives and restoration projects, may seem unusual because it focuses less on Ismailism and more on the recontextualization of wider Islamic elements. But, he concludes, it does concord with Ismaili traditions of opposition to mainstream discourses of Islam as well as its promotion of an alternative vision of the religion and its history.[26] More importantly, however, it sets up the Imam as a leader of the Islamic world in general: "it articulates with an image of the Isma`ili imam as a leader (and *the* true leader, at that) of the Islamic world, an author of the meaning and history of Islam itself; in his involvement with AKTC, he intertwines his position with the heritage of Islam at large."[27]

We are returned here to the perennial revolutionary aims of the Ismailis to establish their Imam at the head of the Muslim community. In the modern context, though, the role becomes ethicospiritual; the Imam appears now as the definer of an Islamic ethic that supports a Qur'anic vision for coexistence in a globalized world. To this end, the AKTC constructs "an official *culture*," which, by its choice of projects that "bear more than a tangential relationship to Isma`ili identity and metacultures of history," exhibits a "clear concern with the past, and more specifically, with the way that history is told."[28] For Steinberg, then, Ismaili institutions like the AKTC are "involved in the creation of alternative historical counterdiscourses, in the recasting and retelling of history."[29] In the contemporary context, the semiology of those institutions appears to Steinberg to reveal "an intense interest on their part in Enlightenment discourses and modernism and in their corresponding values of individualism, cooperation, rationalism, democracy, and industriousness (with reward)."[30]

While these values are consistent with the themes explicated by the IIS and articulated publicly by the Imam as Islamic/Ismaili values, Steinberg acknowledges that the institutions are not dedicated solely to socializing Ismaili communities to liberal values and consolidating the communities into a centralized, loyal structure.[31] He recognizes that the Aga Khan Foundation "has been lauded for its efforts in sustainable, participatory development," and that "the institutions serve many, and in the process, the survival of thousands of poor people is ensured."[32]

Nevertheless, he concludes that while the AKDN does not serve Ismailis exclusively, it typically works in areas where there is a receptive Ismaili community or Ismaili elite. He quotes personal communication with Tom Kessinger, AKDN's general manager in 2004, as defining AKDN's mandate as "development, in the broadest sense of the word, *for* Isma`ilis."[33] In the end, though, that is in line with the Imam's stated objective for establishing the network, which he articulates as a function of his office as Imam to improve the lives of his followers, an ethic that he believes informs the work of the AKDN, as articulated in the "Ethical Framework" document prepared by the IIS, an Imamate institution.

PART II: THE AKDN IN AFGHANISTAN

Perhaps it is typically Ismaili that a practical organization such as the AKDN articulates a complementary exposition of its ethics and motivations, such as in the "Ethical Framework" document. It seems to fulfill the oft-repeated Ismaili ethic of *din wa dunya*—the dual-edged principle that faith and action are interdependent.

On this view—considering both the stated ethical impetus and the practical work of the AKDN—the network appears as a carefully planned organization that is well respected for its socially concerned and often innovative work, especially in postconflict areas like Afghanistan, where the network was the first agency to begin operations after 9/11. Considering the amount of work the network does in Afghanistan, that country provides a useful example for a survey of how some of its projects are implemented. Along with the support of its donors and partners, more than US$700 million has been channelled through the AKDN for Afghanistan's reconstruction.[34] The stated goal of the AKDN's work in Afghanistan (and elsewhere) is to ensure stability and security. Recalling the ethics explained in its mandate, the various comments of its founder, as well as the needs of Afghanis, the network seems to be working toward the inculcation of a citizenry that is ethically educated, positively pluralist, and democratically inclined.

On July 20, 2010, in his statement at the Kabul Conference on Afghanistan, the Aga Khan once again stressed the importance of pluralism for the development of a stable and progressive Afghanistan; "in diversity lies strength," he said.[35] Further: "Pluralism—ethnic, linguistic, cultural and confessional—is critical for this country: mutual trust and respect amongst ethnic groups are essential if peace, stability and equitable development are to be achieved."

In his view, it is essential that Afghans take increasing responsibility for their affairs. It is vital, he says, for local government and development actors to work with local communities in order to identify pressing needs. He stresses the importance of local mechanisms for the success of future development projects: "The Government's ability fruitfully to absorb outside funding is dependent on the creation of Afghan-driven mechanisms to address security, justice and socio-economic growth." As well, in order for civil society to function and to ensure civilian order, it is necessary to strengthen and equip the police force. "It is my personal view," he says, "that military withdrawal and meaningful reintegration can only take place when Afghanistan has a sufficient and sufficiently equipped police force." Finally, he is concerned about reports from residents in stable areas of the country that resources are being directed away from them toward less secure parts of the country: "We believe that ensuring equity of investment across the country is essential."

As he continues, he discusses the particular role of the AKDN in Afghanistan. One concept he highlights as being increasingly utilized by the network is Multi-Input Area Develoment (MIAD). In their experience, working on multiple fronts (economic, social, cultural) "simultaneously and synergistically" is an effective way to spur progress on all fronts. To show how this works, he provides the example of the network's work on restoring historic monuments: "while undertaking the restoration work of, say, a monument or an historical building, one can create nearby a minor medical facility, launch educational programmes for adult education, literacy and early childhood education, undertake to improve the infrastructure around that monument, provide microfinance to the local citizens, help them maintain or upgrade their dwelling, and their shops, etc." In this way, he says, MIADs repeated in other areas can have an immediate impact on quality of life and, importantly, generate confidence in the future, as well as the inputs that have created positive change.

Another important way to create growth for the poor, he says, is willingness to support unconventional small- and medium-scale investments in the short term. Such investments "may not immediately be considered financially sustainable by conventional measures," he says, but "experience demonstrates are necessary to achieve medium to long-term returns and benefit." Perhaps an example of this sort of approach is the AKDN's recognition and utilization of Afghanistan's potential as a regional land bridge, which he says few other projects have realized: "the AKDN, in partnership with the Governments of Afghanistan and Tajikistan and the provincial governments of the Badakhshans of the two countries, has taken a regional approach to health, education, tourism, trade, energy and infrastructure, which has begun to yield tangible improvements in the lives of the local communities. Surely connecting Kabul to China through Tajikistan should open new trade corridors and multiply social and economic fallout benefits for the communities of those areas and thereby for the country as a whole."

Democracy

The Community Development Councils (CDCs)—established throughout Afghanistan under the government's National Solidarity Programme (NSP)—are democratically elected bodies charged with carrying out small development projects approved by the community. Funding is provided by a government grant, with 10 percent of the cost of projects (cash, labor, or materials) being provided by the community. The AKDN's Aga Khan Foundation (AKF) supports 1,254 councils in five provinces across Afghanistan. These councils, say the AKF, represent an institutional basis for more effective governance at the local level across rural Afghanistan, effectively extending democratic control and accountability.[36]

Leaders in Afghanistan complain about corruption and lack of accountability as one of the major obstacles to rebuilding their society after years of conflict. To tackle this issue, the AKF introduced the "social audit", in which public meetings are called to assess the success of development projects carried out by the Community Development Councils. In these public meetings, individuals who have never had the opportunity to publicly question their leaders ask pointed questions about where and how the money was spent. As well, it is noteworthy that in a country where the role of women in public life is normally restricted, women also ask questions and raise issues regarding their welfare and education. Social audits are undertaken voluntarily, with the joint agreement of the council and the community, but the pressure for fair play has become so strong that they are rarely refused. It is hoped that while social audits change attitudes at the local level, they will eventually help change attitudes in the higher strata of government, as players at the community level will come to expect the same levels of accountability at regional and national levels.[37]

The *Christian Science Monitor* (*CSM*) calls the social audit a "groundbreaking" program that brings accountability to a country ranked by Transparency International as among the world's five most corrupt.[38] The *CSM* article outlines the process of the social audit, which begins with the selection of a social audit committee, comprising individuals the community considers the most honest and industrious. Since most of the villagers are either illiterate or unfamiliar with accounting, the AKDN trains the committee on how to inspect the council's financial transactions. The fact-checking process is rigorous, with committee members "following the money trail." For example, in the village of Kalan Guzar, the council had been charged with building a microhydroelectric generator and arranging a tailoring course for local women and girls. The Social Audit Committee checked the materials used, interviewed laborers to ensure they were paid, and even made a two-hour journey to see the merchants who had provided the materials for the projects, to ensure their prices matched those quoted by the council. The process culminates in a village-wide assembly in which the committee presents its findings and invites the community to question the council, after which the village votes on whether or not it is satisfied with the council's dealings. In Kalan Guzar, fraud was not an issue and the locals largely approved of the council's work.

This is not always the case, the article reports. In one village, the committee found that its council had paid $1,000 for a kebab. In another, the committee forced its council to stay in more modest accommodations during future trips, after finding out that the councillors had stayed in a nice hotel in Kabul. Because the committees complete their work in a matter of days and present their findings to the public, there is little opportunity for the council to intimidate the committee members. One government official in the Baghlan province said this is creating fear among the councils, as it puts pressure on them to limit abuses of power. The article concludes by cautioning that although the AKDN has implemented the program in over 400 villages, they are mostly in the peaceful northern regions and security issues in southern and eastern Afghanistan prevent its operations there.

But, in his statement at the Kabul Conference, the Aga Khan said that initiatives like the NSP, in promoting direct community involvement, have "demonstrated tangible progress" in improving Afghan lives.[39] In addition to rebuilding state institutions, investment in the institutions of civil society deserves greater attention, he says, as they are well placed to take into account specific local or provincial political and socioeconomic needs and opportunities: "They are well placed to ensure that progress is both public and transparent, that good governance is observed as the norm, just as they are the best tools for ensuring better impact and for hastening visible socio-economic development."[40] Such programs, he continues, need not undermine central authority. Rather, programs synchronized with subnational governance and policies need to be implemented, such as the CDC program under the NSP. It is vital, he says, for local government and development actors to work closely with local communities to identify their needs, and communities themselves need to be involved in the process of program development and implementation. Thus, locally democratic initiatives like the CDC make an essential contribution to human development and nation building and ensure that "an insurmountable gap" does not develop between government on the one side and private enterprise on the other.[41]

Pluralism

In his address to the Nobel Institute in Oslo in 2005, the Aga Khan identified once again the three mutually reinforcing essential conditions necessary for developing societies to become "masters of the process" and to make it self-sustainable. He said, "I put it to you that no human development initiative can be sustainable unless we are successful in achieving three essential conditions. We must operate in an environment that invests in, rather than seeks to stifle, pluralism and diversity. We must have an extensive, engaged civil society. And we must have stable, competent democratic governance."[42]

In achieving this goal, he recognizes the importance of partnerships in building the indigenous capacity of civil society in developing countries, and highlights the alliances made by the AKDN with various international governments. In collaboration with the Government of Canada, the Global Centre for Pluralism in Ottawa seeks to provide permanent institutional capacity, "drawing on Canada's successful record in constructing and sustaining pluralist civil society," with the aim of fostering "legislation and policy to strengthen developing countries' capacity for enhancing pluralism in all spheres of modern life."[43]

In other parts of the world, the AKDN seeks to create practical enabling environments for enhancing pluralist civil society: "through a great variety of village and community organizations, we encourage people to overcome their antagonisms and work together to find solutions to common problems in the search for a better life."[44] The overall goal of the AKDN Civil Society Programme is to ensure a sufficient number of civil society organizations (CSOs) exist as functional components of societies and impact positively the lives of the members of the societies in which they operate. The program in Afghanistan has five main goals: (1) the creation of a baseline of information about the civil society sector; (2) increased systematicness of work to build the capacity of high-quality sustainable CSOs; (3) a better appreciation by government, business, CSOs, and citizens of the need for integrity and good governance; (4) better understanding in the government about the possibility of mutually advantageous relationships created by working with CSOs; and (5) better understanding among businesses about the usefulness of corporate social responsibility.[45]

But achieving long-term positive change is complicated and multifaceted. Thus, AKDN adopted the Multi-Input Area Development (MIAD) strategy outlined above. Acknowledging the fact of pluralism in all facets of life, AKDN recognized that overall quality of life requires more than simply increased income. A lack of access to education, the inability to effectively manage the outfall of disasters, and the absence of good civil society organizations are all examples of issues that need to be tackled together in order to improve quality of life. The AKDN Development Blog states that, for AKDN, "successful development occurs when a continuum of development activities offers people in a given area not only a rise in incomes, but a broad, sustained improvement in the overall quality of life."[46]

The various agencies of the AKDN in Afghanistan work simultaneously to achieve such improvement in quality of life. The Aga Khan Foundation's Rural Support Programme works in partnership with the government's Rural Solidarity Programme to help bring roads and microhydroelectric power to regions like Badakshan and Damyan. The Aga Khan Trust for Culture restores dozens of historic houses, monuments, landmark buildings, and public spaces—such as the Baghe Babur in Kabul—leading to the revitalization of local economies and urban areas surrounding such projects. The Aga Khan Fund for Economic Development seeks to create economic engines that provide jobs, set service standards, and stimulate economic activity through local sourcing, through such projects as the Serena Hotel, which works to revitalize tourism and building and related industries; as well as the Roshan mobile network, which revitalized trade in the country when there were no operational telephone lines. Focus Humanitarian Assistance combines food aid programs with the rehabilitation of schools, infrastructure and health clinics. Aga Khan Education Services helps to develop skills in English language and information technology, as well as tutorial assistance programs for schoolgoing children. Aga Khan Health Services operates seventeen Basic Health Centres and five Comprehensive Base Centres in the provinces of Badakshan, Baghlan, and Bamyan, as well as the provincial hospital in Bamyan. The Aga Khan Agency for Microfinance administers thousands of new microfinance loans and pioneered microinsurance for the poor through the establishment of the First MicroFinance Bank Afghanistan (FMFB-A) in 2003, the first bank to be licensed under Afghanistan's new legal framework on microfinance.

All these projects, working in tandem, seek to invigorate civil society and create a respect for pluralism and cooperation.

Education

Caroline Arnold, the former Senior Programme Officer for Education at the Aga Khan Foundation (AKF) in Geneva, says that children of different ethnicities have a sense of boundary and even animosity toward each other ingrained in them by age three. One project implemented by the AKF to help counter this situation and promote pluralism is the development of children's literature that deliberately features a group of friends from multiple ethnic backgrounds. In an interview with Arnold, she commented that many of the books available for children in Central Asia are either "absolutely terrifying, really, really frightening, bloodthirsty stories," or "very sugary" and have little solid content. So, she says, "we wanted this set of stories to have the children having adventures, but also getting into disagreements, like children everywhere do, but resolving them effectively, [thereby] giving them some sort of idea about conflict resolution and pluralism."[47]

Educating people in pluralism has been a long-term goal of the AKF. An AKF draft concept note from 2006 entitled "Education for Pluralism: Explorations & Avenues for Future Programming" investigates the strategies for embedding pluralism into educational practices. The paper's author, Zahra Kassam Mamdani, argues that in a time when there is deep ignorance and resentment between peoples and countries, "educators cannot be ethical bystanders."[48]

Addressing pluralism in schools, she says, relates to a vision of both education and the world in which we want to live. In order for students to become ethically grounded and active citizens, they must receive a broad and inclusive education that "provides them with the knowledge, skills, and values necessary to succeed in and contribute toward a society characterized by difference and change."[49] Finally, she says that with its long and broad experience, AKF can play a unique role: "given the AKDN's broad experience in the field of education, the Imamat's commitment to pluralism, and the relative lack of attention given to this issue worldwide, AKF can play a unique role in advancing peace and pluralism in the schools, communities, and countries in which we work."[50]

An intentional focus on pluralism and social justice is important for several reasons, she says. First, it challenges the notion that any specific worldview should be considered inherently superior. "It requires that students be taught that the contemporary world is, in reality, a product of contributions from many different entities and that this rich tapestry of people, faiths, cultures, nations, and traditions should be celebrated and valued."[51] Further, it recognizes and validates the existence of different peoples and identities, as well as their contributions to the global community. Finally, it acknowledges that plurality enhances and strengthens society and social unity.

Most importantly, such an ethic has to be inculcated at a young age. She provides research that indicates young children are more open to diversity and learning about others, but between ages six to nine years children begin to view their own race and culture as better than others, and by the age of nine or ten years children have well-established racial prejudices that are highly resistant to change. "For all of these reasons and others," she concludes, "it is critical that an education program focused on pluralism begin in the early years—when curiosity, creativity, and energy are in abundance."[52]

Indeed, close to half of the education budget of AKF goes to early childhood development (ECD), which, says Arnold, is "unusual," since most agencies devote only 5 to 10 percent of their budgets to ECD. One of AKF's primary projects is the Girls Education Support Programme (GESP) in Afghanistan. Implemented in partnership with CIDA, the GESP "supports the enhancement of girls' education through activities aimed at increasing access to quality learning opportunities and at promoting secure and supportive learning environments for girls."[53] Working closely with the government of Afghanistan, the GESP is expected to benefit more than one hundred thousand girls in more than three hundred schools.

AKF claims that breaking the cycle that limits girls entering school requires a comprehensive focus on promoting gender equity, through education programming.[54] The GESP is "tackling the physical, cultural, and administrative constraints particular to Afghanistan, and supporting an enabling environment which encourages girls to enter and stay in school longer."[55]

To achieve this end, GESP has developed a number of focused program components, as outlined in its press kit, "Canada and the Aga Khan Foundation in Afghanistan."[56] ECD is one of the main program components of GESP, which works to ensure that both girls and schools are ready for each other. Through directed training, GESP also works to eliminate gender stereotypes by aiming to instill an ethic whereby education is recognized as a right for all children. Further, by providing young mothers with basic literacy skills, GESP aims to increase female participation in communities as well as active participation in children's education. As well, GESP's reference schools will be outfitted with the appropriate facilities necessary to meet girls' education in Afghanistan;

these schools will serve as models and encourage replication. Finally, GESP will prepare teachers and parents to manage issues arising in transition years between grades and between primary and secondary school, in order to encourage girls to stay in school longer.

Girls' education is vital in Afghanistan, says Richard Phinney in his documentary, *Change in the Making: a Journey in Afghanistan*. He interviews Farima Begum, a woman who has benefited from the Women's Savings Group, a microinvestment scheme initiated by the AKDN. She sees a brighter future for her daughters: "Look at me," she says, "I can't read or write. But they will get an education." In a country where only 10 percent of adult women can read or write, almost half their daughters are in school. "That," says Phinney, "is a revolution waiting to happen."[57]

CODA

According to Ruthven, "the Aga Khan firmly believes that in Islam *din* and *dunya*—'religion and world'—are not to be treated as separate realms but constantly intersect and interact, with the pursuit of material gain framed within the calculus of ethical concern."[58] Indeed, this is the Imamate's stated impetus for the establishment of the AKDN, which sees institutionalized development as the contemporary embodiment of a timeless Qur'anic concern for social action. This is an essential point; in the Ismaili interpretation of Islam, social action is a necessary part of faith, and the AKDN is the practical, institutional expression of that faith.

Ruthven captures the Ismaili position on this score:

> "for Ismailis the Imam of the Time facilitates the imperative of social action by providing the appropriate institutions—a duty the present Imam takes very seriously. He seeks out the best advice for his projects, regardless of the religious orientation of his advisors, and finds ways of including that advice in his programmes. As the sole authoritative interpreter of the tradition, he sees to it that those programmes are underpinned by the ethics of Islam. Service to God, in his view, is not just to be made through religious worship but through service to humanity."[59]

The benefits of the AKDN for Ismaili communities around the world are both practical and notional. The complex of programs implemented by the various AKDN agencies in rural areas offers freedom from poverty. This was the case in post-9/11 Afghanistan, where trucks emblazoned with the FOCUS Humanitarian Assistance logo—the only providers of support and sustenance in that region—were literally the symbols of survival for all rural communities in that country.

Importantly, part and parcel of the AKDN's presence is, as Steinberg puts it, the "dissemination into those communities of the language of liberal humanism couched in the lexicon of Isma`ilism."[60] For Ruthven, the current and previous Aga Khans "have proved remarkably successful in adapting an ancient tradition to modern conditions," which he says is a result of their conception of themselves "as exemplars of a model of leadership which stretches back 14 centuries."[61] On this view, the establishment of the AKDN and the elaboration of Jamati institutions allowed for a centrally directed transnational community-building project that created the global Ismaili community, which is now assured continuity through a complex process of institutionalization and consolidation under an allegiance to a renewed conception of Imamate wedded to liberalizing commitments to democracy, civic education, multicultural pluralism, social justice, and sustainable development.

PART II

6

DEMOCRACY, SECULARISM, AND SOCIAL ETHICS

Our central challenge in this new century, as leaders and
future leaders of our world, is to renew the democratic promise.
The saving grace democratic systems are most likely to possess,
after all, is that they are self-correcting. A system of public
accountability still provides the best hope for change without
violence. And that virtue alone redeems the entire concept.
    —Aga Khan IV, *Where Hope Takes Root*

If the nobility of secularism resides in its quest to enable multiple
faiths to exist in the same public space, its shallowness resides
in the hubris of its distinction between private faith and public
reason.
    —William E. Connolly, *Pluralism*

I

For Pericles, democracy's promise was equal justice for all. The Athenian's oration on democracy's virtues, delivered in the fifth century BCE—perhaps significantly, in the midst of a struggle for survival, just like its literary descendant, Abraham Lincoln's Gettysburg Address—can perhaps be hailed as the ideological inspiration for all future tyranny-toppling movements from the French Revolution to the Arab Spring. Certainly, the Periclean vision captures the spirit of the Aga Khan's support for the democratic promise, which, as the head of a development network, he sees as liberating societies from both tribal and global violence.

Perhaps it is predictable that the Aga Khan, as chief of the long-persecuted minority Ismaili community, would strive to institutionalize in all societies the civic safe havens offered by the liberal democratic state. But Aga Khan IV claims his support for democracy derives directly from the tenets of Islam: "I am a democrat not because of Greek or French thought," he declares, "but primarily because of principles that go back 1,400 years, directly after the death of Prophet Muhammad."[1] This is the typical line taken by liberal Muslims all over the world who find in the Qur'an and the Prophetic tradition a democratic vision that staunchly supports the safe civic space that attends the separation of powers.

The failure of democratic institutions to engender its promised social progress—in both the developing and the developed world—is the Aga Khan's stated impetus to take up the challenge to "find more and better ways to make democracy work."[2] For Sajoo—one of the Ismaili institutions' most prolific interlocutors with liberal political theory—the public spaces offered by separated powers to accommodate minorities is the starting point, but the ideal of separation cannot, he insists, lead to a cleavage between ethics and the rule of law. He emphasizes the role of social ethics, arguing that "the formal commitments of the law alone cannot deliver pluralist culture."[3]

He is not alone in this assertion, and he lists an array of Muslim intellectual activists stretching from Indonesia to Syria and Nigeria whom he articulates as "striving for secular spaces while invoking ethical as well as human rights critiques of the failings of their governing elites and institutions."[4] Reflecting Sajoo's thought, the work of Abdou Filali-Ansary, Abdullahi an-Na'im, and Tariq Modood is representative of contemporary North Atlantic English-speaking liberal Muslim scholars who advocate secular culture as creating safe civic space. These scholars argue that the separation of powers—the bedrock of a secular democracy—is not only necessary in the modern world but is also not incompatible with Islam, despite assertions to the contrary.

Indeed, the Aga Khan comments that "sometimes I read that Islam is in conflict with democracy."[5] But, as Carl Ernst puts it, to question whether "Islam" is compatible with democracy is "unusual." Not only does such an assertion seem to deny the democratic expressions of Muslim countries from Turkey to Bangladesh to Afghanistan and Indonesia, but it also puts undue pressure on an ethical framework, Islam, that posits no real political system,[6] to conform to a specifically post-Enlightenment construction. This, says Ernst, is tantamount to asking whether or not "Christianity" is compatible with democracy, though it has not given much indication in that direction.[7]

Nevertheless, liberal Muslim scholars will insist that democratic values have been present throughout Muslim history, exemplified, at the very least, by the Prophet's respect for consultation. And, they contend, democracy's core feature, secularization—the separation of powers to secure civic space from coercion—has been a feature of most historical Muslim societies. Thus, some scholars argue that the perceived incompatibility of contemporary times is simply a matter of perception, deriving from misunderstandings of the "Islamic" and "liberal" conceptions of secularism.

II

José Casanova configures secularism into constitutive elements, arranging it as a triptych: "the secular" as a modern epistemic category differentiating a realm separate from "the religious"; "secularization" as an analytical conceptualization of the historical processes of the modern world; and "secularism" as an ideology or worldview.[8] Certainly, says Talal Asad, "the secular" predates the political doctrine of "secularism,"[9] but, says Casanova, rather than being a residual category as originally intended, the secular has come to represent all of reality, encompassing the religious,[10] thus dominating the concepts and sensibilities of modern lifeworlds.

At first blush, then, we seem to be inhabiting the world predicted by theorists of modernity like Emile Durkheim and Max Weber, in which religion, though necessary during humanity's social evolution, is increasingly displaced by modernity. This "naturalization of 'unbelief,'" as Casanova puts it, is a foregone conclusion of dominant theories of secularization, which fuse the modern and the secular to posit that the more modern/secular a society is, the less religious it is supposed to become.[11] But, as Charles Taylor clarifies, this conception of society is bound to particular histories, in which "unbelief and exclusive humanism defined itself in relation to earlier modes of belief," and later societies with different histories define themselves in relation to contemporary societies of unbelief.[12] For Casanova, this explains why there are some modern non-European societies, such as the United States and South Korea, which are fully secular but have conspicuously religious populations.[13] Thus, he concludes, the fact that modernization is accompanied by religious revival in so many non-Western societies "puts into question the premise that the decline of religious beliefs and practices is a quasi-natural consequence of processes of modernization."[14]

For Muslim societies, then, the path to modernization/secularization need not imply a compulsion toward unbelief. The Casanova/Taylor notion of "varieties of secularism" opens the door to varieties other than the sort of "closed secularism" that proves so problematic for liberal Muslim thought, with which contemporary Ismaili thought identifies. Indeed, many influential Muslim thinkers advocate secularism, such as Iran's Abdolkarim Soroush, who comments: "as to the separation of powers I do not think that any serious scholar in the world of Islam would find any 'unislamic' element in it. I am not saying that it can be derived from the Quran and sunna, all I am saying is that it is compatible with the corpus of Islamic teachings."[15]

In the same vein, Asghar Ali Engineer also declares that "we cannot say that secularism is essentially un-Islamic or anti-Islamic in any fundamental way."[16] And Abdulaziz Sachedina observes that the concept of separate jurisdictions is acknowledged in the Shari'a and is not an imposition on the Islamic tradition.[17]

Such assertions by modern Muslim scholars contrast sharply with the writings of Bernard Lewis's ilk, whom Wilfred McClay quotes in support of the argument that Islam is hindered from adapting to a secular modernity by its "rigid, poorly developed understanding of the world, and of its relationship to the ultimate."[18] For Sachedina, though, Islam has no such intransigent predilections. The interaction between religion and history in Islam, he says, reveals a sophisticated public religion that runs contrary to modern popular impressions of religion in the public sphere. "Islam has been a faith in the realm of the public," he writes, using liberal terminology to further contend: "considering the historical development of Islamic tradition, and contrary to our modern perceptions of the role of religion, one is struck by a religious tradition that has been a source of a public project founded upon the principle of coexistence, recognizing self-governing communities that are free to run their internal affairs under a comprehensive religious and social political system. Of all the Abrahamic religions based on the biblical ethos of shaping its public culture, Islam has been from its inception the most conscious of its earthly agenda."[19]

In this view, Islam is "compatible" with the essential values of modernization/secularization and, indeed, has even been its exemplar. To be sure, Engineer argues that "Islam upholds the values of what we call today democratic governance,"[20] and he finds in liberal political ethics the Qur'anic concepts of reason, justice, and wisdom.[21]

Despite such assertions, there remains a perceived incompatibility between Islam—indeed, religion generally—and secularism. But the idea of securing civic space from coercion—the essential mandate of secularism—is not the preserve of post-Enlightenment societies; and historical Muslim societies, influenced by Qur'anic ideals, separated powers in order to fulfill that essential mandate. To be sure, the modern period has been witness to stifling authoritarianism in many Muslim-majority countries, but this was the consequence of the socioeconomic breakdown wrought by the end of colonialism and has, as the Aga Khan says, "nothing to do with the faith of Islam."[22] For Engineer, it is the postcolonial Arabization of Islamic culture and Muslim societies that "has eroded and disfigured the fundamentally democratic and egalitarian ethos of Islam."[23]

The existence and persistence of the democratic ethos in Islamic tradition and Muslim history is consistently endorsed by liberal Muslim scholars around the globe, from Ebrahim Moosa in the US to Abdolkarim Soroush in Iran and Nurcolish Majdid in Indonesia. It is perhaps not the place, then, of the outside observer to deny the tradition's compatibility with the modern world. Indeed, the problem at the heart of the discussion seems not to be the compatibility between "Islam" and "secularism," but rather knowledge about the relationship between "Islam" and "secularism."

Neither concept is absolute, but much of the discussion tends to universalize both, thereby limiting Islam to a strictly soteriological system and secularism to a strict separation between religion and state. The reality, of course, is not so absolute: the religious and the secular intermingle in all societies and individuals, across time and geography. The notion of dichotomy is a forced one, because individuals, groups, and societies are all comprised of diverse and conflicting components that are being constantly negotiated.

III

For Abdou Filali-Ansary—founding director of the Aga Khan University's Institute for the Study of Muslim Civilisations (AKU-ISMC) in London (UK)—the opposition between secularism and Islam is "completely artificial."[24] He explains that Arab scholars in the nineteenth century translated the English word "secularists" into Arabic as "temporalists," a word that in the Qur'an has associations with "atheists." Thus, the feeling among Muslims is that to be a secularist has meant to abandon not only the religious faith of Islam but also the attendant morality and traditions that are perceived to compose Muslim societies. Secularism, writes Filali-Ansary, "has been understood as a total alienation from the constituent elements of the Islamic personality and as a complete surrender to unbelief, immorality, and self-hatred, leading to a disavowal of the historic identity and civilisation inherited from illustrious ancestors."[25] He argues that previous translations have scarred the Muslim imagination and rather than trying now to reconcile ideologies the best course of action would be to eliminate the misunderstanding.[26]

The choice of terminology had the effect of strengthening the perceived dualism between Christian and Muslim societies. This was aggravated in the colonial period, since the colonial powers were seen as the harbingers of Christian proselytism as well as the new secularism.[27] One of the most striking consequences of this evolution, writes Filali-Ansary, is that Islam now appears as the religion most hostile to secularization and to modernity in general, but "intrinsically Islam would seem to be the religion closest to modern views and ideals, and thus the one that would most easily accommodate secularisation."[28] As endorsement, he furnishes Ernest Gellner's observation that Islam is endowed with a number of characteristics that are presumably congruent with modernization, such as individualism, egalitarianism, a rule-ethic, and an aversion to hierarchy and magic.[29]

Filali-Ansary proposes an approach that avoids the implementation of a "utopianized" democracy in favor of inculcating conceptions and systems that are constituent to democracy.[30] In support, he quotes Tim Niblock, who writes that a focus on democratization in general detracts from the more specific and critical issues for people, such as corruption, freedom of expression, an effective bureaucracy and independent judiciary, minority and human rights, and other inequalities that lead to social disorder.[31] While these ideas are important for policy-makers, says Filali-Ansary, they must be complemented by an approach that takes into account the attitudes of Muslims themselves. He articulates at least three conditions that seem to be required for the particular case of contemporary Muslim societies: (1) the updating of religious conceptions, (2) the rule of law, and (3) economic growth.[32] "For this purpose," he writes, a "more 'conceptual' approach is required, one that would help present democracy in terms understandable and acceptable to Muslim publics, and thus bridge the gap between a 'mystical' representation and a more realistic comprehension."[33]

Part of this comprehension entails coming to a deeper understanding of secularism and democracy, and that they cannot be transplanted wholesale. This is the thrust of Abdullahi An-Na'im's argument, who writes that the two concepts must be understood by every society in a "*dynamic and deeply contextual*" sense, "rather than preconceived notions, such as the so-called strict separation of 'church and state,' to be transplanted from one setting to another."[34] An-Na'im also grapples with terminology, arguing that a major barrier is the contemporary definition of secularism, which tends to limit it to Europe's experience with Christianity since the eighteenth century. "Whether viewed as 'separation of church and state' or 'dis-establishment of religion,'" he writes, "such definitions are obviously specific to certain situations, and do not address the continuing social and political role of religion in public life."[35] Thus, he argues, secularism should be viewed as the *type* of relationship between religion and the state, rather than a specific way in which that relationship has evolved. Furthermore, the form that that relationship takes in any society has to be the product of "organic development"[36] and has to be given time to be accepted as legitimate by the population, instead of expecting drastic change by constitutional fiat.

For An-Na'im—a non-Ismaili political thinker engaged by Ismaili theorists—the basic limitation of secularism is that its appeal to political pluralism is based on its limited view of the social good; it is able to unite diverse communities into one political community precisely because it makes the least moral claims on the community and its members.

Thus, the most serious objection to secularism is its inability to inspire or motivate believers, who are the vast majority of the world population. What is not sufficiently appreciated, therefore, is the importance of a religious justification and rationale for secularism.

IV

Calls for greater recognition of religion are often inspired by a perceived need for greater ethical responsibility when confronted with the vagaries of modern life. Indeed, the Aga Khan asks: "how can we inspire people to reach beyond rampant materialism, self-indulgent individualism and unprincipled relativism?"[37] One answer, he offers, is to supplement individual rights with a greater understanding of personal responsibilities and communal goals—"not merely the absence of negative restraints on individual freedom, but also a set of positive responsibilities, moral disciplines that prevent liberty from turning into license."[38] The spiritual, he says, is central to this endeavor; "a deepening sense of spiritual commitment, and the ethical framework that goes with it, will be a central requirement if we are able to find our way through the minefields and the quicksands of modern life."[39]

Strengthening religious institutions are vital to this process, he argues, which should lead, he hopes, to a universal ethical sensibility and moral outlook shared across denominational lines. In the end, he contends that an ethical sensibility buttressed by spiritual commitment is vital to public life because it inspires people to uphold the moral imperatives that undergird the ideology of pluralist society: justice, equality, tolerance, and dignity. To be sure, freedom of religion is a benchmark value of that society. But, he muses, "if freedom of religion deteriorates into freedom from religion, then societies will find themselves lost in a bleak, uncompromising landscape, with no compass, no road map and no sense of ultimate direction."[40]

The call for greater ethical commitment is shared in the West, too. Charles Taylor, for example, argues on similar lines, calling the relativism of today a "profound mistake" because "the culture of self-fulfillment has led many people to lose sight of concerns that transcend them,"[41] and he further laments that "the dark side of individualism is a centring on the self, which both flattens and narrows our lives, makes them poorer in meaning, and less concerned with others or society."[42] His comments echo the initial impulses of European secularism, which, while promoting separated powers, did not promote religion's removal from public life. Indeed, many scholars—such as the nineteenth-century political thinker Alexis de Tocqueville—argued that the morality taught by religion keeps in check the individualistic passions championed by democracy. This is the ethical upshot of religion that many scholars today do not wish to jettison.

Democratic life, says Sajoo, is empowered by public trust, and while it "assumes the existence of the rule of law," it "depends on the ethical sense to drive the everyday acts of civility that make citizenship worthwhile."[43] It is the reason, he writes, that Islam is said to merge the secular and the religious—"the point of which is to have a constant ethical critique of the secular."[44] Indeed, in this sense, the Islamic conception of secularism is more complex than the simple separation of religion from the state. To be sure, while many Muslim scholars support separated powers, they argue that a strict distinction between the religious and the secular is not only unattainable but also undesirable.

Thus, while separating powers is accepted in practice, Islamic theory is not willing to adopt secularism as ideology—with its "autonomous agentic individual"—since "Islam is both *din* and *dunya*, spirit and matter, distinct but linked, neither to be forsaken."[45] It is this latter part that is the key—neither faith (*din*) nor world (*dunya*) are to be forsaken; they are interlinked, and success in both is a believer's responsibility. To be sure, this does not translate into an automatic partnership between state and religion. After all, says Sajoo, the point of separating powers is to ensure that individuals are able to pursue their goals without coercion. This, of course, is an ethic that is central in the Qur'an, which declares unassailably that "no coercion is there in religion" (Q. 2:256).

The Qur'an itself endorses no particular system of governance (though both historical and contemporary Muslim societies have run the gamut of options). Rather, it propounds a vision of humankind as a pluralist community of individuals who strive to ennoble both themselves and each other in whatever system best provides dignity and freedom. Tunisian scholar Muhammad Talbi asserts that "Islam has no intrinsic political principle or organisation." He argues that "in light of Islam's inherent liberal values and practices such as freedom, love, tolerance and pluralism, it may then be inferred that Islam preferred a form of government which exemplified these; as it happens, democracy, in our time, is just that system and thus should it be seen for now as the best political system for Muslims, despite its human imperfections."[46]

In the minds of many scholars, what we today call democratic expression runs deep in Muslim history and Islamic theory. According to Sajoo, the point of separating powers is to protect the weak (whether in numbers or status) from the tyranny (ideological, legal, economic) of the strong,[47] and this was certainly an ethos that motivated Muhammad in the establishment of his "ideal community" (Ummah) in seventh-century Medina, where he put to vote every major decision that affected his community. In Islam's minority, says the Aga Khan, "Muslims debated how best to implement the premises [Muhammad] had established for being qualified for leadership. The principle of wide public consultation for selecting leadership for matters relating to affairs of state and civil administration was adopted." He further notes: "Muslims of the time also established that leadership in social governance was to be selected on the basis of merit and competence. These principles, cemented 14 centuries ago, are consistent with democratic models that exist around the world today."[48]

These principles were derived from the Qur'an's overarching concern for social justice, which sought to mirror on earth the Justice (*'adl*) and Unity (*tawhid*) of the Divine. Thus, they perpetuated in later Muslim societies, wherein separated powers were a fact of life: in the theory and practice of medieval Muslim polities, the caliph was subject to the Divine Law (Shari'a), which itself was promulgated by the religious scholars (*'ulema'*), who thereby provided a check on the coercive power of the state.

But democratic expression is not confined to the past. It is, according to Mohamed Abed Jabri, the only legitimately acceptable political principle in present-day Muslim societies.[49] Robert Hefner, among others, argues that contemporary Muslim societies exhibit Habermasian public spheres, helping to create an open and egalitarian culture of participation, a vital precedent for democratic representation.[50] Certainly, many activists invoke the idea of Islam as "religion and state" to justify coercive policies. Typically, they insist that the only method of enforcing high standards of Muslim morality is the dissolution of the public/private boundary and the use of the state's disciplinary powers to police both spheres.[51] But, Hefner proclaims, the Qur'an itself knows of no such concept of a coercive, Islamic state.[52]

V

Muslim democrats "deny the need for an Islamic state,"[53] declares Hefner. But what *is* insisted upon is that society comprises more than autonomous individuals and democracy comprises more than markets and the state. Democracy relies on a noncoercive public culture in which citizens' rights are respected. This public culture, says Hefner, depends on mediating institutions in which citizens learn the democratic habits of free speech, participation, and toleration. For Hefner, "there is nothing undemocratic about Muslim voluntary associations (as well as those of other religions) playing a role in the *public* life of civil society as well as in personal ethics."[54]

The core issue here is the role religion can play in the public sphere. While religion is a vital identity in Muslim societies, in closed secularist societies the value of religion is often downplayed or denied. Indeed, George Marsden opined in his 1993 plenary address to the American Academy of Religion that "voicing a religious perspective is just not intellectually respectable."[55] Despite this, however, religious identity seems to play an indispensible role in the public life of Western states.

For example, the 2007 Canadian Survey of Giving, Volunteering and Participating showed that "Canadians who are religiously active are more likely than other Canadians to be donors,"[56] and that religious organizations are the biggest beneficiaries of giving, receiving 46 percent of all donated dollars.[57] As well, in his study on civic activity in America, Robert Putnam wrote that "faith communities in which people worship together are arguably the single most important repository of social capital in America."[58] Religious identity, he argues, is essential for civic engagement: "regular worshippers and people who say that religion is very important to them are much more likely than other people to visit friends, to entertain at home, to attend club meetings, and to belong to sports groups; professional and academic societies; school service groups; school fraternities and sororities; farm organizations; political clubs; nationality groups; and other miscellaneous groups."[59]

Religious affiliation, however, can be seen as a competitor for the individual's affiliation to the state, which is why the public sphere is formulated as an objective, neutral space for public debate. But many scholars of multiculturalism, like Will Kymlicka and Tariq Modood, argue that the public sphere is not morally, ethnically, or religiously neutral, because a public order will reflect the culture and principles from which it derives.[60] This will have the important implication, Modood argues, that citizens whose identities are reflected in the public order will not feel the rigidity of an enforced public/private division, because they will never be aware of its coercive influence—until they have to share the public domain with persons from other communities, who may wish the identity of the political community to reflect something of their own community as well.[61]

The lack of public recognition for religion has deep implications for the multicultural state, he warns, as it results in discrimination. For example, because of the conceptualization of discrimination in legal and policy framework as based on ethnicity, "it is lawful to discriminate against Muslims *qua* Muslims because the courts do not accept that Muslims are an ethnic group."[62] For this reason, he argues, "the goal of democratic multiculturalism cannot and should not be cultural neutrality but rather inclusion of marginal and disadvantaged groups, including religious communities in public life."[63] And thus, "institutionalizing some public space for religious groups in a broadly secular framework is the appropriate multicultural response."[64]

Eva Schubert, writing in the IIS volume *Muslim Modernities*, agrees, saying that "engaging religion in pluralist civic space moderates authoritarian religious impulses."[65] For her, to contend that religious loyalties are incompatible with civic identity, or that strong religious belief neutralizes moderate political views "creates the danger it tries to avoid."[66] Creating civic space for religion is important, she writes: "*it creates a 'stake' for religious groups in maintaining a plural civil society, because their own freedoms depend on it.* Competing in public for legitimacy invites peaceful engagement; exclusion generates defensive and condemnatory reactions. Attempting to restrict religious voices to the private sphere alone fails the test."[67]

The role of civil society here is essential, says the Aga Khan, since a democratic society requires much more than democratic politics. "Governments alone do not make democracy work,"[68] he says, and the array of private civil society institutions driven by public motivations are vital for moving beyond policy makers' tendencies to get preoccupied with politics. He suggests thinking beyond political preoccupations, as "a thriving civil sector is essential in renewing the promise of democracy."[69]

Part of that promise includes "rigorous, responsible and relevant education," with the goal of training leaders and shaping institutions toward higher levels of competence and excellence. He bemoans the sort of education that "made our students less flexible—confident to the point of arrogance that they now had all the answers—rather than more flexible."[70] Thus, he stresses quality education, the goal of which is "to equip each generation to participate effectively in what has been called 'the great conversation' of our times." But, he concludes, "it also means being sensitive to the values and outlooks of others," since "in a pluralistic world, the consequences of ignorance can be profoundly damaging."[71]

To cap this point, he draws attention to the Danish cartoon controversy, in which the editors claimed ignorance of the sensitivities involved, in which case it would be less a clash of civilizations and more a "clash of ignorance," as he puts it. "Perhaps," he reflects, "it is ignorance that has allowed so many participants in this discussion to confuse liberty with licence, implying that the sheer absence of restraint on human impulse can constitute a sufficient moral framework."[72]

This is not to say that governments should censor speech or people should resort to violence, but, he suggests, "freedom of expression is an incomplete value unless it is used honourably and that the obligations of citizenship in any society should include a commitment to informed and responsible expression."[73] To this end, he argues that the educational enterprise can be "an effective antidote" to what he terms as the "great public enemies of our time": ignorance, arrogance, and insensitivity.[74]

Building on these two requirements for democracy—the need for civil institutions and educational excellence—is a third: a renewed commitment to ethical standards. "What I am calling for," he says, "is an ethical sensibility that can be shared across denominational lines and can foster a universal moral outlook."[75] Public ethical sensibility offers a check against the abuse of power, while democracy increases the number of people who share social power; greater public integrity keeps watch over how that power is used.

VI

Sajoo follows this line of thought, arguing that "the rule of law needs the support of public ethics for civil society to deliver a meaningful pluralism."[76] He insists that the rule of law alone does not ensure fundamental human rights, as was evinced in the United States and Canada by the racial profiling of citizens from predominantly Muslim countries as part of the war on terrorism; or the refusal of the École de Technologie Supérieure in Montreal to provide prayer spaces to Muslim students, arguing that the request would violate the separation of church and state, despite the requirement of "reasonable accommodation" in Canadian human rights law.[77] These cases, he says, raise fundamental questions about the integrity of the rule of law, which requires equal treatment of individuals in public policy,[78] and illustrate an "abuse of the separation of Religion and State, whose purpose is to safeguard secular space for pluralism."[79]

He quotes Canada's Chief Justice, Beverley McLachlin, who contends that "inclusion and equality cannot be achieved by mere rights." It is only "when we add to the mix attitudes of tolerance, respect and generosity," she concludes, that "the prospects become bright for the inclusive society of which we dream."[80] These "attitudes of tolerance, respect and generosity" resonate loudly with the Muslim understanding of social ethics—*adab* and *akhlaq*, custom and propriety—that ground Islamic civilization. "They not only are the handmaiden of the rule of law, but the underlying ethos which gave birth to those entitlements that privilege human dignity and which we now cherish as human rights."[81] But this is not an endeavor that is restricted to Muslim thought. As mentioned earlier, contemporary liberal thinkers, too, "share the concern over the distancing of ethical principles from the public square in the name of secularism as ideology."[82] Sajoo lists Charles Taylor, Jose Casanova, Hans Kung, Amitai Etzioni, Richard Falk, Michael Sandel, and Amartya Sen as some of the most prominent who he says argue that "there has been a withering critique of the old liberalism on behalf of a turn—some would say a return—to civic ethics."[83] This is more than "elitist discourse," says Sajoo; this sense of the malaises of closed secularism is one that contemporary Ismaili thought shares with the likes of Taylor and Casanova, and it echoes a general public discontent with the alienations of secularist modernity.

Although the institutional separation of religion and state is considered necessary to foster and support public spaces that accommodate all minorities, this is not tantamount to building a wall of separation between ethics and the rule of law. Muslim intellectual activists like Mohsen Kadivar and Abdolkarim Soroush in Iran, Nurcolish Majdid and Abdulrahman Wahid in Indonesia, Sadiq Al-Azm and Mohammed Shahrur in Syria, Saad Eddin Ibrahim and Nawal Sadawi in Egypt, Daulat Khudanazarov in Tajikistan, Chandra Muzaffar and Farish Noor in Malaysia, Sima Samar in Afghanistan, and Ayesha Imam in Nigeria strive for secular spaces while invoking ethical and human rights critiques of the failings of their governing elites and institutions.[84] Sajoo argues that "social ethics not only lends legitimacy to their critiques in the eyes of fellow citizens, it also avoids depending on the formal commitments of the law alone, which cannot deliver pluralist culture."[85]

He details three important features that distinguish a positive transition to a democratic society: (1) a commitment to *civility*, the "concern for the good of the entire society";[86] (2) the creative energy to *institutionalize* values into action; and (3) the readiness to enlarge social welfare, "so that inclusion is genuine."[87] A sense of civility inculcates a social conscience that prescribes dialogue as the solution to conflict and abjures violence as the "ultimate denial of a civil ethos."[88] By institutionalizing civic values into the justice system, the rule of law becomes a supporter of civic ethics rather than its repressor. Redressing large-scale poverty is an essential precursor to inclusion. Economic inequity, and its attendant denial of liberties, is a scourge not limited to the developing world, as attest minority ghettos from Detroit to Manchester.

But what, asks Sajoo, "turns normative values into lived experience?"[89] Here Sajoo, like Taylor, emphasizes the crucial role played by educators, writers, artists, and public intellectuals in shaping the public worldview, which in turn affects public actions. "Shared public images," writes Sajoo, "lie behind how we understand ideas like 'democracy,' 'justice' and 'religion'—*and act accordingly*."[90] It is these images that compose our *social imaginaries*: "the way in which we picture the world we inhabit."[91] In his article "Civil Imagination after September 11, 2001," Sajoo writes:

Social imaginaries know no borders. They are local and global, drawing on traditions in which cherished values come alive. Attar, Rumi and Ibn Tufayl knew this, as did the musicians, painters and traders who trekked the transcultural pathways of the medieval Silk Road. Among their creative heirs today are Saadi Youssef and Naguib Mahfouz, Abbas Kiarostami and Samira Makhmalbaf, Khaled Hosseini and M.G. Vassanji, all of whom sculpt the landscapes of our minds and influence the way we see the world. This civil imagination is where an ethos of pluralism ultimately takes root, against the dire tides of chauvinism.[92]

VII

It is in the public sphere, then, where pluralist values take root. Bhiku Parekh advances (after Habermas and Rawls) the notion of a society of individuals with a common affiliation to common citizenship. "In this view," he says, "a political community is a voluntary association of free and equal citizens held together by principles of justice as embodied in the structure of public authority and a regime of rights and obligations."[93] This is not aimed at conflating diversity, but rather at strengthening bonds between diverse groups: a society's cohesion is threatened by the coexistence of strong group identities with weak common identities. "Strong multicultural identities are a good thing," says Modood, "but they need a framework of vibrant, dynamic, national narratives and the ceremonies and rituals which give expression to our common citizenship."[94]

Still, this cannot be a solely legal endeavor. As admits Parekh, the law "cannot compel a passenger not to leave her seat or mumble abuses when an immigrant of a different colour sits next to her, or require a bank clerk not to keep an immigrant waiting for an unduly long period of time."[95] The law cannot eliminate discrimination by formalizing equality. It cannot inspire quotidian kindnesses or metaphysical notions of common humanity. It cannot motivate people to conquer indigence, which is one of the most serious undercurrents of civic tension. Only a lived ethic of engagement can.

This is the basis for the support by so many scholars for faith-based public ethics. Sajoo argues that while democratic life is buttressed on the rule of law, it is *empowered* by the ethical sense that drives the everyday acts of civility upon which meaningful citizenship relies. Indeed, as Bruce Lawrence asks in the IIS volume *Muslim Modernities*, can modern-day citizenship even be defined apart from religious categories? He answers in the negative and quotes Charles Taylor for support: "religious language is the one in which people find it meaningful to code their strong moral and political experience."[96]

But this does not translate into the merging of church/mosque and state. Rather, in Filali-Ansary's articulation, it demands a "conceptual" approach to secularism that recognizes the diversity of human experience and the impossibility of transplanting preconceived notions, such as the strict separation of church and state, from one setting to another. In the Islamic conception, argues An-Na'im, there is an inherent synergy between the religious and secular spheres of life, which is naturally opposed to the sort of unilateral secularism in which the notions of faith and ethics simply disappear from society. Faith is vital to the vast majority of humanity, and thus, argues Modood, it cannot be ignored by democratic multicultural society, in which it should have institutionalized public space.

However, public integrity must extend beyond the sphere of government, argues the Aga Khan. Ethical lapses in medicine and education, malfeasance in business and banking, and dishonesty among journalists, scientists, and scholars all undermine the most promising democracies. In the final analysis, he argues, a healthy sense of public integrity is difficult to nurture without a strong religious underpinning:

> In the Islamic tradition, the conduct of one's worldly life is inseparably intertwined with the concerns of one's spiritual life. One cannot talk about integrity without talking about faith. ... From that perspective, I would put high among our priorities, both within and outside the Islamic world, the need to renew our spiritual traditions. [...] If modernism lacks a spiritual dimension, it will look like materialism. And if the modernizing influence of the West is insistently and exclusively a secularizing influence, then

much of the Islamic world will be somewhat distanced from it.[97]

He cautions that "spirituality should not become a way of escaping from the world but rather a way of more actively engaging in it."[98] He cites Imam 'Ali, who wrote: "no belief is like modesty and patience, no attainment is like humility, no honour is like knowledge, no power is like forbearance, and no support is more reliable than consultation."[99] Keeping this in mind, the Aga Khan concludes that "Hazrat Ali's regard for knowledge reinforces the compatibility of faith and the world. And his respect for consultation is, in my view, a commitment to tolerant and open-hearted democratic processes."[100]

Thus, in the contemporary Ismaili conception, religion can provide a moral check and a moral impetus for responsible and effective democratic citizenship, and while Islam does not call for the unification of the secular and religious, it does call for a cooperative society founded on the principle of social justice. This is what Hefner calls civil Islam, "a public religion that makes itself heard though independent associations, spirited public dialogue, and the demonstrated decency of believers." The conclusion here, perhaps, is that although religion is not the *only* source of ethics, it is the source for so much of humankind and thus should not be discounted.

7

PLURALISM AND CIVIC CULTURE

At last, made perfect in Reality
You will be gone, and only God will be.
　　　　　—Farid ud-Din 'Attar, *The Conference of the Birds*

I know a woman here in Toronto who is very dear to my
heart. [...] Though she has lived in Toronto for over thirty
years, her French-speaking mind still slips on occasion on the
understanding of English sounds. And so, when she first heard
of Hare Krishnas, she didn't hear right. She heard 'Hairless
Christians', and that is what they were to her for many years.
When I corrected her, I told her that in fact she was not so
wrong; that Hindus, in their capacity for love, are indeed
hairless Christians, just as Muslims, in the way they see God
in everything, are bearded Hindus, and Christians, in their
devotion to God, are hat-wearing Muslims.
　　　　　　　　　　　　　　　　—Yann Martel, *Life of Pi*

I

Why pluralism? For Martha Nussbaum, writing in a 2007 volume titled *Democracy and the New Religious Pluralism*, the liberal commitment to equality and justice requires democracies "to support an idea of toleration, understood as involving respect, not only grudging acceptance, and to extend toleration to all religious and secular doctrines, limiting only conduct that violates the rights of other citizens."[1] Writing in the same volume, Thomas Banchoff points out that Nussbaum's last requirement is the only "normative undertone"[2] for the sociopolitical phenomenon of religious pluralism, which itself is a crucible for pluralism since it promotes no particular epistemic truth or political philosophy.

Filali-Ansary makes a similar observation in the 2009 Aga Khan University Institute for the Study of Muslim Civilisations (AKU-ISMC) volume *The Challenge of Pluralism* when he says that "in even discussing a concept like pluralism, we have already moved away from the idea that what is true, or good, can be defined and expressed in a single, 'unorthodox' way."[3] The fundamental question then becomes not "what is true?" but, rather, "how do we live with multiple truths?" In response Filali-Ansary goes beyond Nussbaum above and employs Diana Eck to argue that toleration is "too thin a foundation for a world of religious difference and proximity."[4]

II

In her conceptualization of pluralism on Harvard University's The Pluralism Project website,[5] Eck makes four essential points: (1) Pluralism is *"the energetic engagement with diversity,"* which is required because diversity without relationship-building leads to increasing tension: "today, religious diversity is a given, but pluralism is not a given; it is an achievement." (2) Pluralism is *"the active seeking of understanding across lines of difference."* Tolerance may be a necessary public virtue, but it "does nothing to remove our ignorance of one another, and leaves in place the stereotype, the half-truth, the fears that underlie old patterns of division and violence." (3) Pluralism is *"the encounter of commitments,"* and requires us to bring along our identities and differences in the relationship-building exercise. (4) Pluralism is *"based on dialogue,"* which is a two-way process that reveals both commonalities and differences and, essentially, "involves the commitment to being at the table—with one's commitments."

To some extent, the Aga Khan's commitment to pluralism appears to build upon a similar conceptual infrastructure. As a point of departure, he declares, "pluralism [is] essential for peace, a statement that is unfortunately documented by armed conflict in contexts of cultural, ethnic or religious differences on almost every continent."[6] He adds elsewhere, "the rejection of pluralism plays a significant role in breeding destructive conflicts."[7] To this effect, Ashutosh Varshney demonstrates an inverse link between civil society and civic conflict and argues that ignoring the fact of diversity risks the type of conflict such as those between the Protestants and Catholics in Northern Ireland, or the blacks and whites in the United States and South Africa, or the Tamils and Sinhalas in Sri Lanka, or the Shias and Sunnis in Pakistan.[8] According to Varshney, "forms of engagement, if robust, promote peace: contrariwise, their absence or weakness opens up space for ethnic violence."[9]

This lack of active understanding and engagement, says the Aga Khan, is the source of conflict. He is "convinced" that "many of today's problems could have been avoided if there had been better understanding," and asserts that "what we have been observing in recent decades is not a clash of civilizations but a clash of ignorance."[10] Arguing that both the Afghan and Iraqi situations resulted from a lack of precise understanding, he concludes that the 9/11 attack was a "direct consequence of the international community ignoring the human tragedy that was Afghanistan at that time"[11] For this reason, he proclaims, like Eck above, that "pluralist societies are not accidents of history. They are a product of enlightened education and continuous investment by governments and all of civil society in recognizing and celebrating the diversity of the world's peoples."[12]

Thus, for the Aga Khan, "the effective world of the future will be one of pluralism,"[13] in which diversity will be understood and appreciated. In this conception, education in pluralism becomes integral for the positive restructuring of all global communities, for it is only by embracing pluralism as an essential civic building block that they will be able to emerge as positive partners in a global system of cooperating and converging civilizations.

These convictions are relevant for today's forty-some Muslim-majority countries, which, says Filali-Ansary, "have found themselves, in an age of globalisation and mass communication, projected into and confronted with a world in which they realise their difference as a group, as well as the fact of diversity within their own ranks."[14] Most Muslim-majority countries—suffering, as they do, from the postcolonial malaise—have low levels of economic and social development, are subject to political oppression, and lack the necessary administrative, legal, and economic mechanisms to sustain properly functioning political and civic systems. The consequence of these confused circumstances is weak rules of law, which results in destructive conflicts and persecution of minorities.

The cessation of conflict, then, appears as the Aga Khan's central concern when he touts pluralism as the key to survival and human progress—not only in war-torn societies, but in all societies where different groups coexist. Basing himself on the forty years of development work of the AKDN, he concludes that institutional development is the essential requisite to engendering a sustainable pluralist civil society, because, he says, "no country, to my knowledge, can achieve stable, continuous growth if its civil society is constrained by inherent institutional instability."[15] Furthermore, he argues that "without support for pluralism, civil society does not function."[16] Thus, a diverse and engaged civil society and an environment that respects and encourages pluralism are complementary, making up—along with competent democratic governance—the "three essential preconditions for the successful transition of the poorest areas of the world into modern, peaceful societies."[17]

III

Perhaps reflective of the tenor of our times, "pluralism" as a term of distinction came into its own only in the twentieth century, evinced by the appearance of philosophical works dedicated to the subject. Whereas "diversity" is the presence of heterogeneity, "pluralism"—as a sociopolitical philosophy—is the *valuing* of human diversity to the extent that it promotes the existence and promulgation of various internal groups and their differing ethnic, religious, or political backgrounds within a society.[18]

At the Annual Meeting of the European Bank for Reconstruction and Development in Tashkent, Uzbekistan, on May 5, 2003, the Aga Khan defined pluralism as "the recognition that people of diverse backgrounds and interests, organizations and projects of different types, and different kinds and forms of creative expression are all valuable and therefore deserving of recognition and support by government and society as a whole."[19]

Robert Hefner, speaking more specifically about the liberal context, defines "civic pluralism" as "a public culture and social organization premised on equal rights, tolerance-in-pluralism, and a legally recognized differentiation of state and religious authority."[20] We may speak of civic pluralist democracy, he writes, when "such a civic pluralism is in turn linked to a system of free and fair elections, a separation of powers in the state, the rule of law, and human rights."[21]

However, pluralism itself is a pliable concept with diverse forms of pluralistic theory and practice. Contemporary liberal political thought has generated plural conceptions of pluralism, such as *modus vivendi*, overlapping consensus, convergence pluralism, and agonistic (or conflict) pluralism. Our concern here is with the particular conception of pluralism that the Aga Khan and contemporary Ismailism espouse. Ismailism gravitates toward deep-diversity forms of multiculturalism that accommodate and celebrate a wide range of deeply divergent religious and nonreligious communities. However, it steers way from agonistic or conflictual versions of deep-diversity pluralism that would envisage a more combative political interaction between diverse ideological and religious parties. The constitutional order of the society should work to facilitate collaborative rather than conflictual interaction.

The Aga Khan has, in effect, attempted to institutionalize and advance this evolving Ismaili conception of pluralism by establishing the Global Centre for Pluralism in Ottawa, a joint project between the Aga Khan and the Government of Canada. In January 2012, the Global Centre published on its website a document entitled "Defining Pluralism," which articulates pluralism as (1) an ethic of respect that values human diversity, and (2) a set of practices and outcomes, as well as a set of intentions.[22] Perhaps what is most emblematic of the Ismaili approach to pluralism is that it views pluralism as a "process, not a product": "it is a series of choices informed by the desire to balance equality of treatment with equity of outcome. Although a journey, pluralism is not a fixed destination. The work of seeking pluralism is never ending."[23] The Global Centre conceives of the pluralist society as constructed on a public investment in "good governance, strong civic institutions, and sound public policy choices that promote respect for diversity, whereby diversity itself becomes a public good and citizens are enabled to realize their rights as well as their obligations."[24]

The "Defining Pluralism" document argues that "respect for diversity transcends tolerance to embrace difference as an engine of commonwealth," and that, in contrast to multiculturalism, "pluralism emphasizes individual choices as well as collective compromise and mutual obligation as routes to peace, stability and human development."[25] The document further contends that the political and economic benefits of a society based on a pluralist ethic are obvious: through enhanced intergroup cooperation, governments are able to build loyalty and mobilize networks of support for their citizenry; such stability, in turn, leads to a positive and thriving economic environment, which is a requisite for a strong civil society. However, it recognizes that "policies to support pluralism must address the relationship of the state to groups as well as the dynamics among groups," and "a commitment to pluralism often necessitates adjustments in the principles, institutions and procedures of the state."[26]

Following this, it articulates certain drivers of pluralism:[27] (1) economic well-being—*Poverty impedes pluralism through exclusion*; (2) law and politics—*Institutional mechanisms preempt violence by managing conflict through political means*; (3) citizenship and civil society—*To support pluralism, citizens must enjoy the freedom to meet their civic obligations as well as exercise their rights*; (4) education and culture—*Education is a route to intercultural literacy and communication as well as sustainable human development*; (5) history and memory—*Historical literacy is a route to reconciliation and the past is a key to predicting pluralism failure*.

In the context of religion and the interactions between religious groups, we may define "pluralism" as the idea that (1) different religious groups practicing their own religions can coexist in society, and (2) no one group has a monopoly on salvation. "Pluralism" is differentiated from "inclusivism" as such: while a proponent of the former *recognizes* the validity of difference, the latter *tolerates* the existence of differing opinion but believes itself superior. "Exclusivism," on the other hand, rejects divergence of opinion and asserts its own as true.

We may also speak here of a theological "ethos of pluralism" in contemporary Muslim thought. Shah-Kazemi, in an article published on the Institute of Ismaili Studies website, writes that "it is not so much 'religious pluralism' as 'metaphysical unity' that establishes a deep-rooted and far-reaching tolerance," and thus "what emerges is a mode of tolerance that is organically related to an awareness of the divine presence in all things, an apprehension of the inner holiness of all that exists."[28] Thus, the "ethos of pluralism" refers here to the *idea* that different groups and individuals can/must coexist and respect each other's beliefs because there persists between humans an intrinsic, metaphysical unity—that there is within each human a spark of the divine flame that links them both to the Divine and to each other. This notion of unity propounds a respect for the other on the basis of a common humanity, which in turn promotes a shared appreciation for common goals and interests.

IV

A common critique against pluralism-in-Islam is that Muhammad did not know of or use the term "pluralism," and thus to suggest that he implemented pluralist policies is anachronistic as well as historically and academically fallacious. But supporters of Islamic pluralism argue that the *fact* of pluralism existed in Muhammad's Arabia, exemplified by the cooperation of the different religiocultural groups referred to in the "Constitution of Medina". They further argue that certain Qur'anic verses, as well as the inclusion of various religious groups in the Prophet's Community, the *Ummah*, suggest that the *ethos* of pluralism was both understood and practiced by Muhammad as part of his policy at Medina.

To be sure, while examples of pluralism in classical Muslim historical experience are widespread, these are not identical to modern notions of pluralism and their related notions of common citizenship or equality of opportunity. Indeed, Aziz al-Azmeh, writing in the AKU-ISMC volume mentioned above, argues that the policies of historical Muslim societies would appear inequitable to the modern mind and thus not be understood today as "pluralistic". "All in all," he argues, "classical Muslim historical experience presents us with a set of precedents of plurality and pluralism which would not be recognisable to modern notions of pluralism, or which would provide 'sources of inspiration' for them."[29]

Contemporary Ismailism, however, does look to the past as a source of inspiration, and it does choose to locate pluralism in Qur'anic ethics, Islamic doctrine, and Muslim history, as is evinced by the writings of scholars such as Azim Nanji, Ali Asani, and Amyn Sajoo, who dedicates a chapter in his book *Pluralism in 'Old Societies and New States'* (Singapore, 1994) to "The Islamic Heritage in Pluralist Perspective."

Despite al-Azmeh's assertion that supporting "indigenist pluralism" with "shadowy historical memories, real or contrived, is not useful for the present purposes of any Muslim society,"[30] it persists among liberal

Muslim scholars from doyens like Seyyed Hossein Nasr to apologists like Ahmad Moussalli and all the Nurcolish Majdids, Abdolkarim Soroushs, Bassam Tibis, and Hasan Hanafis in between. It persists even in the social imaginary, from William Dalrymple's exposition of the mingling of religions/cultures at the end of Muslim rule in nineteenth-century India in *The Last Mughal* (Bloomsbury, 2008) to Tariq Ali's vivid description of the end of Andalusian pluralism with the eighth-century Christian conquest of Iberia in his *Shadows of the Pomegranate Tree* (Verso Press, 1997).

What, then, we may ask, makes the idea of Islamic pluralism so persistent? The response, simply, is that mediaeval Muslim societies were more "pluralistic" than other contemporary civilizations. Al-Azmeh admits here that "Muslim polities were benign and tolerant and knew little of the long-term hysterical fear and persecution of outsiders experienced by their European contemporaries obsessed with demons, witches, Moors, Saracens, Cathars, Jews and lepers".[31]

To be fair, these sorts of accounts belie a widely held scholarly assessment. Even Bernard Lewis acknowledges in his *Jews of Islam* that Muslim societies were egalitarian and afforded the individual far greater social mobility than the rule of aristocratic privilege in Christian Europe or the caste system in Hindu India.[32]

Contemporary Ismaili thinkers, like other liberal Muslim scholars, would argue that these historical Muslim societies were influenced by the Qur'an's promulgation of an ethos of pluralism and resulting position toward the other, as well as the practical example of Muhammad's policies toward other religious groups. Here, they seem to be making a rhetorical point about Islam's "ethos of pluralism," which, in any case, supports their construction of a vertical history that bridges past and present via an ethical Bifröst.

V

Aside from the critique of anachronism, the most widespread criticism against an Islamic pluralism is that Islam is a religion and therefore must have "special problems"[33] in granting salvation to nonmembers. But, for contemporary Ismaili thought, the Qur'an is explicit in its religious pluralism, offering salvation to all humans who believe, regardless of their religious affiliation. Abdulaziz Sachedina, for example, argues that "Islam has never harboured a widespread belief that Jews and Christians are to be denied salvation if they do not first convert to Islam."[34]

Advocates of pluralism-in-Islam cite a matrix of key Qur'anic verses that they suggest supports a Qur'anic ideal of pluralism. In their view, the Qur'an recognizes and promotes diversity by proclaiming to the Prophet Muhammad that if God had willed "He would have made you [all] a single people" (Q. 5:48). But humankind was made into "nations and tribes" so that they may come to "know one another" (Q. 49:13). Thus, the Qur'an encourages individuals to come to know people, both Muslim and non-Muslim, who believe differently from themselves, and to "vie with one another in good works" (Q. 5:48). This fraternal ethic, it is argued, is rooted in the Qur'anic notion of a common humanity, which stresses that all humans, regardless of ideological persuasion, were created "from a single soul" (Q. 4:1) and thus have within them the spark of the Divine. In this conception, it matters not whether one is a Jew, or a Christian, or a Sabaean, since those who do right "shall have their reward with their Lord" (Q. 2:62). Indeed, the Qur'an seems to universalize salvific opportunity, since "the noblest of you in the sight of God is the best in conduct" (Q. 49:13).

In this way, the Qur'an appears to decree that humankind's judgment depends on its righteousness, not its allegiance to this or that creed. Certainly, this idea is a cardinal crux of the AKDN: the IIS article articulating the AKDN's ethical framework states that "service of God is not only worship, but also service to humanity, and abiding by the duty of trust toward the rest of creation."[35] Thus, the idea of social responsibility is, for the Ismaili institutions, tied intimately to the notion of Islam's universality, which the IIS's work endeavors to show is buttressed on an ethos of pluralism that suffuses the Qur'an. The article, "AKDN: An Ethical Framework," continues, articulating its conception of Islam as a system that requires human action for divine salvation: "Righteousness, says the Quran, is not only fulfilling one's religious obligations. Without social responsibility, religiosity is a show of conceit. Islam is, therefore, both *din* and *dunya*, spirit and matter, distinct but linked, neither to be forsaken."[36] On this view, the call for social justice is the foundational impetus for Muhammad's inclusive *Ummah* ("Community of Believers"), composed of diverse and different human beings joined together by the twin human responsibilities to ennoble both Self and Society.

In short, Qur'anic pluralism is soteriological in nature. The Qur'an extends its salvational invitation to all nations, whom it says have all received prophets from God (Q. 10:47), who, in turn, makes no distinction between those prophets (Q. 3:84). Furthermore, says Muhammad Asad, by insisting that salvation is to be achieved by righteous deeds, not allegiance to creed (Q. 2:62), the Scripture shifts the focus toward the universal—the promise of salvation is a gift to *all* humans, not *some* humans:

> Lo! Those who believe (in that which is revealed unto thee, Muhammad), and those who are Jews, and Christians, and Sabaeans - whoever believeth in God and the Last Day and doeth right - surely their reward is with their Lord, and there shall no fear come upon them neither shall they grieve (Q. 2:62).

According to Asad, this is a fundamental doctrine of Islam and is "unparalleled" in any other faith:

> [T]he idea of "salvation" is here made conditional upon three elements only: belief in God, belief in the Day of Judgment [i.e., individual moral responsibility],[37] and righteous action in life.[38]

Indeed, says Asani, the Qur'an "[repeatedly] declares that on the Day of Judgment all human beings will be judged on their moral performance, irrespective of their formal religious affiliation."[39]

Other Qur'anic verses cited by scholars to espouse a universalist position include 28:88[40] and 2:115, the latter of which reads: "Unto God belong the East and the West, and whithersoever ye turn, there is God's Countenance."[41] Through such verses, it is argued, the Divine comes to be seen not as the property of any individual or creed, but rather as a mercy to each individual seeker, and, says Shah-Kazemi, makes possible "a particular mode of self-knowledge."[42] In this conception, says Nasr, the word "God" is transformed into an ideal, or an idea, that relates to the personal philosophy of each individual. Salvation, he concludes, is therefore open to "anyone who accepts a Divine revelation [in] its most universal sense, be he a Muslim, Christian, Jew or Zoroastrian."[43]

The Qur'an here limits its salvational promise to those who believe; atheists are not included. This is the sort of "special problem" that some argue applies to the notion of religious pluralism. But all comprehensive doctrines have their limits: the liberal state, for all its inclusive tolerance, draws the line at behavior that threatens its core commitments—what it defines as illiberal. The Qur'an's soteriological pluralism appears to draw the line at unbelief.

So, in the pluralist conception of Islam, creedal allegiance is not a determining factor for salvational success. Shah-Kazemi draws attention to the Qur'an's repeated exhortations against the exclusivist claims of pre-Islamic traditions, and argues that the Qur'an "does not contradict the exclusivist claims of the Jews and the Christians[44] with an exclusivism of its own, that is, with a claim that only 'Muslims,' in the specific sense,[45] go to Paradise."[46] Access to salvation, he argues, is broadened—"faithful submission, allied to virtue: such are the two indispensible requisites for salvation."[47]

In this account of the Qur'anic worldview, diversity is posited as both divinely willed as well as humankind's natural state. Verse 3:84, mentioned above, is held up as exemplary, since it charges Muhammad to "make no distinction" between the prophets of God, among whom the verse lists Abraham, Moses, and Jesus. Going beyond this short list, however, the Qur'an further asserts that God's prophets are not restricted to the Abrahamic traditions and that while God inspired Muhammad just as He did previous messengers, the Prophet is unaware of the identities of the full spectrum of God's messengers: "Lo! We inspire thee as We inspired Noah and the prophets after him, as We inspired Abraham and Ishmael and Isaac and Jacob and the tribes, and Jesus and Job and Jonah and Aaron and Solomon, and as We imparted unto David the Psalms; *And messengers We have mentioned unto thee before and messengers We have not mentioned unto thee*" (Q. 4:163–4).[48]

Aga Khan III, in his memoirs, mentions by name some of these messengers and argues that Islam's universalism in this regard is a matter of course:

All Islamic schools of thought accept it as a fundamental principle that, for centuries, for thousands of years before the advent of Mohammed, there arose from time to time messengers, illumined by Divine grace, for and amongst those races of the earth which had sufficiently advanced intellectually to comprehend such a message. Thus Abraham, Moses, Jesus, and all the Prophets of Israel are universally accepted by Islam. Muslims indeed know no limitation merely to the Prophets of Israel; they are ready to admit that there were similar Divinely-inspired messengers in other countries—Gautama Buddha, Shri Krishna, and Shri Ram in India, Socrates in Greece, the wise men of China, and many other sages and saints among peoples and civilizations of which we have now lost trace.[49]

Thus, in the modern Ismaili interpretation of Islam, non-Abrahamic traditions are viewed as valid recipients of God's universal Revelation.

Asani draws attention here to the term used in the Qur'an to refer to communities who have received revelation in the form of scripture—the *ahl al-kitab* or "People of the Book"—as evidence of the Qur'anic belief in the truths of other religious traditions. While commonly used to refer to Abrahamic traditions, Asani argues that "the pluralistic nature of this term is evident in the use of the noun *Book* in the singular rather than the plural," thus emphasizing that the different traditions "follow one and the same Book, not various conflicting scriptures."[50]

The concept of the People of the Book referred originally to the major monotheistic traditions of the Arabian milieu, exemplified by the inclusion of Jews and other religious groups in the Constitution of Medina as part of the Muslim *Ummah*. But, says Asani, when Muslim armies encountered groups such as the Zoroastrians in Iran and the Hindus and Buddhists in India, all of whom claimed to have received revelation, the term was expanded to include the scriptures of those religious groups under the umbrella term "Book." Here, he argues that the Muslim encounter with other traditions was deep, and he provides the example of the seventeenth-century Mughal prince, Dara Shikoh, who declared the Hindu scriptures to be the "storehouse of monotheism" and claimed that they were the *kitab maknun*, or "hidden scripture," referred to in the Qur'an (Q. 56:77–80).[51]

Certainly, Asani admits, not all Muslims were ready to broaden the category of People of the Book to traditions not mentioned specifically in the Qur'an. Nevertheless, he concludes, "the fact remains that these types of interpretations were made possible by the pluralistic nature of the Quranic worldview."[52] Asani is a staunch supporter of a Qur'anic pluralism, an opinion he expresses outright in his article "On Pluralism, Intolerance, and the Quran" when he says, "my contention is that the Quran essentially espouses a pluralist worldview, one that promotes peace and harmony among nations and peoples."[53] And "it is only by completely disregarding the original historical contexts of revelation," he concludes, "that the exclusivist Muslim exegetes have been able to counteract the pluralist ethos that so thoroughly pervades the Quran."[54]

Doubtlessly, religions and their scriptures have been interpreted in different ways in different times to produce often contradictory political or social readings. Asani says that anti-pluralist or exclusivist readings were conjured in order to advance hegemonic political or religious goals.[55] Here Shah-Kazemi admits that "a truly inclusivist metaphysical perspective must recognize the validity of the exclusivist, theological perspective," but nevertheless also "uphold as more compelling, more convincing, and more 'true,' the universalist understanding of Islam."[56]

Thus, proponents of a Qur'anic pluralism contend that the Qur'an's *overall orientation* is toward the promotion of a pluralist society—harmony of existence between diverse peoples. These scholars, then, argue that the proper consideration of historical contexts would reveal a universalist message whose aim is to establish amid humankind's diversity a justice and unity that reflects on Earth the divine qualities of *'Adl* (Justice) and *Tawhid* (Unity).

VI

For Sajoo, the Qur'an's ethos of pluralism is no mere abstraction—it pervades Muslim lifeworlds. This is exemplified, he says, in the life of Muhammad, who once rose to his feet while in midconversation to offer respect to a Jewish funeral in progress; upon being asked why by his companions, the Prophet retorted, "Is he not a human soul?"[57]

Sajoo argues that the Qur'an's ethos of pluralism instilled in the Muslim consciousness the recognition of an intrinsic human unity, regardless of creedal allegiances. This ethos is avouched, for example, in the verse that circumvallates the Aga Khan's Golden Jubilee emblem, which declares that all of humankind was created from "a single soul" (Q. 4:1). The ethos of pluralism, declares Sajoo, is "hard-wired" into the Qur'an and is thus a motivator of Muslim decisions. In his view, "pluralism is hard-wired into the Qur'an, which time and again proclaims that an inclusive *umma* is the only legitimate community of the good, that the very idea of 'Islam' encompasses the Judaeo-Christian heritage, and that there can be no compulsion in religion."[58]

The definitive proof of the Qur'an's pluralist tenor, says Shah-Kazemi, is its affirmation that a diversity of ways (and its resultant interfaith dialogue) is divinely ordained (Q. 5:48, 22:67).[59] Diversity among peoples is a celebration of divine mercy and grandeur, says the Qur'an, and the difference of humanity's languages and colors is among God's signs (Q. 30:22).[60] For Shah-Kazemi, this worldview is reflective of the pluralist tenor of Islam, which envelops previous revelations and their followers into a unified human community, despite their chronological differences. He quotes the thirteenth-century Andalusian thinker Ibn al-'Arabi to show how this ethos informed and inspired Muslim lifeworlds and luminaries: "Beware of being bound up by a particular creed and rejecting others as unbelief! Try to make yourself a prime matter for all forms of religious belief. God is greater and wider than to be confined to one particular creed to the exclusion of others. For He says, Wherever ye turn, there is the Face of God."[61]

Asani, like others, sees peaceful pluralistic coexistence as the original motor of Islam. He traces the ideals of unity and coexistence through Muslim history as undergirding the policies of early Muslim communities, exemplified, he says, in Imam 'Ali's seventh-century letter to his governor of Egypt, which instructed him to "incline your heart to show clemency, affection, sympathy, and beneficence to your subjects"—after all, concludes the caliph-Imam, "either they are your brothers in religion or your equals in creation."[62]

Nanji draws attention to Farid-ud-din ʿAttar's twelfth-century Persian poem, *The Conference of the Birds*, as revealing the notion of unity in diversity through the allegory of thirty birds (*sih murgh*) questing to find their teacher, the Simurgh. For Nanji, the poem expresses concerns about "human conflict, human distinctions, the meanings of the self in a community,"[63] through the birds' journey over seven valleys and mountains in the quest to understand the nature of their "birdness." Once the birds reach their goal and find no Simurgh, they realize that they themselves are the "*sih murgh*," bound together as one in a common metaphysical unity: "When [the birds] sit in contemplation and awaken from that contemplation, they looked around and they awaken to a profound act of understanding. The word in Persian for thirty is '*sih*' and the word for bird is '*murgh*'. They are the *Simurgh*. There was no *Simurgh* outside of them. Their experience, their quest, their origin had brought them to their beginning."[64]

"Similarly," Nanji concludes, "it is through the discovery of our common, shared heritage that we will learn to define our shared humanity."[65] So, it is argued, the metaphysical concept of apprehending the innate divinity and commonality among humans informed the foundational ethos of Muslim society.

To be sure, writes one scholar, Muslims "have always understood—and constructed—their 'Islams' in a context of pluralism."[66] Muhammad's Medina was comprised of a diversity of socioreligious groups who united under Muhammad's direction to form one Community (*Ummah*). That partnership was formalized in the 622 CE Constitution of Medina, which states that "the Jews ... are a community (*ummah*) along with the believers (*muʾminun*)."[67] For Sajoo, the founding of this "civic *umma*" was necessarily guided by the pluralist ethos of the Qurʾan. In his view, "the ethical imperative is distinguished by its pluralism, religious and civic, as in the oft-quoted verses, 'We have made you into nations and tribes that you may know one another' (49:13), and 'If God had pleased He would have made you a single people' (5:48). Specific moral lessons are drawn from universals, and universal inferences from the particular."[68]

Later Muslim civilizations, says Asani, took up these lessons and based their policies toward minorities on the Qurʾan's intrinsically humanist ethos and the Prophet's example at Medina: "such tolerance is later reflected in the policies of the Arab dynasties of Spain, the Fatimids in North Africa, and the Turkish Ottomans in the Middle East, granting maximum individual and group autonomy to those adhering to a religious tradition other than Islam."[69]

Indeed, for Daftary, the successes of the Fatimids were "in large measure due to the remarkable ethnic and religious tolerance of the dynasty and the administrative stability of the Fatimid state."[70] In Jiwa's conception, the Fatimid caliph-Imams purposefully connected themselves with the Prophetic example of pluralism, "self-consciously bypassing its various other political and theological expressions over the course of centuries, some of which were less favourable to [other religious] communities."[71] She quotes G. E. von Grunebaum's bold remarks as support: "All praise is due the Fatimids for having known how to induce the communities under their sway to develop their courage and enterprise and to preserve their intellectual élan without damaging that unity of the larger community which hinged on the dynasty's sense of purpose."[72]

Critics may argue here that things were not as rosy as pluralism's proponents propound. Sajoo acknowledges that examples of intolerance exist in all societies, but, he says, this is evinced even in the legacy of modern Western civilization, which includes "two world wars and the Holocaust, the genocide of native populations in grand colonial ventures,"[73] among other such events. But, he concludes, "the object here is not to set up a normative or historical contest among the ethical traditions of Christianity, Islam and Judaism,"[74] all of whose scriptures contain bloody examples of exclusivism. The point made by Ismaili advocates is that there is a pervasive ethos of pluralism in the Qur'an that can be a source of inspiration for creating peaceful, pluralist societies that aim toward meaningful coexistence with the other.

VII

That ethos of pluralism is the essential philosophical buttress upon which rests civic culture in general. Through involvement in civic life, one is obliged to come to terms with the beliefs, attachments, and concerns of the other; through the bond of common citizenship, both one and the other begin to reconcile their differences in favor of an overarching appreciation of commonality in interests, goals, and humanity. Civil society, then, is an important facet of the pluralist endeavor—it is the vehicle through which knowledge of the other is actualized.

For the Aga Khan, "civil society makes an enormous contribution to human development, filling the gaps between government, the business sector and the family. It does things the state cannot and thus supports citizens in nation building. Most important, civil society underwrites human progress. It acts as a stabiliser or buttress in times of economic slowdown or social stress. When democracies are failing, or have failed, it is the institutions of civil society that can carry an added burden to help sustain improvements in quality of life." Thus, he concludes, a robust civil society "is critical to supporting pluralism and ultimately, effective democracies."[75]

Beyond the assumed practical benefits of safeguarding the individual from the power of the state, at the heart of discussions about civil society is the notion of "civility." This, says Edward Shils, is the "conduct of a person whose individual self-consciousness has been partly superseded by his collective self-consciousness,"[76] which means "regarding other persons, including one's adversaries, as members of the same society, even though they belong to different parties or to different religious communities or to different ethnic groups."[77] This is the basis of the pluralist project, in which the recognition of the other is vital to the subsistence of peaceful and fulfilling civic life.

For Augustus Norton, civility refers to that everyday cooperation and civic friendship, which "implies tolerance, [and] the willingness of individuals to accept disparate political views and social attitudes."[78] Such willingness allows individuals to express their attitudes and orientations *civilly* through a network of autonomous institutions—such as those of market economy, competing political parties, independent judiciary, free press, voluntary associations, etc.—that facilitate participation in civic life.

However, for scholars like Şerif Merdin, "civil society is a Western dream," and thus "does not translate into Islamic terms."[79] But Aziz Esmail, writing in the IIS volume *Civil Society in the Muslim World*, posits that such assertions carry the underlying assumption that "civil society is one phenomenon, and Muslim societies, another; and that these two may be matched against each other."[80] This, he concludes, is asymmetrical, because "civil society" is a philosophical/sociopolitical concept, while "Muslim societies" is at least a geographical one and at most a religiocultural one.

For Sajoo, it is untenable to suggest that civil society—as the "space of uncoerced human association"—is limited in practice to segments of the European or American continents, especially when put in the light of historical and contemporary cross-civilizational realities. He asks: "if civil society is wedded exclusively to the particular unfolding of North Atlantic/West European history, why the readiness to acknowledge the prospect of Czech, Hungarian, Polish, Rumanian, Slovak ... Argentine, Brazilian, Chilean, Mexican ... Chinese, Philippine, South Korean and Vietnamese dreams of institutionalising the legal, economic and political frameworks of civic culture?"[81]

At this juncture, Sajoo critiques Mardin's assumption that the Muslim dream is a "social equilibrium created under the aegis of a just prince" in which the authority of the ruler trumps the rule of law. Sajoo contends that, from the outset, Islam provided for society an "uncoerced space" in the institution of the *Ummah*. He recalls that the initial Western conception of civil society was essentially an ethical one, not a political one, and thus shares much with the Islamic conception of the "good society" as captured in the appellation "Ummah"[82] Though perhaps different from European forms or developments, he concludes, elements of civic culture abound in Muslim societies and are central to their functioning. This contention appears to be part of an overarching Ismaili concern with civic culture, evidenced by the publication of IIS volumes such as *Civil Society in the Muslim World* (London, 2002) and *Muslim Modernities: Expressions of the Civil Imagination* (London, 2008), both edited by Sajoo.

In any case, it is a contention shared by a wider spectrum of contemporary Muslim scholars, such as Hasan Hanafi, who argues that "if civil society means a system of checks and balances that prevent a preponderance of power residing in either the state or societal institutions, then Islamic theory from the earliest period demonstrates similar concerns."[83] Typically, these scholars argue, like John Esposito, that "Islamic history provides examples of many nonstate actors, institutions, and organizations that served as intermediaries between the ruler/government and the people, between state and society."[84] In mediaeval Muslim societies, the mercantile class, Sufi orders, and perhaps most importantly, the religious scholars (*ulema*) all represented autonomous groups that provided a check to the power of the rulers, who were themselves subject to the law. Although rulers in Muslim societies were, in practice, often able to assign high office or distribute personal favors to their advantage, this does not negate the ethical obligation felt in their societies to provide checks to the rulers' power. Indeed, we are provided with numerous accounts of rulers' agitation with the autonomy of Sufi orders, which offered important mediating roles between families or tribes and the state mechanisms. As well, there are regular instances of a caliph's will being dashed by the resoluteness of his chief *qadi*.

Sajoo makes the connection here between the autonomous power of the *ulema*, who were the promulgators of law, and the church/bourgeois resistance that fuelled the rise of Western civil society.[85] The authority of the legal scholars in Muslim societies resonates soundly with the type of state-society tension that is the fundamental characteristic of modern articulations of civil society, says Sajoo, who quotes one study to say, "the scholarly conception of Prophetic sunna was … a threat to caliphal authority from the moment of its appearance."[86] Sajoo's point here is that indigenous expressions of civic life and the state-society tension existed and were at play in historical Muslim societies.

In contemporary Muslim contexts, however, the discussion on civil society (as well as its attendant themes of pluralism and the rule of law) has grown ever louder. According to Farhad Kazemi, this has been a result of a number of developments, including the fall of the Soviet Union, the end of the Cold War, and the movement toward democratization, as well as rapid urbanization, increased literacy, and increases in electronic communication.[87] But, he says, attempts to create uncoerced civic space in contemporary Muslim societies has been obscured in recent decades by a substantial shift toward authoritarianism in Muslim-majority countries, occasioned in the main by postcolonial and post-Cold War economic realities.[88]

Adding to the obscurity, says Sajoo, is the tendency of many critics, such as Ernest Gellner, to wilfully overlook "the disempowering effects of underdevelopment on effective citizenship."[89] Sajoo writes, "the sociology of diversity, poverty, and demographic shifts has not figured meaningfully in assertions about the 'fated' obstacles to civil society in the Muslim world. The latter shares not only 'Islam,' but also the hard realities of underdevelopment and its negative impact on the conditions for civic culture."

Thus, it is argued—while different from the European *form* of civil society—the desire for an uncoerced civic culture is in *fact* a part of both historical and contemporary Muslim experience. But, contrary to the arguments supporting an intrinsic Islamic aversion to freedom, the desire for uncoerced civic space in contemporary Muslim contexts seems most often to be stifled by socio-politico-economic realities.

VIII

Ultimately, this seems to be the Aga Khan's motivating concern in promoting pluralism and civic culture. There is a general unawareness, he says, in both developed and developing countries of the wealth of global resources; these resources, he contends, will be preserved only by the recognition of the value of pluralism. He cautions that "the inability of human society to recognize pluralism as a fundamental value constitutes a real handicap for our development and a serious danger for our future."[90] He recognizes in post-Cold War conflicts a number of common factors and causes, most notable and common among which is the "failure of those involved to recognize that human society is essentially pluralist."[91] Thus, he declares: "Peace and development require that we seek, by every means possible, to invest in and enhance that pluralism."[92]

But, he observes, "developing support for pluralism does not occur naturally in human society."[93] This is where the significance of inculcating civic culture enters the equation. Pluralism, he says, "is a concept that must be nurtured every day, in every forum—in large and small government and private institutions; in civil society organizations working in the arts, culture and public affairs; in the media; in the law, and in the areas of social justice, such as health, social safety nets and education, and economic justice, such as employment opportunities and access to financial services."[94]

To further the pluralist cause, he argues for systematic efforts to identify and promote pluralist "best practices," and he asks, "as we extract lessons and identify models, should we not put a process in place to share them widely for replication?"[95] To be sure, this is the mandate of the

Global Centre for Pluralism, whose website argues that "Canada is one of the world's most successful pluralist societies."[96] The Centre grew out of the Aga Khan's questions to Canadian leaders in the 1980s and 1990s to explain Canada's successful management of its own diversity, which led eventually to the 2001 launch of a formal Pluralism Initiative "to understand how and why Canada's unique experiment works and how its lessons might be shared with other culturally diverse societies around the world."[97]

Here the twin roles of institutionalized education and development are made essential for enhancing pluralism. He says that "even the most developed countries will need a massive effort to educate the world's youth in a more thoughtful, competent and complete manner to prepare them for the global responsibilities they will be expected to fulfill."[98] And, "the actions to enhance pluralism have to be matched in the developing world by programmes to alleviate poverty because, left alone, poverty will provide a context for special interests to pursue their goals in aggressive terms. Urgent humanitarian assistance is indispensable, but should be conceived as part of a long-term strategy of helping the recipient community develop its own resources that can support the improvement of the socioeconomic conditions of the poorer segments of the population, and charitable support for those unable to work."[99]

Thus, in the contemporary Ismaili conception, what is paramount for developing countries to emerge as effective players in a world of globally converging civilizations is strong civic institutions buttressed by the rule of law, which will engender informed and educated citizens participating fully in a global pluralist society. For the Aga Khan, then, the pluralist project is both an essential precondition for survival and a determined dream for the future.

IX

In contemporary Ismaili thinking, the pluralist ethic is hardwired into the Qur'an, and it instructs believers to come to know one another through civic interaction and thereby construct on Earth a global community of cooperating and converging civilizations. Taking this to heart, the Aga Khan exhorts the global community repeatedly on the dangers of ignoring pluralism and the strength inherent in harnessing humankind's diversity.

Emphasizing the role pluralism can play in conflict-ridden societies, he promotes education about pluralism as part of his mandate as Imam, and, in typically Ismaili fashion, institutionalizes it by developing secondary school curricula and, more grandly, establishing the Global Centre for Pluralism in Canada, a country he believes is exemplary for its management of diversity and promotion of pluralism. The goal of the Centre is to explore and export the Canadian model to societies in both the developed world and the developing world, where most Muslim-majority states are.

A large component of successful pluralism, in his view, is a strong civil society, as it creates the civic interactions that allow pluralism to take hold. Thinkers like Gellner, however, articulate the pervasive perspective that Muslim societies cannot provide civic space because Islam is resistant to secularism. In his address at an IIS conference titled "Civil Society in the Maghreb," held at The Ismaili Centre in London in June 2001, Filali-Ansary comments on two symmetrical views about civil society in Muslim societies.[100] He says that Gellner argues in his 1994 *Conditions of Liberty: Civil Society and its Rivals* that civil society is the preserve of the West and it cannot be extended into non-Western areas. He contrasts this with the view of Wajih Kawtharani, who argues in his 1996 *The Project of Arab Renaissance: The Crisis of Evolution From Sultanian to National Social Forms* that public services managed independently from the state in premodern Muslim societies were a precursor to civil society.

Filali-Ansary believes that both Gellner and Kawtharani have misinterpreted the evolution of civil society in Muslim societies, and he uses the Maghreb as an example to argue against both their propositions. He points to the networks of active associations and organizations in the Maghreb as examples that civil society is "clearly flourishing in areas from which the state has withdrawn," but, he argues, "it is not a reincarnation (or revitalisation) of traditional forms of social action, nor of self-help organisations of the past."[101] To this end, he concludes that forms of spontaneous organization are context-specific and volatile, and they may thus be expressions of other things, rather than forms of social order. Thus, he asks: "Is 'civil society' not an arbitrary concept?"[102]

For the Ismailis, though, an active civil society exemplifies the notion of "doing pluralism," which seems to be essential to the interpretive framework that unifies faith and world. This, again, is exemplary of the

Ismailis' ethical Bifröst—the bridging of the Qur'anic Revelation to the mission of liberal pluralism. In this conception, the pluralist tenor of the Qur'an must be realized in the world of man, where diversity, though willed by God, must be harnessed skilfully by humankind, His vicegerent on Earth.

8

KNOWLEDGE AND LEARNING

*From the very beginnings of Islam, the search for knowledge has
been central to our cultures. I think of the words of Hazrat Ali
ibn Abi Talib, the first hereditary Imam of the Shia Muslims,
and the last of the four rightly-guided Caliphs after the passing
away of the Prophet (may peace be upon Him). In his teachings,
Hazrat Ali emphasised that 'No honour is like knowledge.' And
then he added that 'No belief is like modesty and patience, no
attainment is like humility, no power is like forbearance, and no
support is more reliable than consultation.'*

*Notice that the virtues endorsed by Hazrat Ali are qualities
which subordinate the self and emphasise others—modesty,
patience, humility, forbearance, and consultation. What he thus
is telling us, is that we find knowledge best by admitting first
what it is we do not know, and by opening our minds to what
others can teach us.*

—Aga Khan IV, Commencement Address at the American
University, Cairo, 15 June 2006

*It is necessary to have a master who by his teaching and precepts
stirs and awakens the moral virtues whose seed is enclosed and
buried in our souls.*

—Baldesar Castiglione, *How to Achieve True Greatness*

I

The first revelation received by the Prophet Muhammad was—"Read!" As he sat in meditative contemplation in the cave of Hira about two miles from Mecca, he heard what would later become verses 96:1–5 of the Qur'an: "Read! In the name of your Lord, who created man from a clot … Who taught man by the Pen, taught man what he knew not." Thus, from its outset, the Islamic Revelation linked the spiritual with the intellectual.

In the Ismaili perspective, the Qur'anic text underscores the conviction that the reality of the Divine can be understood and perceived by humans through rigorous use of the intellect. God is perceptible through comprehensive arguments and self-evident facts, and it is the responsibility of the individual believer to pay attention to the "signs." Arguably, this is a widely shared perspective in the Islamic tradition, as explained in the *Encyclopaedia of the Qur'an*: "Unbelief is in the first place not attributed to a lack of will but to a lack of intellectual ability and perception—the unbelievers fail to see and understand the signs 'in the world at large or in themselves' (Q. 41:53)."[1] Signs, says the Qur'an, are self-evident for those given knowledge (Q. 29:49), to whom God's ordinances are made plain (Q. 2:230) and parables are made comprehensible (Q. 29:43).[2] Knowledge is thus made the requisite for understanding God's truth (e.g., Q. 22:54, 17:107, etc.).

Knowledge, says Franz Rosenthal, gave Muslim civilization its "distinctive shape and complexion." In fact, he writes, "there is no other concept that has been operative as a determinant of Muslim civilization in all its aspects to the same extent as *'ilm* [knowledge]."[3] The acquisition of knowledge was perceived not only as a divine imperative but also part of daily life. "Faith and learning," writes Nanji, "were seen to be interactive and not isolated from each other."[4]

In his article "Learning and Education" in his edited volume *The Muslim Almanac*, Nanji argues that the Qur'an itself provided the initial impetus for learning and for educational institutions. Typically, the mosque would be the place for the study of the Text, the Prophet's life, and the Arabic language. In time, informal gatherings of learning on law and theology developed at the mosque, in public places, and in private homes. Increasing encounters with other cultures and their various methods of learning, however, provided incentive for the establishment of more formal systems of education, culminating in the *madrasa*, the primary institution of learning in Sunni Islam.[5] Cities like Cairo, Baghdad, Cordova, Bukhara, and Samarqand became centers of learning, with large libraries and renowned intellectual institutions where scholars of diverse ethnic and religious backgrounds would come to share knowledge.

Contemporary Ismaili thought builds on this widely held account of the constructive relationship between faith and reason in Islam. According to the Institute of Ismaili Studies article on the AKDN's ethical framework, these early Islamic centers of learning were marked by a spirit of openness, and acknowledged and assimilated truth, whatever its source.[6] Echoing these comments, the Aga Khan—in a speech at an IIS Qur'anic arts colloquium—noted the trace of this same spirit in the famous maxim of the ninth-century philosopher al-Kindi, who "saw no shame in acknowledging and assimilating the truth, whatever its source," since he argued that "truth never abases, but only ennobles its seeker."[7] Furthermore, the Aga Khan asserts that it is the Qur'an's exultation of knowledge that inspires Muslims to seek knowledge: "The Qur'an itself acknowledges that people upon whom wisdom has been bestowed are the recipients of abundant good; they are the exalted ones. Hence Islam's consistent encouragement to Muslim men and women to seek knowledge wherever it is to be found."[8]

Thus, it is argued, it was Islam's pluralist approach to knowledge that gave rise to centers like the Dar al-'Ilm ("House of Knowledge") in Cairo and the Bayt al-Hikma ("House of Wisdom") in Baghdad, where sciences of all stripes flourished: mathematics, astronomy, botany, medicine, optics, pharmacology, zoology, and geography.[9]

Developed by the Abbassid caliph al-Ma'mun (r. 813–833)[10] the Bayt al-Hikma was an institution where key Greek philosophical and scientific works were translated into Arabic. These texts, previously lost to Europe, now found their way back in the form of Arabic translations and commentaries, paving the ground for the European Renaissance. According to Ted Thornton, "original research in medicine was conducted in the *Bayt al-Hikma*": the Christian physician Yuhanna dissected apes; Al-Razi built a hospital and wrote a medical encyclopedia cataloging Greek, Indian, and Persian medicine; and Persian-born Ibn Sina (Avicenna) "codified Greek and Arabic medical knowledge into a volume that became the standard medical textbook in Europe as well as the Arab world for five hundred years."[11]

II

For the Ismailis, education is portrayed in Islam as a religious imperative and thus bears a mystical dimension: "The key to the nature of society that Islam espouses is an enlightened mind, symbolized in the Quran's metaphor of creation, including one's self, as an object of rational quest."[12] The metaphor of the self as both the subject and object of the rational-spiritual quest is taken up by those specialists in allegory, the Ikhwan al-Safa ("Brethren of Purity").

Nanji analyzes one of the parables of this tenth-century group of apparently Ismaili intellectuals in which a wise king seeks to educate his children and thus builds them a palace, writing on its walls every science he wished to teach them and portrayals of correct behavior, and establishing small study groups. In this parable, the wise king is God, the young children are humanity, the palace is the firmament, the study groups are the human form, the illustrated rules of conduct are the composition of the body, and the inscribed sciences are the faculties of the soul and its knowledge.[13]

Nanji explains that this parable is part of a chapter that describes human beings as a microcosm: "It is clearly stated that since life is short, and the scope of knowledge of the world too large, individuals must learn to attain a realisation of the whole creation by studying themselves, since persons epitomize the universe."[14] Rationally, it is argued, a comprehension of the smaller model lends itself to a comprehension of the larger one.

Thus, says Nanji, just as a place of learning is the preparatory ground where one acquires the tools to face life, the body is seen as the preparatory place for the soul to acquire what it needs to perfect itself.[15] The school in the story symbolizes the body and the various subjects are the knowledge the soul must acquire before it reaches its ultimate destination, the "Court of the King." The model is pragmatic: it divides knowledge into various fields, such as the celestial spheres, Earth's geography, and life's physicocultural aspects; as well, it makes room for a proper enabling environment for learning by requiring a suitable physical structure as well as the amenities of good living.[16] Thus, concludes Nanji, the Ikhwan recognizes the balance of faith and world—the philosophy of education as acquiring self-knowledge is balanced with the recognition that one must acquire skills needed to live in the world.[17]

III

In the Ismaili conception, the individual on his quest for self-knowledge has unlimited capacity for development—in potentia. Crucially, the individual *potential intellect* needs the assistance of one who is an *actual intellect* to access the intellectual/spiritual realm. Like all Ismaili thinkers, the *da`i* (missionary-scholar) Nasir Khusraw argues that direct access to intellectual/spiritual knowledge is not possible through solely personal endeavor.[18] In his eleventh-century treatise, *Knowledge and Liberation*, he substantiates this argument using verse 55:33 of the Qur'an: "O assembly of *jinn* and men, if you can penetrate the bound of the heavens and the earth, do so, but you cannot without the proof (*hujjah*)." This, he says, establishes clearly the necessity for the Imam's guidance: "*jinn* and men cannot conceive anything in their souls other than what they see in the heavens and the earth, and they cannot go beyond what is under the heavens and time unless they receive nurture [of true knowledge] from the Imam of the time who is the proof of God (*hujjat-i Khuda*) on earth."[19]

The Ismaili position—that the individual only becomes recipient to divine knowledge and spiritual perfection through the Imam of the time—has been widely criticized, most vociferously by the famous Sunni theologian al-Ghazali (d. 1111), who argues that the Ismailis invalidate the exercise of intellect because of their reliance on the *ta`lim* (teaching) of the infallible Imam.[20]

According to Hunzai, though, Ismailism is often described in contradictory terms, as an "anti-authoritarian philosophical movement" or an "anti-rationalistic authoritarian movement."[21] This, he says, is because of the lack of understanding by others of Ismaili doctrines and their conception of reason and authority. Reason and authority are necessary together, he explains, citing the famous eleventh-century *da`i* al-Shirazi:

> The lamp is useless to the blind who has lost his eyesight
> and similarly the guidance of prophethood is useless to the
> one who is blind of intellect and insight.[22]

In Ismailism there is no mutual exclusiveness between reason and authority, he concludes; the individual intellect simply requires the assistance of the actual Intellect in its striving toward perfection:

> The Ismaili doctrine of the necessity of the Imam is based on the belief that the nature of human intellect is imperfect or potential and that it requires a perfect or actual Intellect to attain perfection or actuality.[23]

This was the central argument of the thirteenth-century Ismaili thinker Nasir al-Din al-Tusi. In his spiritual autobiography, *Contemplation and Action*, al-Tusi says that the philosophers with whom he conversed blundered at the question of the recognition of the True One, since they were relying on their own intellects to comprehend something not within their scope. The following principle, he tells us, is the seminal lesson gleaned from his association with philosophers: "if in any existing thing perfection is potential, it cannot change from potentiality into actuality by itself without being affected by something outside itself."[24] If it could, he reflects, the change would not be delayed and the existing thing would be perfect already. For al-Tusi, this proposition leads naturally to the conclusion that the attainment of perfection requires a perfect teacher:

> It thus becomes clear that without the instruction (*ta`lim*) of a teacher (*mu`allim*), and the bringing to perfection (*ikmal*) by an agent of perfection (*mukammil*), the attainment of the truth is not possible.[25]

Thus, he writes, mankind is mistaken when it claims that the truth can be had solely through reason and intellect, and the "believers in instruction" (*ta`limiyan*)—the Ismailis—are therefore correct. He goes on in this vein of rational argumentation, coming finally to his major conclusion:

> As for the word of the exalted Creator … if it had no connection (*ta`alluq*) to the sensible world, the latter would have never come into existence. Since there is such a connection, which is of the same kind and therefore has to be perceptible to the senses, the command and

the word must inevitably be manifest in this world, and the locus of its manifestation (*mazhar*) must be in the form of an individual human being who appears to be like other humans, [one who] is born, grows old and succeeds to the one before him in a continuous line, so that it [the command] will be preserved in perpetuity [among mankind]: "And had We made him [the Prophet] an angel, We would have certainly made him a man, and disguised [him] before them in garments like their own" (6:9).[26]

Here the command of God is likened to the *mazhar*—the locus of manifestation of the light of God—namely, the Imam, "the possessor of infinite knowledge," from whom "all forms of knowledge and perfections pour forth from it upon the intellects and souls."[27] As with previous Ismaili thinkers, God is outside al-Tusi's system, since He is free of the oppositions of unity and multiplicity, reality and relativity, etc. ("Glory be to thy Lord, the Lord of majesty. [He is] above what they describe" [37:80]). Thus, for Tusi, the individual's potential perfection is made actual only through the instruction of God's *mazhar*, the Imam:

Any perfection that exists potentially in souls and individuals in the two realms is brought from potentiality to actuality by [His command], by the light of its instruction and the illumination of its guidance: "[Our lord is He] who gave everything its existence, then guided it" (20:50).[28]

IV

For the tenth-century *da`i* al-Sijistani, God—while the ultimate ground of reality—is not a root of knowledge. "God is not a knowable existent," explains Walker, perhaps the most prolific writer on al-Sijistani. In al-Sijistani's conception, "God does not respond to temporal appeals, but rather has already put in place an existing structure, a divine hierarchy, that rules the cosmos."[29] It is this structure that must answer the individual's query and that contains all the sources of knowledge.

Walker describes and delineates al-Sijistani's four roots, or "wellsprings," of truth. In descending order, they are: intellect, soul, Speaking-prophet, and the Speaking-prophet's executor (or Founder of interpretation). Intellect here is not human thought; rather, it is the supreme being of the created cosmos. It is not, however, God the creator; nor is it His creative command. It is quite different from ordinary human thinking: "intellect is the rational law that governs and regulates all things."[30]

Together, soul and intellect form the primal pair indicated in the Qur'anic expression of God's fiat, "be and it is" (*kun fa-yakun*), with which creation commences.[31] In al-Sijistani's conception, God originated intellect as a perfect and complete being and as the sum of an existent being; soul came into being when intellect began to regard its own essence. Soul thus proceeded from intellect.[32] Soul ascends to intellect and conveys the benefits of rational order and truth downward, to the natural world, making nature logical. It is intellect incarnate, as Walker puts it: "soul functions to convert the lessons of intellectual life into bodily forms."[33] Al-Sijistani was adamant that human soul is part of universal soul, and universal soul has parts that reside in human soul: "that is why and how humans maintain their link with intellect; why they can think abstract thoughts and perceive the laws of science."[34]

Speaking-prophets are an important Ismaili motif. They are the six prophets mentioned in the Qur'an as founders of new faiths—Adam, Noah, Abraham, Moses, Jesus, and Muhammad. Whereas the legislator of Islamic law is commonly held to be God, in al-Sijistani's Ismaili Shi`ism it is the Speaking-prophet. Thus, while the law for Sunnis is sacred, for the Ismailis it is a reflection of the sacred source from which it derives. While the words of the Qur'an hold a sanctity for the Sunnis, for the Ismailis that sanctity is not true of the Qur'an but rather of an inner meaning that reflects the intellectual reality of which it is a copy.[35] The special skill of the Speaking-prophets is their ability to formulate their unique access to intellect into an intelligible representation of reason in an imperfect and evolving world. In his capacity as the formulator of law for things in the material world, the Speaking-prophet is the deputy of intellect.[36]

Both soul and Speaking-prophets rise to the realm of spiritual things and transform the benefits of intellect into a physical manifestation of reason. The Speaking-prophets, however, are mortal, and so they institute a law that should succeed them. However, humanity is prone to deviation, and thus the fourth source of knowledge, the *ta`wil* of the Founder, acts to protect the instrument of divine purpose. *Ta`wil* is "a living ever-present fountain of knowledge and understanding,"[37] explains Walker. *Ta`wil* means to return something to its origin, to trace it back to its source: "thus it is not simply to interpret something, e.g. some phrase or word, as loosely applied, but instead to seek and find its root meaning, its original essence."[38]

The context for the term *ta`wil* is Qur'anic, as in the important verse 3:7, which states that some verses are ambiguous and, while some persons will find troublesome interpretations, "no one knows its interpretation (*ta`wil*) except God and those who are firmly grounded in true knowledge." The Shi`a have always maintained that the phrase "those who are firmly grounded in true knowledge" refers to the Imams descended from `Ali ibn Abi Talib.

The Qur'an, says Walker, "thus admonishes its readers not to interpret the text by themselves but, rather, to seek the correct interpretation from a proper source," which—because of the organic nature of interpretation—cannot be written down but must be transmitted orally.[39] He continues: "a source for continuous interpretation must exist and, moreover, it must have the authority required to establish certainty and dispel doubt. As with the law of a Speaking-prophet, it must adjust as well to changes in time, place, and situation. But, whereas the law was compiled once at a given moment, the interpretation ought, like the human beings that use that law, to live and respond organically. Above all, it cannot be written down because it must constantly adjust. It is, by its very nature, oral."[40]

The lawgiver was concerned more with the formulation of scripture and less with its interpretation. Nevertheless, the interpretation must outlive him as a continuous operation, and he must thus choose a person to commence the interpretive role. Thus, in al-Sijistani's vision, "the interpretation as *ta`wil* gains its institutional status with the executor of each legislating prophet."[41] `Ali and the Imams following him can fulfill this function because they, like the lawgivers, have the benefit of intellect through *ta'yid* (divine aid) and thus receive support and inspiration.

From the perspective of the individual human, concludes Walker, "a vast universe of uncertain content and unfathomable dimension stands between him or her and an utterly remote God."[42] Now, he asks, there must exist a path from one extreme to the other, from the single human entity all the way to God. The entry point, he says, is clear. It is not intellect, or soul, or the law of a Speaking-prophet. Though they are sources, they are distant and confusing in their complexity: "closer to the individual is an organization that has as its sole responsibility the provision of guidance," who urges upon the individual a course of study which, if followed, leads the disciple up the correct path step-by-step.[43] Access to the interpretation granted by the Founder allows a proper understanding of the law of the Speaking-prophet, which helps one to discern the operations of nature better and thus see the role of soul, of which a part exists in all humans. These three sources then direct the individual to the highest source: the intellect.

The final purpose of the whole system, Walker explains, is to "ensure a true unmitigated recognition of God's incomprehensible splendour."[44] Without a full appreciation or understanding of the system that lies between God and the individual, there is the danger of confusing Him with an aspect of His work. By explaining the system of the four sources, al-Sijistani is in fact demonstrating what God is not. They are but the way to the proper appreciation of God, and all that is encompassed by them is not God: "God is other than they, and that is the final lesson to be learned."[45]

All these ideas are coalesced in his *Kashf al-Mahjub (Unveiling of the Hidden)*, where al-Sijistani explains his vision of the important Ismaili conception of the procession of knowledge from intellect to individual:

> Intellect has yet another [way of] becoming one with the
> Knowledge which is the Command of God, and that is
> the outpouring of [the light of] spiritual support (*ta'yid*)
> upon the hearts of God's chosen ones and His servants.
> This is the Pure Knowledge which belongs exclusively
> to the Prophets, the Legatees and the Imams. It is the

Knowledge of things found with many Prophets, namely, of future events and turns which cannot be perceived through the knowledge of the motions of the planets and the signs of the zodiac, and the knowledge which they need for the administration of the affairs of the Community, which cannot be perceived through the knowledge of the [worldly] administration of kings. [...] Now, the Pure Knowledge which is not contaminated by anything else is the one appropriate exclusively to God. Therefore, of necessity, the Prime Intellect became one with the Knowledge of God and then poured out the light of pure spiritual support upon the hearts of the chosen ones among the Prophets, so that they, thanks to that knowledge [obtained through] spiritual support, revealed for humans the way to live [in this world] and to "return" [to their ultimate home]. Understand this![46]

V

Knowledge appears here as a central pivot of Ismaili doctrine. In the Aga Khan's view, "the Holy Qur'an sees the discovery of knowledge as a spiritual responsibility, enabling us to better understand and more ably serve God's creation." Just as "world and faith are inseparable in Islam," he continues, "faith and learning are also profoundly interconnected."[47] In contemporary Ismaili thought, then, the ethic of learning encompasses both mystical knowledge and civic education. Following this view, education becomes an important focus area for the AKDN, whose self-articulated goal is to realize the social conscience of Islam by enabling the poor to achieve self-reliance.

In his speech to the Association of American Universities on April 22, 2001, the Aga Khan argues for the necessity of quality education, which he says has always been a critical component in the development of any society: "In the developing world education offers the poor -- opportunities for new futures, women -- higher status, and new roles in their families and communities, migrants -- an asset that is portable, and refugees -- an asset that is both portable and secure."[48] This is why, he says, the Aga Khan

Education Services has been operating hundreds of schools in Eastern Africa and Central and South Asia, often in isolated regions.

The AKDN describes its education programs as covering a wide spectrum of activities ranging from early childhood care through to degrees in medicine. The lead organizations in education are the Aga Khan Education Services (AKES), the Aga Khan Foundation (AKF), Aga Khan University (AKU), the Aga Khan Academies, and the University of Central Asia, but, according to the AKDN website, "all institutions are involved in some form of training or education, whether it is through curriculum reform, exhibitions of Islamic art or literacy programs for employees of economic project companies."[49] As well, professional teacher development and school improvement programs play a central role in strategies designed to improve access.

Indeed, says the Aga Khan, access to quality school-level education is particularly important in the developing world, where only a small percentage of the population will ever be able to attend university, and where the population growth is much more rapid than the capacity of its universities.[50] The school system has a vital role, as it is the "supply system" for higher education. But higher education is especially important, he says, because it arms students with a framework for critical thinking and develops their sense of ethics. He argues that "higher education has a special importance because of the difference it can make by developing new models and standards for other institutions in society, and by inculcating in its students the skills of critical thinking, analysis and problem solving, under-pinned by a strong grasp of moral reasoning, ethics and respect for others."[51]

He has, however, observed that there is an enormous knowledge deficit in numerous countries in Africa, Asia, and the Middle East. Men and women in public office who seek to build well-governed and competent states and economies simply do not have access to individuals sufficiently educated to operate the institutions of the state. In his remarks to the Academy of Sciences in Lisbon on May 8, 2009, he concluded that the deficit of knowledge that pervades many areas of education is due to a tendency to rely on the past and a lack of novel thinking: "because what have been inherited are curricula of the past, reflections of the past, attitudes of the past, rather than looking forwards, asking what do future generations **need** to know."[52]

Further, the Aga Khan identifies three areas of knowledge that will be necessary in these environments in order to inculcate stable governments in the future. Firstly, he observes that all these societies are pluralistic in nature. Thus, if pluralism is not part of the educational curriculum in these societies from the earliest stages, then they will always be at risk of conflict because they are unused to pluralism and thus do not value it:

> The failure of different peoples to be able to live in peace amongst each other has been a major source of conflict. Experience tells us that people are not born with the innate ability nor the wish to see the Other as an equal individual in society. Pride in one's separate identity can be so strong that it obscures the intrinsic value of other identities. Pluralism is a value that must be taught.[53]

Ethics in civil society is another critical aspect, because when governments fail in these parts of the world, he says, it is civil society that sustains development:

> And when ethics are not part of education, teaching, examinations; when they are not part of medicine, the quality of care; when they are not part of financial services, then civil society is undermined.[54]

This is especially true in rural environments, where the majority of the people in the developing world live, but where fraud is not reported or corrected and is simply accepted as inevitable.[55]

The third area is constitutionality. Teaching in areas such as comparative government is critical, because, he says, "so many countries which I have visited have stumbled into, run into difficulties in governance, because the national constitutions were not designed and conceived to serve the profiles of those countries."[56] Education in governance is therefore essential so that people in the developing world will be able to make competent judgments about their political systems and actors: "public referenda, to sanction new

Constitutions, for example, make little sense when they call for judgments from people who do not understand the questions they are being asked, nor the alternatives they should be considering."[57]

These concerns undergird the essence of the Aga Khan Academies and also guide their curriculum. When addressing the Annual Meeting of the International Baccalaureate in Atlanta on April 18, 2008, the Aga Khan articulated that the "Academies Program is rooted in the conviction that effective indigenous leadership will be the key to progress in the developing world."[58] But, he argues, educating for leadership requires more than the development of rote skills, which is altogether different from schooling in the art and science of thinking. In his view, the most important measure of the quality of education is no longer what students know, but rather the ability to engage what they do not know and work out a solution. Thus, he concludes, the ability to reach conclusions, make judgements grounded in solid information, and employ careful analysis should be among the top priorities for any educational endeavor:[59]

> In a world of rapid change, an agile and adaptable mind, a pragmatic and cooperative temperament, a strong ethical orientation - these are increasingly the keys to effective leadership. And I would add to this list a capacity for intellectual humility which keeps one's mind constantly open to a variety of viewpoints and which welcomes pluralistic exchange.[60]

The curriculum he outlines—one of pluralism, ethics, global economics, world cultures, and comparative political systems—impacts a large number of countries across the world and addresses problems that will take decades to resolve. Nevertheless, he says that "as we work together to bridge the gulf between East and West, between North and South, between developing and developed economies, between urban and rural settings, we will be redefining what it means to be well educated."[61]

After all, he asks:

> Should we not expect a student at an IB school in Atlanta
> to know as much about Jomo Kenyatta or Muhammad Ali

Jinnah as a student in Mombasa or Lahore knows about Atlanta's great son, the Reverend Doctor Martin Luther King, Jr.? Should a Bangladeshi IB student reading the poems of Tagore at the Aga Khan Academy in Dhaka not also encounter the works of other Nobel Laureates in Literature such as the Turkish novelist Orhan Pamuk or America's William Faulkner or Toni Morrison?[62]

"It is one thing," he concludes, "to talk about cultural understanding when 'the Other' is living across the world. It is often a different matter when the 'Other' is living across the street."[63]

VII

The *da`i* al-Shirazi expresses poetically the core Ismaili doctrine that the path to knowledge cannot be traversed without a guide:

Similarly, the intellect,
> during reflection by itself,
remains in the throes of
> doubt and bewilderment.
Except when it is helped
> by a light from the outside;
then it ascends the ladder
> of enlightened contemplation. [64]

The focus of contemporary Ismaili thought, however, seems to have shifted from mystical hermeneutics to emphasizing the need for active and engaged civic education. This is not to say that they have abandoned their core doctrine. Rather, contemporary Ismaili scholarship does seek to enrich that core by excavating Ismaili mystical and intellectual traditions, but the thrust of modern Ismaili thought seeks to link the ethic of learning to practical civic education.

To be sure, the Ismailis argue that the mystical and the practical have always cohabited their tradition—exemplified here by the founding of institutions of learning throughout their history. This observation raises interesting questions for the contemporary period. We may ask, perhaps, does Ismailism's mystical tradition allow it to have a less doctrinaire approach to civic values? More pertinently, does the Ismaili hermeneutic allow more pliability for the tradition to pursue the cause of civic education, as opposed to that of a more rigid tradition that may have an obligation to promote doctrinaire public policies? These, of course, are questions that require deeper probing.

For now, it suffices to observe that the contemporary Ismaili self-narrative presents its modern focus on educational development as derivative of its traditional commitment to knowledge as a founding ethic of Islam. In this view, the Qur'an commands the believer to seek out knowledge, because the active use of intellect is the path to knowing God. Furthermore, the faithful believer seeks to engender for his fellow man an enabling environment for learning in order to realize the social conscience of Islam that undergirds the ethic of *din wa dunya*—recalled by Imam 'Ali's exhortation that "faith without action is like an archer without a string to his bow." In effect, this conception reflects the distinctive ethical Bifröst, or "bridging," evident in contemporary Ismaili thought that attempts to connect the historical Ismaili approach to mystical and esoteric knowledge with modern Ismaili commitments to social justice and liberal democracy.

9

CLOSING: THE TRANSNATIONAL
ISMAILI IN CANADA

*The blossoming of the Ismaili community in Canada offers
a ray of hope to the world. By demonstrating that diverse
congregations of the great faiths can co-exist and flourish
peacefully here, we are proving that there indeed can be unity in
diversity.*
—Stephen Harper, 22nd Prime Minister of Canada

Make Canada your home.
—Aga Khan IV, *farman* made in Burnaby,
Canada, 1978.

I

Sitting on the quiet shores of Lake Ontario, the main character in M. G. Vassanji's novel *The In-Between World of Vikram Lall* recalls his life in Kenya as caught between the colonial British and the indigenous Africans. "The feeling of belonging and not belonging is very central to the book,"[1] says Vassanji, one of Canada's most acclaimed authors, and an Ismaili. Vassanji's books chronicle the positioning of African Indians in North America trying to negotiate the warp and woof of modernity while holding on to their traditions and living with the "inescapable presence of the past."[2]

For Ismailis in Canada, says Karim, "the past remains ever present, even in the engagements with modernity and postmodernity."[3] Canadian Ismailis struggle to balance the demands of the workaday world with commitments to communal life, centered around daily attendance and obligations at the *jamatkhana*, the Ismaili congregational house of prayer. "Tradition," Karim observes, "is central to the religious practice of Ismailis in Canada."[4] And, he concludes, it is "deeply imbedded in ritual practices, which are traced to various points in history going back to the time of the Prophet."[5]

Connecting the present to the past via overarching Islamic ethical principles is a key facet of Ismaili doctrine and tradition, which has consistently made the point throughout its history that the entire Ismaili religion derives from Qur'anic principles. Perhaps Ismailism anchors itself to ethics because it has no physical anchor—even during Fatimid times, the religion was transnational. Perhaps, furthermore, connecting to something nonphysical is, arguably, reflective of the tradition's core principle of esotericism, of allegorical interpretation. In any event, the promulgation of a shared history serves to unify the diverse transnational Ismaili community by concretizing the essential doctrines and ethical principles of the religion, whose interpretation is mandated by the Imam of the time.

The current Imam, Aga Khan IV, told his community when they came to Canada as refugees in the 1970s to "make Canada your home." Aly Kassam-Remtulla recalls that when he was a child he heard the Imam repeating this sentiment. He now perceives this as unique among diaspora leaders, who typically urge a nostalgic attachment to the distant homeland. He reflects that "it is probably because there is no homeland to return to that Aga Khan IV's advice is given in the first place, and taken to heart by his *murids* [disciples]."[6] Indeed, heeding that advice enabled the Ismailis to prosper. The transnational character of the Ismaili tradition seems to allow it to embed itself in the particularity of the local. Furthermore, in Karim's view, "Canada's lack of a monolithic and fixed national identity opens up areas in which minority groups can contribute to the common conversation," and it has allowed Ismailis therefore to explore the axes of tradition, modernity, and postmodernity within the country's own wider discussions.[7]

II

Speaking at the 2005 Foundation Ceremony of the Delegation of the Ismaili Imamat in Ottawa, the Aga Khan declared that "the Ismailis [are] a transnational community who are, first and foremost, active and loyal citizens of the countries where they live, though in outlook they transcend the divisions of North and South, East and West."[8] He affirmed, thus, the nonphysical commitments of the Ismaili tradition, and linked it to the larger Muslim community through what he views as a shared tradition of ethical humanism. "Whatever the context of their lives," he says, the Ismailis "all share, like other Muslims, the commitment to an ethic whose values converge on the inherent dignity of the human person as the noblest of creation."[9]

Connecting to and building bridges with the wider Muslim *Ummah* is important to contemporary Ismailism, whose official institutions and scholars discourse with leading Muslim scholars who share viewpoints relevant to Ismaili concerns, such as "a critical intellectual approach when examining Muslim traditions, a non-adversarial engagement with the West, and respect for both pluralist and universal values."[10] In his chapter in the 2011 IIS volume on Ismaili history, Karim articulates the views of some contemporary Muslim scholars on these issues.

He cites Ebrahim Moosa's argument that "Muslims need to move beyond apologetics that distort those aspects of history and theology which do not appear to conform to contemporary standards"[11]—an approach to Islam that does not insist on entrenchment in the past. Next, Karim quotes Tariq Ramadan as saying that contemporary Muslim intellectuals are increasingly insistent on taking account of "the concrete realities of our societies" and "produce a *fiqh*, a legislation appropriate to our times"[12]— an assertion that fits comfortably within the Shi`i doctrine of Imamate, itself predicated on the requirement that the practice of the faith must be interpreted and updated to suit the exigencies of the day. Karim continues, describing the "essential concerns of progressive Muslims" articulated by Omid Safi: critically reflecting on the Islamic tradition; re-viewing "Islamic scriptural teachings on social justice in the context of the contemporary world"; rethinking anew "Islamic feminism"; and "a pluralistic openness toward human sources of compassion and wisdom that goes beyond Islamic ones."[13] Karim concludes his list with contemporary Ismaili intellectual Aziz Esmail, who proposes a common critical project across communities to assess their cultural assumptions. In Karim's words, Esmail "refers to a 'pluralistic, universal point of view' that safeguards the particularity of the Muslim community and moves 'from the inside to the outside' to gain an awareness of humanity's ethical and spiritual aspirations."[14] Recalling the Ikhwan al-Safa's allegory of the individual as a microcosm for the whole of creation, this is a typically Ismaili articulation that emphasizes the internal (*batin*) search in order to bring order to the external (*zahir*) world.

The Ismaili notion of necessary balance between the esoteric (*batin*) and exoteric (*zahir*) is, in this view, a metaphysical representation of the larger Islamic concern for balance between faith and world—*din wa dunya*—which the AKDN argues is the motivating factor behind its development work. In Steinberg's observation, Ismaili institutions like the AKDN are the locus of Ismaili transnationalism because they teach Ismaili communities "how to be Isma`ili in a modern way, or modern in an Isma`ili way,"[15] and thus help to create the Ismaili identity and formalize the religious structure of Ismailism. Through its rural development programs, the AKDN socializes those communities to modern ideologies by providing a forum for local participation in a global network and introducing them to the tenets of liberal modernity, entrepreneurial capital, rational humanism, and civil society.[16] Perhaps more importantly, the institutions bring disparate Ismaili communities together under the banner of Imamate, creating a global community unified by their loyalty to the Imam.

And the Imam—through the social, educational, health, and cultural development work of the AKDN as well as through his propagation of a shared Islamic ethic that concords with liberal modernity—is portrayed as a modern Muslim leader of the global Muslim *Ummah* at large; expressing in a fluid, contemporary way one manifestation of the perennial aspiration of the Ismailis to establish their Imam at the head of the Muslim Community. Recognizing the sociocultural differences of the *Ummah*—which mirror the internal differences of the Ismaili community—the Imam focuses on the shared religiohistorical, intellectual, and ethical tradition of Muslims everywhere, thus appearing as the definer of a liberal Islamic ethic that supports a Qur'anic vision for coexistence in a globalized world.

Nowhere is this vision endorsed more wholeheartedly than in Canada, where Ismailis energetically pursue social activist voluntarism, and the international work promoted by the Imam—all of which, says Prime Minister Stephen Harper, are core Canadian values. He said as much when addressing the Aga Khan at the opening of the Delegation building in 2008: "Your Highness, Canada is a fitting choice for the Delegation. Our country and the Ismaili Imamat are bonded by our shared values; tolerance, compassion, community service and, especially, our devotion to pluralism—the essential ingredient for harmony in our modern, interconnected world."[17]

By the same token, Canada's unique conception of the world—embodied in its pioneering policy of multiculturalism—allowed a modern Muslim minority group like the Ismailis to flourish. Indeed, says Karim, sociological research shows that Canadian multiculturalism has played a critical role in establishing the Ismaili community and allowing young Ismailis to mediate smoothly the confluence between Canadian and Ismaili values.[18] Furthermore, he says, Ismailis have learned from Canada's modernist project and are applying the multiculturalist approach to their own community's diverse traditions,[19] implementing a deliberate policy to incorporate non-Khoja Ismailis, mainly from Afghanistan, into the community.[20] "An indicator of the success of the community's internal policy of pluralism," he concludes, "is that Khoja Ismailis are beginning to sing Farsi *qasidas* (poetic hyms) from the Central Asian Ismaili traditions while the Afghan members of the *jamat* recite *ginans*."[21]

The gusto with which the Ismailis have integrated themselves into Canadian life is exemplified by the fact that the term "Ismaili" is now widely recognized and is provided in media coverage without any background explanation.[22] Karim surveys key points of public Ismailism in Canada reported by the press: the annual World Partnership Walk organized by the Aga Khan Foundation Canada to raise funds for development; stories commemorating the anniversary of the Ugandan exodus in the early 1970s; the election of Ismailis to federal and provincial parliaments, the appointment of an Ismaili senator, and the awarding of national honors like the Order of Canada to Ismailis; and, additionally, the Aga Khan's public visits to Canada.[23]

To be sure, Canadian multiculturalism has provided the space for Ismailis to succeed in the country's civil society, but Zahra Jamal offers the perspective that the ethic of voluntarism—a spur for civic responsibility—is emic in Ismailism. Volunteering, she says, is for the Ismailis neither voluntary nor obligatory; it is, rather, a natural, commonsensical action. "Unlike their Sunni counterparts," she writes, "most of my Ismaili informants spoke of voluntarism not in terms of alms (*zakat*) or charity (*sadaqah*), but rather in terms of balancing the spiritual (*din*) and material (*duniya*) worlds."[24] For these Ismailis, she concludes, "voluntarism is a 'means of keeping ethics in dynamic motion.'"[25]

On this view, active participation in civil society is reconfigured as an ethical imperative—a contemporary method of balancing faith and world. Certainly, the invitational openness of Canadian multiculturalism allows communities and traditions to thrive, and, for the Ismailis, it provided the necessary space to adapt their religion to the contemporary world without persecution. Indeed, the decision to establish the Global Centre for Pluralism in Ottawa—a joint project between the AKDN and the Canadian government to map and share insights into Canadian pluralism—derives from the Ismailis' positive experience with Canada's policy of multiculturalism.[26] As Karim puts it, "they are now working with the Canadian state to harness their own transnational postmodernity, using pluralism as a human resource in the quest to enhance the quality of life in other regions."[27]

But, while Canada may have provided a unique space for Ismailis to explore pluralism without persecution, Karim quotes the Aga Khan to emphasize the point that this approach is perceived to be part of an Islamic tradition "in which pluralism has 'profound roots.'"[28] Thus, Karim reminds us of history's centrality in the Ismaili worldview, asserting further that "tradition remains deeply implicated in Ismaili encounters with modernity and postmodernity."[29]

III

Ismailism is, after all, a religion first. Only secondarily can it be viewed as a sociological constellation of diverse cultures and traditions trying to make it in a pluralist world. Indeed, the amalgamating element in that diverse Ismaili constellation is its central and definitive religious tenet—the institution of Imamate. It is, in Steinberg's articulation, "constitutive of Isma'ilism."[30] The Ismailis, he says, are devoted not to any singular Imam, but rather to the institution of the Imamate—"to the reality that underlies any particular imam who is but a manifestation of that institution."[31] Thus, devotion to the Imam is a "central pillar of horizontal Isma'ili fraternity," and the defining criterion of membership, while "nondevotion is by definition nonmembership."[32]

That devotion brought the Ismailis to Canada, bade them heed the Imam's *farman* to "make Canada your home," and brought them to the eudemonia that followed. Because of its role in the creation of Ismaili transnationalism, Steinberg calls the *farman* "the signature instrument of modernization"—"it is through the *farman* [directive] more than anything else that the imam fulfils his mandate to continually update and interpret, through *ta'wil* [esoteric Qur'anic exegesis], the meaning of Islam."[33]

The Imam's role as authoritative interpreter of the faith is the core doctrine of Shi'ism, predicated on the idea, says Canadian Ismaili scholar Khalil Andani, that the Qur'an provides only the ethics of the faith; it does not define its practice—that is left to the Prophet and, later, to his heirs.[34] S. H. Nasr describes the Sh'i and Sufi notion of a prophetic Light as the source of all prophetic knowledge—the "Muhammadan Light" or "Muhammadan Reality," identified as the Logos—which continues through prophetic cycles and which exists within the Imams, by whose virtue they are the Prophet's heirs and authoritative interpreters of the faith.[35] In the foreword to a book about the Prophet Muhammad, Aga Khan III affirmed the principle of an ever-changing faith as a central Islamic tenet:

> If, rightly, the Muslims have kept till now to the forms of prayer and fasting at the time of the Prophet, it should not be forgotten that it is not the forms of prayer and fasting that have been commanded, but the facts, and we are entitled to adjust the forms to the facts of life as circumstances changed. It is the same Prophet who advises his followers ever to remain *Ibnu'l-Waqt* (i.e., children of the time and period in which they were on earth), and it must be the natural ambition of every Muslim to practice and represent his Faith according to the standard of the *Waqt* or space-time.[36]

The notion of change, says Steinberg, is part of the contemporary Ismaili self-image. It impacts "nothing less than the transformation of the lifeworld and experience of the Isma`ili subject," and, reflecting upon the effect of the contemporary Ismaili institutions, he declares that "a global assemblage with neither parallel nor precedent should impact so profoundly the formulation of self and the structure of locality is remarkable indeed."[37]

IV

Steinberg observes two "simultaneously occurring, overlapping, historically inflected Isma`ili globalities":[38] the dispersed diasporic Khoja community and the remote and vulnerable Central Asian communities. Both, however, are directed by the "transnational Isma`ili institutional assemblage" centered in Europe.[39] This locational spread is important, says Kassam-Remtulla, since part of the transnational Ismaili community's success is that it is nonnational and expresses no appeals for an Ismaili nation.

A transnational commitment to the local seems to be a distinctive characteristic of the contemporary Ismaili self-identity. In his Stanford University AB honors thesis on Ismaili transnationalism, Kassam-Remtulla argues that "Ismailism does not pose a threat to hostlands or homelands" because "Ismailis are able to balance their local obligations as citizens of a nation, and their other obligations as members of a transnational community."[40] He draws attention to the 1986 Ismaili Constitution, which "lays out clear guidelines about the allegiance of a *murid* [disciple] to the Imam, but warns that this allegiance 'is distinct from the allegiance of the individual *murid* to his land of abode.'"[41]

For the most part, he says, Ismaili loyalties to location and religion do not clash. For example, issues typically raised between other religions and the state—prayers in school, abortion, homosexuality—have been avoided by Ismailis and by the Imam, with the understanding that "these decisions must be made individually and within the local legal structure."[42] Importantly, he says that the Ismaili tradition of adaptability is essential here, as it allows Ismailis to live comfortably within a society without feeling as though they are compromising their faith—"Ismailis value the essence of spiritual practice over the ritual surrounding it."[43] He does, however, note that this adaptive attitude is also typical of a minority group attempting to be unobtrusive. Nevertheless, he says, the necessary balancing of the transnational community and the nation-state has been relatively easy for Ismailis because of their wealth, status, and education, as well as the Aga Khan's leadership, which has allowed them to live as nontraditional Muslim citizens.[44] Kassam-Remutulla describes this conception of Ismaili transnational citizenship: "transnational Ismailism emerges as a unique community which defies traditional notions of diaspora, nation and religion. Ismailis are a multiracial diaspora that is not limited by the trope of the tribe; a stateless nation without a desire for territory; an imagined community that is transnational; and a sect of Islam that does not rely on the Qur'an and is headed by a monarch. These unique and seemingly contradictory traits describe a remarkably complex and coherent community, which has been crafted and maintained by the central figure of the Imam."[45]

The Imam, he concludes, has played a critical role in transnationalizing the Ismaili community, through his efforts to change Ismaili religious practice to align it with wider Muslim practice, to have the religious hymns of the various Ismaili traditions recited in the *jamatkhanas*, to establish organizations in the developing world through which *murids* practice philanthropy, and to create institutions that teach a standard Ismaili history in religious education classes worldwide.[46] Thus, the Imam has managed to link Ismailis through religious practice, shared institutions, philanthropy, and capital flows—"the imagined community that has resulted," concludes Kassam-Remtulla, "incorporates elements of a diaspora, stateless nation, and religion."[47]

V

The Canadian Ismaili diaspora's engagements with its past and current surroundings have begun to have a noticeable impact on the wider society.[48] This is Karim's observation, who argues further that Canada has provided the space for the Ismaili community to be involved continually in an evolving discursive relationship between their religion and the norms of Canadian society. In some ways, he says, this recalls the community's historical encounters with external influences that led to a reexamination of Ismaili traditions.[49]

In this view, then, Ismaili history is repeating itself in the present. Contemporary Ismailism, however, emphasizes this notion of continual adaptability as a defining principle of the tradition—deriving less from the necessity to adapt to external factors like demographics and economics—and, rather, as a defining principle of the religion, embodied in the mandate of the Shi`i institution of the Imamate to perpetually redefine the faith.

Indeed, for Karim, although the Ismaili interaction with Canadian society is simultaneously reliving the past and redefining the present, they are doing so through the lens of their religion: "their traditional acknowledgement of the need to respond to changing conditions has been manifested in the value they place upon the importance of continued religious guidance from the Imam of the time as well as the believer's use of intellect."[50] This approach, in his conception, has been instrumental in the community's survival on its journey from Alamut to Aiglemont, and, importantly, it has persisted only because of its ability to hold fast to the rope of Imamate. Thus, he echoes a fundamental contemporary Ismaili view of itself when he says that the Ismaili tradition "has continually adapted itself to contemporary conditions while holding fast to its Islamic heritage."[51]

This habit of the Ismailis to bridge past principles to present practice embodies the ethical Bifröst. Like the rainbow from which that allegorical bridge takes its name, the Ismaili tradition has an elusive feel: though it is always present, it is not always perceptible. Though it is visible at certain times and stands more prominently, it is not anchored to a solid place and can only be seen in certain climatic contexts. Canada seems to provide that unique climatic context: in the Canadian multicultural project, contemporary Ismaili adaptivity and transnational locality has found a uniquely compatible partner. Its stated values and policies give wide berth to minority communities like the Ismailis, who have found a way to revise their tradition so as to bring an unexpected dose of religious passion to the deep Canadian commitments to pluralism, democracy, and multiculturalism.

Postscript: Whither Neutrality?

Perhaps the most salient point that contemporary Ismailism is making about itself is that it is a tradition with roots. Through the creation of a self-narrative that sees certain Islamic ethics guiding the tradition through history, and by articulating those ethics in contemporary times as support for core liberal values, the tradition is creating relevance for itself as a modern, liberal Muslim community, to be seen by the world as part of a wider Islamic idiom and not as a completely disconnected, newborn cultural movement. The tradition is reworking history to make sense of and give meaning to the new form of Ismailism that has taken on new dimensions in the contemporary context but that also makes the case that those dimensions are part of its legacy, rooted in the past. What is thus central to its modernization project is the claim that it is *not* a modern movement, born of the postcolonial soup.

In a sense, this approach might exemplify the typical pattern of religious modernization movements, because it is precisely their sense of communal history that vivifies their contemporary identity. A modernizing community has to think seriously about the construction of its history; unless the tradition wants to be perceived as newly invented, it must undertake significant historical spadework to make the case that its revised forms of communal life and values are marks of development, not revolution or radical innovation. In the Ismaili case, this is made plain by the efforts of the IIS and the Imamate to engage a fairly high level of reconstruction.

In this way, academic scholarship becomes part of the construction project; it becomes part of the tradition it studies because it is rethinking the past. Whom, we may ask, is that rethinking serving? In the case of contemporary Ismailism's self-contemplation, the answer is clear. But the question certainly bears pondering in the broader domain of religious studies. Scholarship on religion itself is more complex than it may seem, because it is feeding into religious constructions of religion. This was, in a sense, Edward Said's critique of orientalist scholarship, echoed most recently by the ongoing debate in the study of Hinduism in which certain strains of North American scholarship are viewed as imposing on the tradition a reconstruction colored by the exotized gloss of the "Western gaze."

In some sense, all historical scholarship is reinvention. And all traditions undergo a process of reconfiguration in the face of a new modernity. The project of contemporary Ismailism to unify and articulate its tradition is a fairly sophisticated attempt, offering, in its view, a reenvisioning more than a reinvention. Emerging from the fog of *taqiyya*, contemporary Ismailism uses the open spaces offered by liberal democracy to reenvision itself—not in Sunni-majority countries, but in the West, where they reenvision *taqiyya* itself.

Taqiyya is a method used to preserve alternative forms of identity in authoritarian cultures, where dissimulation is used as means to camouflage difference and to create a pretence of being part of the commonality. However, in pluralistic societies that prize difference, dissimulation becomes inculturation. Dissimulating in authoritarian, monistic societies means masking one's identity; but dissimulating in open multicultural societies involves a showcasing of identity that is sensitive to the public pluralistic ethos. Being pluralistic, together with respectful disclosure of one's identity, is the pathway to effective incorporation into multicultural liberal democratic societies.

This is part of the unique paradox that is Ismailism today. Another part is the role of the contemporary Imamate as a driver of modernization that also accents, perhaps in new ways, the authority of the Imam. Interestingly, similar patterns are observable in other contemporary traditions that work with a religious authority, like the papacy, in which the authority itself can become a force for modernization. It may be a paradox peculiar to the particular modernity we inhabit, but religious groups without an authority seem to have trouble modernizing. Having more democratic structures, it seems, cannot be equated with having more liberal outlooks; certain fundamentalist Protestant or Sunni groups, for example, despite their more congregational and decentralized forms of authority, tend to drift toward fundamentalism as a reaction to modernity.

It may be argued that religious groups without a religious authority can become reactive and they thus need the strong arm of religious leadership to move forward into modernity. It has certainly been noted that without strong direction there is a tendency toward antimodernism, which might be illustrated by the American example of the rise of fundamentalism as a rejection of modernity. This is certainly a line of inquiry that bears further investigation, but that, in the Ismaili case, would require a rather rigorous investigation of the Aga Khan's personal and intellectual history as well as a deep examination of his conception of the institution of Imamate and the reconstruction of the role of the Imam as a force of ongoing modernization throughout history. This is certainly beyond the scope of our current project.

It does, however, brush up against one of the subtler ideas undergirding the present work, which is the notion that all scholarly reconstructions of history are implicated in the modernization processes of religious movements. There is no vantage free from normative content; our interpretations are laden with it, and the academy cannot escape it. There is no innocence of scholarship; it is enmeshed in the process of a tradition's revision, reinvention, and reconfiguration. In this way, the academy is part of the process of modernization; it cannot be a neutral observer. The question that looms spectrally over all contemporary discourse, then, is, whither neutrality? Can we ever escape the complex project of modernity in which we are so deeply embedded in multifaceted ways? In the end, we are all implicated.

Appendix A

Preamble to the Constitution of the Shi'a Imami Ismaili Muslims[*]

(A) The Shia Imami Ismaili Muslims affirm the *shahādah lā ilāha illa-llāh, Muhammadur rasulu-llāh*, the *Tawhid* therein and that the Holy Prophet Muhammad (s.a.s.) is the last and final Prophet of Allah. Islam, as revealed in the Holy Quran, is the final message of Allah to mankind, and is universal and eternal. The Holy Prophet (s.a.s.) through the divine revelation from Allah prescribed rules governing spiritual and temporal matters.

(B) In accordance with Shia doctrine, tradition, and interpretation of history, the Holy Prophet (s.a.s.) designated and appointed his cousin and son-in-law Hazrat Mawlana Ali *Amiru-l-Mu'minin* (a.s), to be the first Imam to continue the *Ta'wīl* and *Ta'līm* of Allah's final message and to guide the murids, and proclaimed that the Imamat should continue by heredity through Hazrat Mawlana Ali (a.s) and his daughter Hazrat Bibi Fatimat-az-Zahra, *Khātun-i-Jannat* (a.s).

(C) Succession of Imamat is by way of *Nass*, it being the absolute prerogative of the Imam of the time to appoint his successor from amongst any of his male descendents whether they be sons or remoter issue.

(D) The authority of the Imam in the Ismaili Tariqah is testified by *Bay'ah* by the murid to the Imam which is the act of acceptance by the murid

[*] Available online at http://simerg.com/special-series-his-highness-the-aga-khan-iv/the-preamble-of-the-constitution-of-the-shia-imami-ismaili-muslims/.

of the permanent spiritual bond between the Imam and the murid. This allegiance unites all Ismaili Muslims worldwide in their loyalty, devotion and obedience to the Imam within the Islamic concept of universal brotherhood. It is distinct from the allegiance of the individual murid to his land of abode.

(E) From the time of the Imamat of Hazrat Mawlana Ali (a.s), the Imams of the Ismaili Muslims have ruled over territories and peoples in various areas of the world at different periods of history and, in accordance with the needs of the time, have given rules of conduct and constitution in conformity with the Islamic concepts of unity, brotherhood, justice, tolerance and goodwill.

(F) Historically and in accordance with Ismaili tradition, the Imam of the time is concerned with spiritual advancement as well as improvement of the quality of life of his murids. The imam's *ta'lim* lights the murid's path to spiritual enlightenment and vision. In temporal matters, the Imam guides the murids, and motivates them to develop their potential.

(G) Mawlana Hazar Imam Shah Karim al Hussaini, His Highness Prince Aga Khan, in direct lineal descent from the Holy Prophet (s.a.s.) through Hazrat Mawlana Ali (a.s.) and Hazrat Bibi Fatima (a.s), is the Forty-Ninth Imam of the Ismaili Muslims.

(H) By virtue of his office and in accordance with the faith and belief of the Ismaili Muslims, the Imam enjoys full authority of governance over and in respect of all religious and Jamati matters of the Ismaili Muslims.

(I) It is the desire and *Hidāyat* of Mawlana Hazar Imam that the constitutions presently applicable to the Ismaili Muslims in different countries be superseded and that the Ismaili Muslims worldwide be given this constitution in order better to secure their peace and unity, religious and social welfare, to foster fruitful collaboration between different peoples, to optimise the use of resources, and to enable the Ismaili Muslims to make a valid and meaningful contribution to the improvement of the quality of life of the Ummah and the societies in which they live.

APPENDIX B

AKDN ORGANIZATION CHART[*]

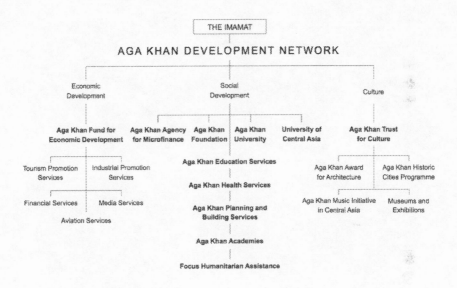

---
[*] Available online at http://www.akdn.org/about_akdn_chart.asp.

ENDNOTES

CHAPTER 1

[1] Paul Evan Ress, "Prince Karim Aga Khan," *Sports Illustrated*, 10 August 1964, http://sportsillustrated.cnn.com/vault/article/magazine/MAG1076226/index.htm. The article's description reads: "A rare portrait of an intent young ruler who rejects the temptations of an idle life in order to carry on his dynasty's sporting tradition. He runs a huge racing stable, is building a vast Mediterranean resort and skis with Olympic skill."

[2] This is Michel Boivin's nomenclature (see his *La rénovation du shî`isme ismaélien en Inde et au Pakistan: d'après les écrits et les discours de Sultân Muhammad Shâh Aghâ Khân (1902–1954)* (London: Routledge, 2003).

[3] See, among others, Richard Kay's *Daily Mail* article, "Divorced? Oh no we're not, says Aga," 9 January 2012, http://www.dailymail.co.uk/news/article-2084107/RICHARD-KAY-Divorced-Oh-says-Aga.html.

[4] Christopher Leake, "More carthorse than racehorse ... the Aga Khan's £100m yacht," *Daily Mail*, 30 March 2008, http://www.dailymail.co.uk/news/article-549352/More-carthorse-racehorse---Aga-Khans-100m-yacht.html.

[5] Seyyed Hossein Nasr, "Introduction," in *Isma`ili Contributions to Islamic Culture*, ed. Seyyed Hossein Nasr (Tehran: Imperial Iranian Academy of Philosophy, 1977), 1.

[6] Ibid.

[7] Farhad Daftary, *The Isma`ilis: Their History and Doctrines* (Cambridge: Cambridge University Press, 1990), 3.

[8] Michael Brett, "The Realm of the Imam: The Fatimids in the Tenth Century," *Bulletin of the School of Oriental and African Studies* 59:3 (1996), 431.

[9] Azim Nanji, "The Imamate in Ismailism," *The Encyclopaedia Iranica*, Vol. XIV (New York: Columbia University Press), http://www.iis.ac.uk/view_article.asp?ContentID=109977.

[10] Jean-Jacques Lafaye, "Interview with His Highness Prince Karim Aga Khan IV: The Power of Wisdom," *Politique Internationale* (Spring 2010), http://www.politiqueinternationale.com/revue/article.

php?id_revue=127&id=909&content=synopsis, trans. Ismaili.net, http://ismaili.
net/heritage/node/30502.

11   Jonah Steinberg, *Isma`ili Modern: Globalization and Identity in a Muslim
      Community* (Chapel Hill: The University of North Carolina Press, 2011), 11.

12   Ibid.

13   Institute of Ismaili Studies, "Aga Khan Development Network (AKDN):
      An Ethical Framework" (2000), http://www.iis.ac.uk/view_article.
      asp?ContentID=101094.

14   Ibid.

15   Steinberg, 72.

16   Ibid., 1.

17   Adrienne Clarkson, "Introduction" (presented at the LaFontaine-Baldwin
      Symposium, Toronto, Canada, October 15, 2010), http://www.akdn.org/
      Content/1019.

18   Jason Kenney, "Statement - Minister Kenney issues statement to recognize
      Canada's Ismaili Muslim Community as they celebrate Navroz," Ottawa,
      Canada (March 19, 2011), http://www.cic.gc.ca/english/department/media/
      statements/2011/2011-03-19a.asp.

19   The Official Website of the Amman Message, "Frequently Asked Questions," http://
      ammanmessage.com/index.php?option=com_content&task=view&id=110.

20   Aga Khan IV, "Message to the International Islamic Conference" (read at
      The International Islamic Conference: True Islam and Its Role in Modern
      Society, Amman, Jordan, July 4–6, 2005), http://ammanmessage.com/index.
      php?option=com_content&task=view&id=57&Itemid=42.

21   The preamble is included in appendix A.

22   The Preamble to the Constitution of the Shia Imami Ismaili Muslims,
      available at http://simerg.com/special-series-his-highness-the-aga-khan-iv/
      the-preamble-of-the-constitution-of-the-shia-imami-ismaili-muslims/.

23   These are listed in the book's inside jacket as the Aga Khan's most abiding
      concerns.

24   Aziz Esmail, "Why History?," *Africa Ismaili* (1970), 20–27, http://www.iis.
      ac.uk/view_article.asp?ContentID=100996.

25   Steinberg, 91.

26   Esmail, "Why History?."

27   Steinberg, 88.

28   Esmail, "Why History?."

29   Aziz Esmail, "The Role of the Institute of Ismaili Studies," *The Ismaili UK*
      (2000), http://www.iis.ac.uk/view_article.asp?ContentID=101010.

30   Aziz Esmail, "Islam and Modernity: Intellectual Horizons," in *The Muslim
      Almanac: The Reference Work on History, Faith and Culture, and Peoples of Islam*,
      ed. Azim Nanji (Detroit: Gale Research, 1995), 486.

[31] Ibid.

[32] Ibid., 487.

[33] Ibid.

[34] Ibid.

[35] Amyn B. Sajoo, "Introduction," in *Muslim Modernities: Expressions of the Civil Imagination*, ed. Amyn B. Sajoo (London: I.B. Taurus, 2008), 11.

[36] Ibid.

[37] Ibid.

[38] Esmail, "Islam and Modernity," 485.

[39] Steinberg, 21.

[40] Q. 4:1: "O mankind! Be careful of your duty to your Lord Who created you from a single soul and from it created its mate and from them twain hath spread abroad a multitude of men and women." All Qur'an quotations are, unless otherwise stated, taken from: Abdullah Yusuf Ali, *The holy Qur'an: Arabic text with an English translation and commentary* (Delhi: Kitab Pub. House, 1973); or Marmaduke Pickthall, *The glorious Koran: a bi-lingual edition with English translation, introduction and notes* (London: Allen & Unwin, 1976); or Muhammad Asad, *Message of the Qur'an: Translated and Explained* (Gibraltar: Dar al-Andalus, 1984).

[41] Aga Khan IV, "Address by His Highness the Aga Khan" (address presented at the Annual Conference of German Ambassadors, Berlin, Germany, September 6, 2004), http://www.akdn.org/Content/583/Annual-Conference-of-German-Ambassadors.

[42] *Today*, MSNBC.com, December 13, 2010, http://today.msnbc.msn.com/id/26184891/vp/40639864#40639864.

[43] The Institute of Ismaili Studies, "The Ismaili Imamat," http://iis.ac.uk/view_article.asp?ContentID=110993.

[44] Ibid.

[45] "The whole becomes greater than the sum of its parts. An example has emerged from our work on restoration and reutilization of historic monuments: while undertaking the restoration work of, say, a monument or an historical building, one can create nearby a minor medical facility, launch educational programmes for adult education, literacy and early childhood education, undertake to improve the infrastructure around that monument, provide microfinance to the local citizens, help them maintain or upgrade their dwelling, and their shops, etc.' (Aga Khan IV, 'Statement by His Highness the Aga Khan" (presented at the Kabul Conference on Afghanistan, July 20, 2010), http://www.akdn.org/Content/1003).

[46] Nicholas Tomalin, Interview with Aga Khan, *The Sunday Times*, December 12, 1965, http://www.nanowisdoms.org/nwblog/1400/.

47   Quentin Skinner represents a school of social and political historiography that includes James Tully, John Pocock, and James Moore. Charles Taylor is a sympathetic interlocutor with this school of thought. For more, see James Tully, ed., *Meaning and Context: Quentin Skinner and His Critics* (Princeton: Princeton University Press, 1988).

48   "[...] In my definition of a state, it cannot fail. What we are observing in reality is the massive failure of democracy around the world. I estimate that some 40% of the states of the United Nations are failed democracies" (Aga Khan IV, "Speech by His Highness the Aga Khan" [statement presented at the Nobel Institute on Democratic Development, Pluralism and Civil Society; Oslo, Norway, April 7, 2005], http://www.akdn.org/Content/599).

49   Aga Khan IV, speech delivered at a dinner hosted by the President of Tanzania, Dar-es-Salaam, November 21, 1982.

50   Ibid.

51   See Azim Nanji, "Khojas," in *Encyclopaedia of Islam and Muslim World*, Vol. II, ed. Richard C. Martin (New York: MacMillan Reference Books, 2003), 393: "Derived from the Persian *khwajah*, a term of honour, the word *Khoja* referred to those converted to Nizari Ismaili Islam in the Indian sub-continent from about the thirteenth century onward. [...] The Khojas live today in East Africa, the Indian sub-continent, Europe and North America, and show a strong commitment to values of Muslim philanthropy in their entrepreneurship and contribution to societies in which they live."

52   Steinberg, 83.

53   Ibid., 16.

54   Frithjof Schuon, *The Transcendent Unity of Religions* (Wheaton, IL: Quest Books Theosophical Publishing House, 1984), 33.

CHAPTER 2

1   Primarily: Farhad Daftary, *A Modern History of the Ismailis: Continuity and Change in a Muslim Community* (London: I.B. Tauris in association with The Institute of Ismaili Studies, 2011); Jonah Steinberg, *Isma`ili Modern: Globalization and Identity in a Muslim Community* (Chapel Hill: The University of North Carolina Press, 2011); and Malise Ruthven, *The Children of Time: The Aga Khan and the Ismailis* (I.B. Tauris, 2012).

2   Anne Edwards, *Throne of Gold: The Lives of the Aga Khans* (London: William Morrow & Co, 1996), 137.

3   Ibid., 262–3.

4   Aga Khan III, writing in *The Memoirs of Aga Khan: World Enough and Time* (New York: Simon and Schuster, 1954), cites the desire to correct these sorts of "gross fictions" about his wealth as the reason for writing his memoirs. He

writes on page 1: "There are certain obvious and gross fictions that need to be corrected—the grandiose estimates, for example, of my own and my family's wealth. I have seen estimates both of my capital and my income so inaccurate that not one but two noughts at the end should be knocked off." Interestingly, he is shocked in 1954 to see writers making biographical mistakes, an error that Edwards seems to be repeating over three decades later. He concludes that such basic errors should intimate larger ones: "Not long ago an alleged biography was published; in the matter of dates the margin of error in it was anything from one to ten years. If there is this amount of misinformation on simple, easily discoverable fact, what sort of veracity is likely in wider, more profound and more intangible matters?"

5 Review of *Throne of Gold: The Lives of the Aga Khans*, by Anne Edwards, *Publisher's Weekly*, April 3, 1996, http://www.publishersweekly.com/978-0-688-08838-5.

6 Ibid.

7 'Le Prince Aga Khan recrute,' *Le Cantilien*, January 6, 2009, http://lecantilien. blogencommun.fr/2009-01-le-prince-aga-khan-recrute/; Jon Henley, 'Aga Khan gives £27m to Chantilly restoration,' *The Guardian*, March 3, 2005, http://www. guardian.co.uk/world/2005/mar/03/france.jonhenley.

8 *Le Monde*, published in the November 1, 2001, edition, http://www.lemonde. fr/rech_art/0, 5987,239159,00.html.

9 "Interview with Aga Khan," *Der Spiegel*, December 10, 2006, http://www. spiegel.de/international/spiegel/0,1518,442180,00.html.

10 AKDN Press Centre, "His Highness the Aga Khan receives 'Prix de l'Entrepreneur philanthropique de l'année 2009,'" December 17, 2009, http:// www.akdn.org/Content/925.

11 Aga Khan IV, "Speech," Nobel Institute.

12 Aga Khan IV, "Remarks by His Highness the Aga Khan" (presented at the Academy of Sciences, Lisbon, Portugal, May 8, 2009), http://www.akdn.org/Content/741/ Remarks-by-His-Highness-the-Aga-Khan-at-Portugals-Academy-of-Sciences.

13 Aga Khan IV, "His Highness the Aga Khan's Statement" (presented at the London Conference on Afghanistan, January 28, 2010), http://www.akdn.org/ Content/955/Statement-Issued-at-the-London-Conference-on-Afghanistan.

14 Yoweri Kaguta Museveni, "Speech by H. E. Yoweri Kaguta Museveni, President of the Republic of Uganda, at the Laying of the Foundation Stone for the Aga Khan Academy of Excellence" (Kampala, Uganda, August 22, 2007), http://www.akdn.org/speeches_detail.asp?id=615.

15 AKDN Press Centre, "President Mseveni and Aga Khan Inaugurate Kampala Serena Hotel" (November 10, 2006), http://www.akdn.org/Content/563/ President-Museveni-and-Aga-Khan-Inaugurate--Kampala-Serena-Hotel.

16   Sabrina Tavernise, "Afghan Enclave Seen as Model for Development," *New York Times*, November 12, 2009, http://www.nytimes.com/2009/11/13/world/asia/13jurm.html?pagewanted=all.

17   Suleman Saadat, "Helping Hands: America and Aga Khan working for flood relief again," *Express Tribune*, September 22, 2011, http://tribune.com.pk/story/257360/helping-hands-america-and-aga-khan-working-for-flood-relief-again/.

18   "Blasts in Schools and Ismaili Community Center," *My Gilgit*, January 16, 2011, http://www.mygilgit.com/blog/2011/01/16/blasts-in-schools-and-ismaili-community-center-in-chilas/; Editorial, "Chitral trouble is symptom of deeper malaise," *Daily Times*, December 29, 2004, http://www.dailytimes.com.pk/default.asp?page=story_29-12-2004_pg3_1.

19   Justin Elliott, "Shariah foes seize on Perry's ties to Muslims," *Salon*, August 15, 2011, http://www.salon.com/news/politics/war_room/2011/08/15/perry_geller_gaffney.

20   Robert Knudsen, "KN-C17294: President John F. Kennedy Meets with The Aga Khan IV, Prince Karim al-Husseini" (White House Photographs, John F. Kennedy Presidential Library and Museum, Boston, March 14, 1961), http://www.jfklibrary.org/Asset-Viewer/Archives/JFKWHP-KN-C17294.aspx.

21   Richard Reeves, *President Reagan: The Triumph of Imagination* (New York: Simon and Schuster, 2005), 280; Nancy Reagan, *My Turn: The Memoirs of Nancy Reagan* (New York: Random House, 1989), 163. In a footnote in his book *Way Out There In the Blue: Reagan, Star Wars and the End of the Cold War* (Simon & Schuster, 2001), Frances Fitzgerald provides an amusing anecdote about Reagan and Gorbachev's first meeting, held in Geneva in 1985 to discuss international diplomatic relations and the arms race, which was held at the Aga Khan's chateau, Maison de Saussure. He writes (p. 651, n. 58): "The President was staying at the Aga Khan's villa. Informed that one of the goldfish in his host's aquarium had died, he, feeling responsible, sent the Secret Service out for a replacement, and put the dead goldfish in his pocket in a matchbox. He then forgot to discard it, so that during his initial meeting with Gorbachev— one of the meetings on which hung the fate of the world—he was carrying a dead goldfish in his pocket. [...] What happened, apparently, was that Reagan promised the Aga Khan's son, Hussain, that he would take good care of his aquarium, but while he was in residence someone, possibly a Secret Service man, accidentally disconnected the aquarium, killing a multitude of fancy tropical fish. Someone in Reagan's entourage replaced the fish."

22   Tricia Escobedo, "Aga Khan makes rare visit to U.S.," *CNN*, April 15, 2008, http://articles.cnn.com/2008-04-15/us/aga.khan_1_ismaili-community-ismaili-muslims-aga-khan-university?_s=PM:US.

23   Michael Valpy, "The World of the Aga Khan," *Globe and Mail*, February 2, 2002, http://www.theglobeandmail.com/focus/the-world-of-the-aga-khan/

article443054/. Mansoor Ladha provides an amusing, if unverified, anecdote about how the target of six thousand Ugandan refugees was set. In September 1972, while the Aga Khan was delivering a talk to immigration officials about the settlement of Asians in Canada, Canada was simultaneously facing off against Russia in the ice hockey Summit Series. One of the officials had conspired with the headwaiter to signal to him the score at regular intervals with his fingers—left hand for Russia, right hand for Canada. "As dessert drew to a close," writes Ladha, "the Aga Khan popped the question to the distracted Canadians: how many would Canada accept? The officials were authorized to agree to 3000. At that very moment the waiter appeared and held up three fingers on each hand. The lead official relayed the signal to the others and the Aga Khan said, 'Six thousand would be splendid.' The officials were faced with a choice: explain the mistake, prolong the lunch and miss the rest of the game, or, let it pass. Happily, their patriotism overwhelmed their sense of duty and we gained 6000 splendid new citizens" (*A Portrait in Pluralism: Aga Khan's Shia Ismaili Muslims* [Calgary: Detselig Enterprises Ltd., 2008], 72–73).

[24] Valpy, "The World of the Aga Khan."

[25] Adrienne Clarkson, "Introduction," LaFontaine-Baldwin Symposium.

[26] Aga Khan IV, "The LaFontaine-Baldwin Lecture" (presented at the LaFontaine-Baldwin Symposium, Toronto, Canada, October 15, 2010), http://www.akdn.org/Content/1018.

[27] John Stackhouse and Patrick Martin, "Canada: 'A model for the world,'" *Globe and Mail*, February 2, 2002, F3.

[28] Valpy, "The World of the Aga Khan."

[29] Adriana Barton, "Ismaili Success: Made in Vancouver," *BCBusiness*, July 2, 2006, http://www.bcbusinessonline.ca/2006/07/01/ismaili-success-made-vancouver.

[30] Ibid.

[31] Ibid.

[32] See Mohammad Miraly, "Information on Ismailis is widely available," *Vancouver Sun*, June 16, 2005, A13, in which I argue that Doug Todd's argument in his June 11, 2005, column that the sect lacks "openness" requires revision, since "both the basic and advanced tenets and ideas of the sect are available openly on the [IIS] website."

[33] Barton, "Ismaili Success."

[34] Ibid.

[35] Ibid.

[36] Ibid.

[37] Ibid.

[38] Sumayya Kassamali, "Why Canada Doesn't Need an Islamic Art Museum," *Islamic Insights*, June 8, 2010, http://www.islamicinsights.com/news/opinion/why-canada-doesn-t-need-an-islamic-art-museum.html.

[39] Ibid.

[40] Ibid.

[41] Ibid.

[42] Ibid.

[43] Ibid.

[44] Ibid.

[45] For a deeper account of this view of postcolonial Islam, see Mohammed Arkoun, "The State, the Individual, and Human Rights: A Contemporary View of Muslims in a Global Context," in *The Muslim Almanac*, 453–7.

[46] Sudha Ramachandran, "Ismailis in deadly education spat," *Asia Times*, March 11, 2005, http://www.atimes.com/atimes/South_Asia/GC11Df06.html.

[47] Ibid.

[48] Ibid.

[49] The Institute of Ismaili Studies, "IIS Overview," http://www.iis.ac.uk/view_article.asp?ContentID=104413.

[50] Paul Walker, "The Institute of Ismaili Studies," *Encyclopaedia Iranica*, Online Edition, December 15, 2004, http://www.iranicaonline.org/articles/institute-of-ismaili-studies.

[51] Walker, "The Institute of Ismaili Studies."

[52] The Institute of Ismaili Studies, "Graduate Programme in Islamic Studies and Humanities," http://www.iis.ac.uk/view_article.asp?ContentID=104478.

[53] Shafique N. Virani, *The Ismailis in the Middle Ages: A History of Survival, A Search for Salvation* (Oxford: Oxford University Press, 2007), 3.

[54] Daftary, *The Isma`ilis*, 3.

[55] Ibid.

[56] Arzina R. Lalani, *Early Shi`i thought: the teachings of Imam Muhammad al-Baqir* (London: I.B. Tauris in association with the Institute of Ismaili Studies, 2000), 78.

[57] Ibid., 79.

[58] Heinz Halm, *The Fatimids and Their Traditions of Learning* (London: I.B. Tauris in association with The Institute of Ismaili Studies, 1997), 1.

[59] Ibid., 20.

[60] Nader el-Bizri, "Prologue," in *The Ikhwan al-Safa' and their Rasa'il: An Introduction*, ed. Nader el-Bizri (Oxford: Oxford University Press in association with The Institute of Ismaili Studies, 2008), 6.

[61] Ibid., 10.

[62] Daftary, *The Isma`ilis*, 254.

[63] Shainool Jiwa, "Religious Pluralism in Egypt: The Ahl al-kitab in Early Fatimid Times" (paper delivered at the annual meeting of the Middle Eastern Studies Association of North America, November 19, 2001), http://www.iis.ac.uk/view_article.asp?ContentID=101208.

64 Ibid.

65 Ibid.

66 Reza Shah-Kazemi, "The Metaphysics of Interfaith Dialogue: A Qur'anic Perspective" (paper presented at Paths to the Heart: Sufism and the Christian East, conference, University of South Carolina, USA, October 18–20, 2001), http://www.iis.ac.uk/view_article.asp?ContentID=101259.

67 Reza Shah-Kazemi, *Justice and Remembrance: Introducing the Spirituality of Imam 'Ali* (London: I.B. Tauris in association with The Institute of Ismaili Studies, 2006), 73.

68 Ibid., 81.

69 Amyn B. Sajoo, *Muslim Ethics: Emerging Vistas* (London: I.B. Tauris, 2004), xi.

70 Ibid., 74.

71 Amyn B. Sajoo, "Introductory Remarks" (presented at The "Good" Society: An Ethical Perspective, conference, the Institute of Ismaili Studies, London, UK, April 2001), http://www.iis.ac.uk/view_article.asp?ContentID=103808.

72 Sajoo, *Muslim Ethics*, 87.

73 Ibid.

74 Steinberg, 39.

75 Steinberg, 39.

76 Ibid., 44–45.

77 Ibid., 45.

78 Ibid., 45.

79 Ali Asani, "From Satpanthi to Ismaili Muslim: The Articulation of Ismaili Khoja Identity in South Asia," in *A Modern History of the Ismailis*, 96.

80 Sajoo, *Muslim Ethics*, 4.

81 Ibid.

82 Ibid.

83 M Yahya Birt, "The Message of Fazlur Rahman," *Newsletter of the Association of Muslim Researchers*, 27 June 1996, http://www.freerepublic.com/focus/fr/531762/posts.

84 Diana Steigerwald, "Isma'ili *Ta'wil*," in *The Blackwell Companion to the Qur'an*, ed. Andrew Rippin (Malden: Blackwell Pub., 2006), 387.

85 Ibid., 386.

86 Azim Nanji, "Rethinking our World: the Search for a Pluralistic Vision," Peterson Lecture, May 2003, Geneva (International Baccalaureate Association, 2004), 1–3 ff.

87 Aga Khan IV, "The LaFontaine-Baldwin Lecture" (Toronto, Canada, October 12, 2010), http://www.akdn.org/Content/1018/His-Highness-the-Aga-Khan-Delivers-the-10th-AnnualLaFontaineBaldwin-Lecture.

88 Ibid.

89 Steigerwald, 399. Among modern exegetes, she includes Pir Shihab al-Din Shah (d. 1302/1885)—the son of the forty-seventh Imam, Aga Khan II—and Imam Aga Khan III (d. 1376/1957), both of whom are now deceased.

90 Ibid., 397.

91 Asani, "Satpanthi," 96.

92 Aga Khan III, *Memoirs*, 185.

CHAPTER 3

1   Virani, 3.

2   E. G. Browne, quoted in Ibid.

3   Ibid., 4.

4   Ibid.

5   Asani, "Satpanthi," 95.

6   Daftary, *The Isma'ilis*, 3.

7   Asani, "Satpanthi," 95.

8   Ibid., 96.

9   Ibid.

10 Ibid.

11 Ibid.

12 Steinberg, 90.

13 Ibid.

14 Ibid., 100.

15 Virani, 11.

16 For a modern study of this period, see Wilferd Madelung, *The Succession to Muhammad: A Study of the Early Caliphate* (Cambridge: Cambridge University Press, 1997). For a modern exposition on the traditional Shi'i view of the origins of Shi'ism, see Sayyid Muhammad Husayn Tabataba'i, *Shi'ite Islam*, ed. and tr., S. H. Nasr (Karachi: Shia Institute of Pakistan, 1975).

17 Some scholars, like University of Chicago's Wadad Qadi, claim that 'Ali never wrote or dictated such a document to Malik al Ashtar (see Qadi's "An Early Fatimid Political Document," *Studia Islamica* 48 [1978]: 71–108), but this claim has been refuted in more recent scholarship (see Mohammad Ghassemi, "Authenticity of Nahj al-Balaghah" [MA thesis, McGill University, 1994]).

18 See Abu Hanifah Nu'man ibn Muhammad, *The Pillars of Islam: Da'a'im al-Islam of al-Qadi al-Nu'man*, trans. Asaf A. A. Fyzee; completely revised and annotated by Ismail Kurban Husein Poonawala (New Delhi: Oxford University Press, 2002) and Shah-Kazemi, *Justice and Remembrance*.

19 Cyril Glassé, *The New Encyclopedia of Islam* (Walnut Creek: AltaMira Press, 2001), 41.

20 Ibid.

21   "O Messenger! deliver what has been revealed to you from your Lord; and if you do it not, then you have not delivered His message" (Q. 5:67).

22   "[…] but none knows its [the Qur'an's] interpretation except Allah and those who are firmly rooted in knowledge…" (Q. 3:7).

23   "O you who believe! obey Allah and obey the Messenger and those in authority from among you" (Q. 4:59). The Qur'anic text is:

24   According to Ibn Hanbal in his *Musnad*, Vol. 4, p. 281, quoted in Moojan Momen, *An Introduction to Shi`i Islam: The History and Doctrines of Twelver Shi`ism* (New Haven: Yale University Press, 1985), 15: "[…] And then he [the Apostle of God] took `Ali by the hand and said to the people: 'Do you not acknowledge that I have a greater claim on each of the believers than they have on themselves?' And they replied: 'Yes!' And he took `Ali's hand and said: 'Of whomsoever I am Lord [*mawla*], then `Ali is also his Lord [*mawla*]. O God! Be Thou the supporter of whoever supports `Ali and the enemy of whoever opposvoes him.' And `Umar met him [`Ali] after this and said to him: 'Congratulations, O son of Abu Talib! Now morning and evening [i.e. forever] you are the *mawla* of every believing man and woman.'"

25   Ibn Hanbal, *al-Musnad*, ed. A. M. Shakir (Cairo, 1949), vol. 4, pp. 281, 370, 372; vol. 5, pp. 347, 358; al-Tirmidhi, *Sahih*, vol. 5, p. 633; al-Kulayni, *al-Kafi*, vol. 1, pp. 294–5; al-Kirmani, *Masabih*, pp. 112–13, all quoted in L. Veccia Vaglieri, "Ghadir Khumm," *The Encyclopedia of Islam*, CD-ROM edition (hereafter EI), which states, "[It is] certain that Muhammad did speak in this place and utter the famous sentence …"

26   Vaglieri, "Ghadir Khumm," EI. The historical sources reveal that there was a degree of resentment towards `Ali regarding his distribution of booty, which is why according to the Qur'an in verse 5:67 the Prophet was made to stop at Ghadir Khumm and explicitly designate `Ali as his successor, which the Qur'an says is a message that if undelivered would nullify the entirety of the Revelation, and God ensures the Prophet that He will protect him from the resentment of the people.

27   See Mahmoud M. Ayoub, *The Crisis of Muslim History: Religion and Politics in Early Islam* (Oxford: Oneworld, 2003), especially the chapter entitled "'Ali Wasi Rasul Allah"; and Marshall G. S. Hodgson, *The Venture of Islam: Conscience and History in a World Civilization*, vol. 1 (Chicago: University of Chicago Press, 1974), 217 ff.

28   This view is supported by S. H. M. Jafri in his 2009 *Political and Moral Vision of Islam*. For an interesting balance, however, see M. Ayoub and T. El-Hibri in their *Crisis of Muslim History* and *Parable and Politics in Early Islamic History* (New York: Columbia University Press, 2010), respectively.

29   Shah-Kazemi, *Justice and Remembrance*, 84.

30   Ibid., 83.

[31] Ibid., 223.

[32] Ibid., 228.

[33] Ibid., 231.

[34] Ibid.

[35] Ibid., 229.

[36] Ibid.

[37] Lalani, *Early Shi`i thought*, 52.

[38] Mohammad Ali Amir-Moezzi, *The divine guide in early Shi`ism: The Sources of Esotericism in Islam* (Albany: State University of New York Press, 1994), 78.

[39] Lalani, 78.

[40] Ibid., 79. There are, however, various explanations for the quietism of Imams Zayn al-`Abidin, al- Baqir, and Ja'far al-Sadiq, at least from the Twelver perspective (see Hossein Modarressi Tabataba'i's *Crisis and Consolidation in the Formative Period of Shi`ite Islam* (Princeton: Darwin Press, 1994)). As well, Lynda Clarke suggests that *taqiyya* may have played a part and that the Imams may have had political ambitions but chose not to overtly express them, unlike their Zaydi counterparts (see Clarke's "The Rise and Decline of *Taqiyya* in Twelver Shi`ism," in *Reason and Inspiration in Islam: Theology, Philosophy and Mysticism in Muslim Thought*, ed. Todd Lawson (London: I.B. Tauris & Co Ltd in association with The Institute of Ismaili Studies, 2005), 46–64).

[41] Daftary, *The Isma`ilis*, 93.

[42] Ibid., 91.

[43] According to Nader el-Bizri, "Prologue," 5–6, "[I]f the Ikhwan are classified as being Shi`i, as most scholars argue, it is ultimately unclear whether they can be definitively classified as Ithna`ashari (Twelvers) or Ismaili. To further complicate these speculations, even if the Ikhwan are seen to be Ismailis, it is not proven whether they had specific associations with the Fatimids or the Qarmatis, or whether they reflected any of the pre-Fatimid proclivities of Ismailism."

[44] Ibid., 10.

[45] Ian Richard Netton, "The Rasa'il Ikhwan al-Safa" in the History of Ideas in Islam,' in *The Ikhwan al-Safa' and their Rasa'il*, 134.

[46] Daftary, *The Isma`ilis*, 249.

[47] Hamid Enayat, "An Outline of the Political Philosophy of the *Rasa'il* of the Ikhwan al-Safa" in *Isma`ili Contributions to Islamic Culture*, 34.

[48] Ibid., 32.

[49] Ibid.

[50] Ibid., 38.

[51] *Rasa`il*, II, p. 317, quoted in Ibid., 35.

[52] Ibn al-Haytham, *Kitab al-munazarat*, ed. and tr. W. Madelung and P. E. Walker as *The Advent of the Fatimids: A Contemporary Shi`i Witness* (London: I.B. Tauris in association with The Institute of Ismaili Studies, 2000).

53   Abu Hanifah Nu`man ibn Muhammad, *Founding the Fatimid State: The Rise of an Early Islamic Empire: an annotated English translation of al-Qadi al-Nu'man's Iftitah al-Da'wa*, trans. Hamid Haji (London: I.B. Tauris in association with The Institute of Ismaili Studies, 2006).

54   A thorough analysis of the sources on the Fatimids may be found in Paul E. Walker, *Exploring an Islamic Empire: Fatimid History and its Sources* (London: I.B. Tauris in association with The Institute of Ismaili Studies, 2002).

55   For a detailed study of the period, see Heinz Halm, *The Empire of the Mahdi: The Rise of the Fatimids* (Leiden: E.J. Brill, 1996).

56   Daftary writes in *The Isma`ilis*, 153: "Now that the Isma`ili Imam had become a caliph, the *da`wa* could no longer address itself primarily to the overthrow of the Abbasids, as it had done during the $3^{rd}/9^{th}$ century. It was also obliged to defend and uphold the claims of the Fatimids within the world of Islam."

57   Ibid.: "[A]lmost immediately after al-Mahdi's accession, serious disagreements developed between the caliph and his chief lieutenant the *da`i* Abu `Abd Allah al-Shi`i. The *da`i* evidently had ideas of his own regarding the policies of the state, including taxation measures to be employed; he also resented the new limits put on his authority. Under these circumstances, Abu `Abd Allah, who was extremely popular amongst the Kutama, had begun to agitate against his master. But al-Mahdi, knowing that the *da`i* could easily incite the Berbers against him, moved swiftly. In 298/911, both Abu `Abd Allah and his brother Abu'l-`Abbas were murdered on his secret orders."

58   Ibid.

59   In the preceding decades, under the reigns of the first four Fatimid caliph-Imams, the Ismailis attacked Abbasid Egypt numerous times and engaged the Byzantines in Italy and France. In 958 CE, following the Fatimid occupation of Corsica and Sardinia, the Byzantine emperor Constantine VII (913–959 CE) was obliged to send tributes and embassies to al-Muizz. In 967 CE al-Muizz defeated the Byzantines in Sicily, a victory that was celebrated throughout the Islamic world, since the Byzantines were seen as a menace to the Muslims of the Near East (see Daftary, *The Isma`ilis*, 157).

60   Some of the elements contributing to the rise of the Fatimids in the tenth century were the enlistment of the tribal Berbers, the cooperation of the Hanafis of Ifriqiya, the Fatimids' favorable reception in Egypt, and the expanding awareness of their dynasty outside of Africa.

61   Michael Brett, *The Rise of the Fatimids: The World of the Mediterranean and the Middle East in the fourth century of the Hijra, tenth century CE* (Leiden: Brill, 2001), 325. Brett writes: "The climax of that progress, however, the entry of the Imam Caliph into his new abode, was nothing if not a triumphal halt. Mu`izz's arrival as the Second Seventh in line from the Prophet, to take up residence in

this new capital of the world, symbolised the fulfillment of the divine promise which had surfaced with the Mahdi and survived the test of the Dajjal" (325).

[62] Halm, *The Fatimids*, 1.

[63] Farhad Daftary, "The Ismaili *Da`wa* outside the Fatimid *Dawla*," in M. Barrucand, ed., *L'Egypte Fatimide, son art et son histoire* (Paris, 1999), pp. 29–43. Reprinted as "The Ismaili *Da'wa* and the Fatimid *Dawla*" in his *Ismailis in Medieval Muslim Societies* (London, 2005).

[64] Paul E. Walker writes in *Early Philosophical Shiism: The Ismaili Neoplatonism of Abu Ya`qub al-Sijistani* (Cambridge: Cambridge University Press, 1993), 151: "In their approach to scholarship, the earlier *da`is* exhibited little of the hesitation and precautionary secrecy so much a feature of later Ismailism. It was important for them to be seen by opponent and friend alike as comprehensive, as people in pursuit of an inclusive scholarship rather than exclusive."

[65] The *da`is* would enter a town, establish themselves as learned teachers, and hold sessions of learning where they would drop kernels of the secret Ismaili doctrine and identify singular youths who desired to know more. Thereupon, they would begin the initiation process through one-on-one instruction (see Halm, *The Fatimids*, 18–19).

[66] Halm writes in his "The Isma`ili Oath of Allegiance (`ahd) and the 'Sessions of Wisdom' (*majalis al-hikma*) in Fatimid Times," in *Mediaeval Isma`ili History and Thought*, ed. F. Daftary (New York: Cambridge University Press, 1996), 91: "From the authentic literature of the Isma`ilis we know that initiates were pledged to observe the secrecy of the 'inner meaning' (*batin*), and that they were sworn to such secrecy prior to their initiation by taking an oath, called a *mithaq* or `ahd."

[67] See S. M. Stern, "The Book of the Highest Initiation and other anti-Isma`ili Travesties," in his *Studies in Early Isma`ilism* (Leiden, 1983), 56 ff.

[68] According to Walker, in *Early Philosophical Shiism*, Ta'wil is a technique of esotericism that is an exclusively guarded "theory of a secret epistemology" (145) and, as such, the act of applying *ta'wil*—interpretation—"is not ultimately rational at all" (147). Because it seems always to be hypothetical and never actual, the "supposed analytical methodology" of the *da`i* al-Sijistani and the Ismailis "remains suspect" and "refuses to regard philosophy as a real hermeneutical tool" (147). Walker lays a "serious charge" against the work of the *da`wa*: because they sought to bring philosophy into the service of a religious mission, "it could not be free of the narrow, restraining forces that made it serve a particular sacred purpose" (145).

[69] Farhad Daftary, "Intellectual Life among the Ismailis: An Overview," in *Intellectual Traditions in Islam*, ed. Farhad Daftary (London: I.B. Tauris in association with The Institute of Ismaili Studies, 2000), 90.

70   Ja'far b. Mansur al-Yaman, "Kitab al-'Alim wa'-l-Ghulam," in *The Master and the Disciple: An Early Islamic Spiritual Dialogue*, trans. James W. Morris (London: I.B. Tauris in association with The Institute of Ismaili Studies, 2001), 64.

71   Halm, *The Fatimids*, 20.

72   Ibid.

73   See Paul E. Walker, "Fatimid Institutions of Learning," *Journal of the American Research Center in Egypt* 34 (1997): 179–200.

74   See S. T. Lokhandwalla, "The Origins of Isma'ili Law" (DPhil thesis, Oxford University, 1951), p. 21; W. Madelung, "The Sources of Isma'ili Law," *Journal of Near Eastern Studies* 35 (1976): 29–40; and Ismail K. Poonawala, "Al-Qadi al-Nu'man and Isma'ili Jurisprudence," in F. Daftary, ed., *Mediaeval Isma'ili History and Thought*, who writes that "a close scrutiny of early Isma'ili literature reveals that there did not exist a distinct Isma'ili law before the establishment of the Fatimid dynasty" (117), and "the officially promulgated Fatimid code, however, came through the composition of the *Da'a'im*, which was commissioned by al-Mu'izz, who revised it 'chapter by chapter and section by section, confirming what was firmly established and authentic, polishing its rough edges, and filling the gaps'" (126).

75   See Abu Hanifah Nu'man ibn Muhammad, *The Pillars of Islam*. Sumaiya A. Hamdani, in *Between Revolution and State: The Path to Fatimid Statehood. Qadi al-Nu'man and the Construction of Fatimid Legitimacy* (London: I.B. Tauris in association with the Institute of Ismaili Studies, 2006), argues that the *Da'a'im* aimed to reconcile the Shari'a with the sole authority of the Imam by expounding a *zahiri* doctrine of caliphate as distinct from the secret *batini* doctrine of Imamate in order to gain the Imam's acceptance as sovereign of Islam from the majority of Muslims. A. A. Fyzee, however, argues in *A Compendium of Fatimid Law* (Simla: Indian Institute of Advanced Study, 1969) that a legal system that ascribes supreme authority to the monarch as the sole guide is fatally flawed.

76   Halm, *The Fatimids*, 29.

77   Ibid. Because the Imam had to authorize everything, there were sometimes delays in transmitting his knowledge, since *da'is* would have to wait for the busy caliph-Imam to look over their work. As well, it has been noted that *da'is* in Cairo would not publish works of *ta'wil*—presumably because the Imam wished always to have new information transmitted, or out of fear of the Imam—while *da'is* operating outside the Fatimid state would publish works of *ta'wil*, which would take years to reach the caliph-Imam in Cairo (Farhad Mortezaee, verbal communication).

78   For an exploration of the diverse literary and intellectual traditions of the Ismailis of Fatimid times, see Ismail K. Poonawala, *Biobigliography of Isma'ili Literature* (Malibu: Undena Publications, 1977), and Farhad Daftary, *Ismaili Literature:*

A Bibliography of Sources and Studies (London: I.B. Tauris in association with the Institute of Ismaili Studies, 2004).

[79] Walker (*Early Philosophical Shiism*) argues that the Ismaili interest in philosophy was a conscious choice. It was possible, he says, to expound on the *zahir/batin* distinction and provide numerous examples of *ta'wil* without philosophizing, as did al-Nu'man in his *Ta'wil al-da'a'im*. Walker further argues that Neoplatonism was a dubious form of philosophy that provided the Ismailis an easy route to engaging with philosophy: "Neoplatonism, then, gave the Ismailis an alternate road to philosophy—one that they did not need to fear. It did not traverse the formal ground of philosophy as laid down by Plato, and most especially, Aristotle. In fact it may not have carried the label 'philosophy' at all" (152). It was no accident, Walker concludes, that the Ismaili thinkers found what they were looking for in a "limited selection of quasi-philosophical texts"; they "sought to co-opt philosophical knowledge by appropriating that portion of it that was more or less congenial to their own basic outlook" (152). Madelung takes a different view, stating that Isma'ili doctrine "selected what it found congenial to its basic convictions and amalgamated it into a coherent synthesis of its own" ("Aspects of Isma'ili Theology: The Prophetic Chain and the God Beyond Being," in *Isma'ili Contributions to Islamic Culture*, 54). Daftary offers the explanation that the *da'i*s aimed to attract the ruling elite and educated classes, and thus "chose to express their theology in terms of the then most modern and intellectually fashionable philosophical themes, without compromising the essence of their religious message,' namely, the Shi'i doctrine of Imamate ("Intellectual Life among the Ismailis," in *Intellectual Traditions in Islam*, 95). Nevertheless, Ian Netton concludes in his *Allah Transcendent* (London: Routledge, 1989) that the "deep structure" of the "Isma'ili myth" should be analyzed not based on its antecedents, but rather as a product of its own day and age (234–43).

[80] See Paul E. Walker, *Hamid al-Din al-Kirmani: Ismaili Thought in the Age of al-Hakim* (London: I.B. Tauris in association with The Institute of Ismaili Studies, 1999).

[81] See Paul E. Walker, *Abu Ya'qub al-Sijistani: Intellectual Missionary* (London: I.B. Tauris in association with The Institute of Ismaili Studies, 1996); Boustan Hirji, *A study of al-Risalah al-bahirah* (PhD diss., McGill University, 1994).

[82] See Verena Klemm, *Memoirs of a Mission: The Ismaili Scholar, Statesman and Poet, al-Mu'ayyad fi'l-Din al-Shirazi* (London: I.B. Tauris in association with The Institute of Ismaili Studies, 2003); Elizabeth R. Alexandrin, *The "sphere of walayah": Ismai'ili ta'wil in practice according to al-Mu'ayyad (d. ca. 1078 CE)* (PhD diss., McGill University, 2006).

[83] See Faquir M Hunzai, *Knowledge and Liberation: A Treatise on Philosophical Theology* (London: I.B. Tauris in association with The Institute of Ismaili Studies, 1998).

84   See Azim Nanji, "Transcendence and Distinction: Metaphoric Process in Isma'ili Muslim Thought," *God and Creation: An Ecumenical Symposium*, eds. David B. Burrell and Bernard McGinn (Notre Dame: University of Notre Dame, 1990), 304–315.

85   Brett argues that the Ismailis' use of Neoplatonist philosophy to create a theology in which the Imam is placed at the center of the universe and its history, and thus "as propaganda for the Fatimids," may have "limited the wider consideration and contribution of this major school of thought to the philosophical discourse of Islam" (review of *Fatimid History and Ismaili Doctrine*, by Paul E. Walker, in *Journal of the American Oriental Society* 128.3 [2008], 575).

86   Halm, *The Fatimids*, 90–91 ff.

87   Walker, "Fatimid Institutions," 193.

88   Halm, *The Fatimids*, 73.

89   Ibid.

90   Ibid.

91   Walker, "Fatimid Institutions," 190.

92   Similarly, scholars like S. M. Stern (*Studies in Early Shiism*, 85–95) and S. D. Goiten (*A Mediterranean Society* [Berkeley, 1967–88], vol. 1, p. 31) acknowledge the Fatimids' liberal attitude as a function of political reality rather than ethical choice. Goiten writes: "It is reasonable to assume that the Fatimids and their Isma'ili followers did not create the comparatively tolerant spirit of the period, but the fact that they themselves constituted only a small minority within the Muslim population of Egypt and Syria may have contributed to their tolerance in governing and to a general leniency toward other minority groups upon whom they came to rely." Gustave von Grunebaum puts it somewhat differently: "All praise is due the Fatimids for having known how to induce the communities under their sway to develop their courage and enterprise and to preserve their intellectual élan without damaging that unity of the larger community which hinged on the dynasty's sense of purpose" (*Colloque International sur l'Histoire du Caire*, March 27–April 5, 1969 [Ministry of Culture of the Arab Republic of Egypt, 1972], 212–3).

93   Daftary, *The Isma'ilis*, 254.

94   Brett and Halm, among others, posit that the *Aman* document could have been issued by al-Mahdi, possibly with reference to the fatal quarrel with his *da'i* Abu 'Abd Allah.

95   Shainool Jiwa, 'Religious Pluralism in Egypt: The Ahl al-kitab in Early Fatimid Times' (paper delivered at the annual meeting of the Middle Eastern Studies Association of North America on 19 November 2001, http://www.iis.ac.uk/view_article.asp?ContentID=101208).

96   Patricia Crone and Martin Hinds argue in *God's Caliph* (Cambridge: Cambridge University Press, 1986) that the Fatimid attempt to combine political power and

religious authority was archaic. The Sunnis, they write, had 'stripped the head of state of his religious authority,' while the 'Shi`ites had lost such real interest in replacing him with an imam of their own,' and 'only utopianists such as the Isma`ilis refused to concede that political power and religious authority had parted company for good' (99). As it stands, they write, the Fatimid version of state Ismailism did not gain ground among the Berbers of North Africa, who were quickly disillusioned, nor among the local Egyptians, who never converted (108, n. 76).

⁹⁷ Jiwa writes in 'Religious Pluralism in Egypt': 'This exalted rank of the Fatimid *imam*-caliph was clearly articulated and embedded in public consciousness through a variety of measures: the promotion of Fatimid rites and law; the dissemination of learning in Fatimid palaces and mosques; their acknowledgement as true sovereigns of the Muslim world from the pulpits of the mosques in Mecca, Medina and Jerusalem, etc.'

⁹⁸ Ibid.

⁹⁹ Ibid.

¹⁰⁰ Daftary, *The Isma`ilis*, 185.

¹⁰¹ Ibid., 185.

¹⁰² Ibid., 188–189.

¹⁰³ M. Canard, "al-Hakim Bi-amr Allah," *Encyclopaedia of Islam*, Online Edition, 2011, http://www.brillonline.nl/subscriber /entry?entry=islam_SIM-2637: "It is difficult to form an exact idea of his personality, so strange and even inexplicable were many of the measures which he took, and so full of contradictions does his conduct seem. His main characteristic is a tyrannical and cruel despotism, with intervals of liberalism and humility […] He seems to have been several persons in succession or even simultaneously."

¹⁰⁴ Halm, *The Fatimids*, 35–36 ff.

¹⁰⁵ Canard, "al-Hakim Bi-amr Allah": "Hakim ruled as an absolute despot, obeying only his own caprice and mood of the moment… [He] resorted to executions for all kinds of reasons, among them to inspire terror and as a method of government. The number of viziers, high officials and ordinary individuals whom he had put to death is considerable."

¹⁰⁶ Canard, "al-Hakim Bi-amr Allah": "There were occasions on the other hand when Hakim showed remarkable simplicity, humility and asceticism, liberality and sense of justice, so that judgements of him have not always been unfavourable."

¹⁰⁷ Halm, *The Fatimids*, 36. Writing in a somewhat different context, Canard ("al-Hakim Bi-amr Allah") says that "the whole population stood in terrible fear of Hakim." He also writes, however, that accounts of al-Hakim's "liberality" have been preserved in several stories of the 1001 Nights, "such as the story of the Cairo merchant who, having given splendid hospitality to the caliph when he

had stopped in front of his garden during an official procession to ask for a drink, received from Hakim as a reward all the coins struck by the Mint in that year." Famously, al-Hakim's habit of disguising himself as *hoi polloi* was attributed in the 1001 Nights to the 'Abbasid caliph al-Ma'mun.

[108]   Halm, *The Fatimids*, 37.

[109]   Ibid. Ahmad S. Moussalli (*The Islamic Quest for Democracy, Pluralism, and Human Rights* [Gainesville: University Press of Florida, 2001], 138), however, writes that "[the Christians] were forced to convert to Isma'ilism if they wanted to be employed in the state apparatus, and were persecuted if they did not. Al-Hakim bi Amri Allah even tried to demolish al-Qiyyama Church, one of the most important churches and supposedly the place where the crucified Christ was buried....Jews and Christians were also forced to wear distinctive clothing, usually black, and were prevented from celebrating their holidays. Their endowments became part of the official *diwan* or ministry. They were subjected to other prejudices and cruel customs, like having to ride donkeys instead of horses." Canard's article ("al-Hakim Bi-amr Allah") recounts some of these instances in greater depth, offering details lacking in Moussalli's account. As well, Canard admits that some measures may not have been strictly enforced, since they were repeated. Also, he notes that in 1013, al-Hakim allowed the Christians and the Jews to return to their faith and emigrate to Greek territory as well as passing in 1021 a series of measures in favor of the Christians. It does appear that many of the seemingly anti-Christian measures were implemented as a reaction to civic disturbance and not out of caprice, as Moussalli's account might suggest.

[110]   Halm, *The Fatimids*, 37.

[111]   Wladimir Ivanow, *Ismaili Tradition Concerning the Rise of the Fatimids* (London: Islamic Research Association in association with Oxford University Press, 1942), 123. He writes: "The acts of al-Hakim in his attempts at suppressing Christianity were probably not insane, but a direct outcome of this mentality of the masses—a move towards the realisation of their ideals. This is why such eminent intellectuals as Hamidu'd-din Kirmani, and others, could sincerely defend him, and their less balanced colleagues even find in these actions of his a reason for deifying him, as the Druzes did."

[112]   Canard, "al-Hakim Bi-amr Allah."

[113]   Halm, *The Fatimids*, 37–38. An example of this, says Halm, is that "during his rides to the Muqattam mountains near Cairo, [al-Hakim] would even stop for a rest at the Dayr al-Qasir convent, talk with the abbot and inspect the progress of the reconstruction."

[114]   Canard, "al-Hakim Bi-amr Allah."

[115]   Moussalli, *Islamic Quest*, 140.

116 Amyn B. Sajoo, "Beyond The Exotic: The Pleasures of 'Islamic' Art," *The Ismaili United Kingdom* No. 42 (July 2001): 16–18, http://www.iis.ac.uk/view_article. asp?ContentID=101171.

117 Daftary, *The Isma`ilis*, 324.

118 Steinberg, 38.

119 Farhad Daftary, "Hasan-i Sabbah and the Origins of the Nizari Isma`ili Movement," in *Mediaeval Isma`ili History and Thought*, 188. He writes: "Hasan-i Sabbah seems to have had a complex set of religio-political motives for his revolt against the Saljuqs. As an Isma`ili Shi`i, he clearly could not have supported the ardently Sunni Saljuq Turks. Less conspicuously, but of equal significance, Hasan's revolt was also an expression of Iranian 'national' sentiments, which accounts for a major share of the early support extended to this revolt in Persia.... And it was to the ultimate goal of uprooting the Saljuq Turks that he dedicated himself and organized the Persian Isma`ilis of diverse backgrounds as a revolutionary force" (189).

120 Daftary, *The Isma`ilis*, 352.

121 Farhad Daftary, *The Assassin Legends: Myths of the Isma`ilis* (London: I.B. Tauris & Co Ltd., 1995), frontispiece: "European myths and fantasies relating to Isma`ili Muslims originated in the time of the Crusaders and centred on the Isma`ili leadership represented by the 'Old Man of the Mountain'. These fantastic tales culminated in bizarre legends of drug-crazed violence which have survived into modern times when the word 'assassin' from *hashishin*—hashish-users—has entered European languages to mean murderer." See pp. 92–3 for a fuller explanation.

122 Ibid., 34: They utilized assassination "rather openly in a spectacular and intimidating fashion. As a result, almost any assassination of any religious, political or military significance during the Alamut period was attributed to them. This provided a most convenient pretext for other individuals or groups to remove their own enemies, resting assured that the Nizaris would be blamed."

123 Virani, 7.

124 Marshall G. S. Hodgson, *The Order of Assassins* (New York: AMS Press, 1980), 111–2.

125 Their methods were effective, giving rise to the accounts that Daftary explores in his *The Assassin Legends*. By way of example, Bernard Lewis (*The Assassins: A Radical Sect in Islam* (London: Weidenfeld and Nicolson, 1967) recounts the warning of the German priest Brocardus to King Philip VI of France about embarking on a new crusade: "I name the Assassins, who are to be cursed and fled. They sell themselves, are thirsty for blood, kill the innocent for a price, and care nothing for either life or salvation. Like the devil, they transfigure themselves into angels of light, by imitating the gestures, garments, languages, customs and acts of various nations and peoples; thus, hidden in sheep's clothing,

they suffer death as soon as they are recognized" (1). Lewis adds, however, that while "the assassins were criminal fanatics" for their victims, "for the Ismailis, they were a corps d'elite in the war against the enemies of the Imam; by striking down oppressors and usurpers, they gave the ultimate proof of their faith and loyalty, and earned immediate and eternal bliss" (48).

126   Daftary, *The Isma`ilis*, 353.

127   Ibid., 381–2.

128   Hodgson, 119.

129   Ibid., 239.

130   Virani, 8.

131   Ibid.

132   Daftary, *The Isma`ilis*, 367.

133   Ibid., 370.

134   Daftary, *Assassin Legends*, 36: "The Muslim opponents of the Nizaris, whose hostility towards the Isma`ilis in general had now been rekindled at a higher level, were much more successful in their anti-Nizari literary campaign. This vast and semi-official campaign, involving polemicists, heresiographers, thelogians, jusrists and historians, which was rooted in the earlier anti-Isma`ili 'black legend', went a long way towards shaping the anti-Nizari opinion of Mediaeval Muslims. It succeeded in making the Nizaris perhaps the most feared community in the mediaeval Islamic world." One of the earliest and most popular anti-Ismaili books was al-Ghazali's, in which his "objective is to parody the Fatimid *da`wa*'s claim of possessing privileged knowledge in religious matters, and thus for al-Ghazali this process of initiation is based on and culminates in a lie—a lie which masks a political drive in the name of religious learning" (Farouk Mitha, *Al-Ghazali and the Ismailis: A Debate on Reason and Authority in Medieval Islam* [London: I.B. Tauris in association with Institute of Ismaili Studies, 2001], 40).

135   See Nasir al-Din al-Tusi, "Sayr wa Suluk," in *Contemplation and Action: The Spiritual Autobiography of a Muslim Scholar*, ed. and trans. S. J. Badakhchani (London: I.B. Tauris in association with Institute of Ismaili Studies, 1998).

136   Henry Corbin (*Cyclical Time and Ismaili Gnosis* [London: Kegan Paul International in association with Islamic Publications Ltd, 1983] sees the Resurrection as the application of *ta'wil* and the reestablishment of the Imam's priority, thus returning Alamut Ismailism to its origins after the closing of the Fatimid episode, whose political success was a paradox doomed to failure on the spiritual plane, since it presupposed the accomplishment of Ismaili eschatology (117). He writes: "Here precisely is the paradox, the permanent challenge of this Shiite Gnosis: to experience the religion of Resurrection, the religion of the Imam, is to penetrate the hidden sense of the positive religion and at the same time to surpass it. And yet the positive religion must be retained, precisely in

order to constrain men to exceed it, to call forth the resurrection of the adepts" (118).

137 Daftary, *The Isma'ilis*, 388.

138 Virani, 3.

139 Ibid., 21.

140 Ibid., 9.

141 Ibid., 185.

142 Ibid., 12.

143 Ibid.

144 Ibid., 14.

145 For a more detailed Ismaili history of this period, see Nadia Eboo Jamal, *Surviving the Mongols: Nizari Quihistani and the Continuity of Ismaili Tradition in Persia* (London: I.B. Tauris in association with Institute of Ismaili Studies, 2002), and Virani, *The Ismailis in the Middle Ages* (Oxford, 2007).

146 Daftary, *The Isma'ilis*, 437–8. For the evolution of the tradition of the Indian Ismailis, see Azim Nanji, *The Nizari Isma'ili Tradition in the Indo-Pakistan Subcontinent* (Delmar, 1978); Dominique Sila-Khan, *Crossing the Threshold: Understanding Religious Identities in South Asia* (London, 2004); Ali S. Asani, *Ecstasy and Enlightenment: The Ismaili Devotional Literature of South Asia* (London: I.B. Tauris in association with the Institute of Ismaili Studies, 2002); Aziz Esmail, *A Scent of Sandlewood: Indo-Ismaili Religious Lyrics* (London: I.B. Tauris in association with the Institute of Ismaili Studies, 2002); Tazim R. Kassam, *Songs of Wisdom and Circles of Dance: Hymns of the Satpanth Isma'ili Muslim Saint, Pir Shams* (Albany: State University of New York Press, 1995).

147 Daftary, *The Isma'ilis*, 513.

148 Daftary (Ibid.) writes that the Nizari Khojas "did not produce any elaborate theological or philosophical treatises nor did they translate the Persian and Arabic texts of other Nizari communities into their own languages" (442). He continues to say that their distinctive literature, the *ginan*s, conveyed "the post-*qiyama* Nizari doctrines in the light of the tenets of Vaishnavism, and presents the Nizari Imam as the awaited saviour on the basis of Vaishnavite ideas concerning the different manifestations of the Hindu deity Vishnu through the ages.... Such explanations were easily comprehensible to the Hindus, who had been converted to Nizarism" (485). For Kassam (*Songs of Wisdom*, 119), "the syncretism in the *ginan*s is not a haphazard mishmash of Hindu and Muslim ideas," but, rather, "the *ginan*s intricately weave Hindu and Isma'ili ideas together to fashion a religious sensibility that holds them in dynamic and fertile tension."

149 Kassam (*Songs of Wisdom*, 35) writes: "But it is an ironic twist that the very tradition [*ginanic* tradition] that nurtured the religious life of the Satpanth Khojahs for so many centuries, and that had successfully been used to establish

the link of this South Asian Muslim community with the Nizari Isma`ili *imams*, once it became exposed, turned into fodder for ultraconservative Muslim groups wishing to question the community's Muslim identity. To some extent, this reversal of affairs helped to demonstrate the validity of the sect's centuries-long fears of persecution."

150   Ibid., 29.

151   Ibid., 34.

152   Ibid., 7.

153   Amrita Shodhan, *A Question of Community: Religious Groups and Colonial Law* (Calcutta: Samya, 2001).

154   Steinberg, 39.

155   Ibid.

156   Aga Khan I's own account of his early life and conflict with the Qajar establishment can be found in his autobiography, `Ibrat-afza (lithograph, Bombay, 1278/1862), ed. H. Kuhi Kirmani (Tehran, 1325/1946). See also Naoroji M. Dumasia, *A Brief History of the Aga Khan* (Bombay, 1903), pp. 66–95; his *The Aga Khan and his Ancestors* (Bombay, 1939), 25–59; H. Algar, "The Revolt of Agha Khan Mahallati and the Transference of the Isma`ili Imamate to India," *Studia Islamica* 29 (1969), 61–81; and Daftary, *The Isma`ilis*, 463–476. Justice Arnould, in his verdict in the 1866 case, gave the following account of the Aga Khan's departure from Iran: "Mr. Watson (*n*) states somewhat vaguely, as the reason for this rising, that the Aga 'thought the time had now come when he might assert with advantage the religious character of which he was inheritor.' The native Persian historian assigns what is, perhaps, a more probable reason. Hadji Mirza Ahasi, who had been the tutor of [Emperor] Mahomed Ali Shah, was during the whole reign of his royal pupil (from 1834 to 1848) the Prime Minister of Persia. A Persian of very low origin, formerly in the service of the Aga Khan, had become the chief favourite and minion of the all-powerful minister. This person, through his patron, had the impudence to demand in marriage for his son one of the daughters of the Aga Khan, a granddaughter of the late Shah-in-Shah! This, says the Persian historian, 'was felt by the Aga Khan to be a great insult,' and the request, though strongly pressed by the Prime Minister, was indignantly refused. Having thus made the most powerful man in Persia his deadly enemy, the Aga Khan probably felt that his best chance of safety was to assert himself in arms—a course not uncommon with the great feudatories of disorganized Persia. Making Kerman his headquarters, he appears to have kept up the fight with varying fortunes through the years 1838–9 and part of 1840. In the latter year, overpowered by numbers, he was forced to flight and with difficulty made his escape, attended by a few horsemen, through the deserts of Baluchistan to Sind.... In Sind he would, of course, find no money difficulties to contend with. The Khojas of that province (numbering nearly 3,000 houses

or families) have always been among his most zealous adherents, and from them and his other Khoja devotees in various parts of India and the East, there can be no doubt, he received ample supplies" (J. Arnould, *Judgement of the Honourable Sir Joseph Arnould in the Khojah Case, otherwise known as the Aga Khan Case*, Bombay, 1867, in *Bombay High Court Reports: Reports of cases decided in the High Court of Bombay* [Bombay: High Court of Judicature, 1876], 341).

[157] Aga Khan III, *Memoirs*, 182.

[158] Ernest Gellner (*Muslim Society* [Cambridge: Cambridge University Press, 1981], 106) writes that the 1866 judgment legitimized the Aga Khan's tithe collection, and thus, "With the wealth he now controlled, thanks to Shi`a theology and British law, the then Aga Khan had the means to live in a princely Indian style which gave him, and his successors, social access to the British rulers. The third Aga Khan went to Europe in 1897 and dined with Queen Victoria. He maintained his position as somehow a member of the British ruling class, of the international aristocracy of title and wealth, and as the divine reincarnation of his own sect."

[159] Ibid.

[160] Steinberg, 43.

[161] Shodhan, 82–83.

[162] Steinberg, 44.

[163] Ibid.,43.

[164] Asani, 'Satpanthi,' 107.

[165] K. K. Aziz, 'Introduction,' in *Aga Khan III: Selected Speeches and Writings of Sir Sultan Muhammad Shah*, ed. K. K. Aziz (London: Kegan Paul International, 1998), 1.

[166] Ibid., 92.

[167] Ibid.

[168] Ibid., 102.

[169] Aga Khan III, *Memoirs*, 188.

[170] Ibid., 187.

[171] However, under insistence from his followers, he did press the British for a small Ismaili state on the scale of Israel, which was refused.

[172] Aga Khan III, *Memoirs*, 187.

[173] Aga Khan IV, "Speech On Acceptance of the 2009 Nouvel Economiste Philanthropic Entrepreneur of the Year 2009 Award" (presented at the Cour des Comptes, Palais Cambon, December 17, 2009), http://www.akdn.org/Content/924/Speech-by-His-Highness-the-Aga-Khan-at-the-Cour-des-Comptes-Court-of-Accounts-Palais-Cambon.

[174] Aga Khan IV, "Speech at the Graduation Ceremony of the University of Alberta" (presented at the University of Alberta, Edmonton, Canada, June 9, 2009), http://www.akdn.org/Content/767/

Speech-by-His-Highness-the-Aga-Khan-at-the-Graduation-Ceremony-of-the-University-of-Alberta.

[175] Asani, "Satpanthi," 119.

[176] Ibid., 121.

[177] Ibid., 122.

[178] Ibid.

[179] Virani, 50.

[180] Ptolemy Tompkins, "Rumi Rules!" *Time Magazine*, October 29, 2002, http://www.time.com/time/magazine/article/0,9171,356133,00.html.

[181] Heinz Halm, "The cosmology of the pre-Fatimid Isma`iliyya," in *Mediaeval Isma`ili History and Thought*, 83.

[182] Charles Taylor, *The Malaise of Modernity* (Concord: Anansi, 1991), 4.

CHAPTER 4

[1] Daftary, *The Isma`ilis*, 138.

[2] Steigerwald, "Isma`ili *Ta'wil*," 386.

[3] Ibid.

[4] Daftary, *The Isma`ilis*, 138. The *ta'wil* practiced by the early Ismailis, he says, was cabalistic and relied on the symbolism of letters and numbers. Further, he says, similar interpretive and spiritual exegeses existed among the earlier Judaeo-Christian traditions and among the Gnostics.

[5] Ibid.

[6] Steigerwald, 387.

[7] Ibid., 389.

[8] Ibid.

[9] Ibid., 395.

[10] Ibid.

[11] Ibid., 397.

[12] Ibid.

[13] Azim Nanji, "Shi`i Ismaili Interpretations of The Holy Qur'an," *Selected Proceedings of the International Congress for the Study of the Qur'an* (1980): 39–49, http://www.iis.ac.uk/view_article.asp?ContentID=111705.

[14] Bulbul Shah, "Al-Qadi al-Nu`man and the Concept of *Batin*," in *Reason and Inspiration in Islam*, 117.

[15] Nanji, "Interpretations," http://www.iis.ac.uk/view_article.asp?ContentID=111705.

[16] Ibid., 3.

[17] Steigerwald, "Isma`ili *Ta'wil*," 391.

18   Faquir Muhammad Hunzai, "*Ta'wil* of the Qur'an and the *Shari'a* according to Hakim Nasir-i Khusraw," (paper presented at Nasir Khusraw: Yesterday, Today and Tomorrow, conference in Khorog, Tajikistan, September 2–4, 2003), 7.

19   Ibid., 3.

20   Faquir Muhammad Hunzai, "The Concept of Knowledge According to al-Kirmani (d. after 411/1021)," in *Reason and Inspiration*, 135.

21   Ibid., 135–136.

22   Ibid., 136.

23   Nanji,   "Interpretations,"   http://www.iis.ac.uk/view_article.asp?ContentID=111705.

24   Ibid., 4.

25   Nasir al-Din Tusi, *Paradise of Submission: A Medieval Treatise on Ismaili Thought*, a new Persian edition and English translation of Tusi's *Rawda-yi taslim*, ed. and trans. S. J. Badakhchani (London: I.B. Tauris & Co Ltd, 2005), 142.

26   Tusi, *Paradise*, 142.

27   Shah, 120.

28   Steigerwald, 391.

29   Ibid.

30   Hunzai, "Knowledge," 138.

31   Hunzai, "*Ta'wil*," 2–3.

32   Hunzai, "Knowledge," 138.

33   Ibid., 139.

34   Aga Khan III, *Memoirs*, 178–9.

35   Ibid., 172.

36   Ibid., 173.

37   Aga Khan IV, "Opening Address," in *Word of God, Art of Man: The Qur'an and its Creative Expressions: Selected Proceedings from the International Colloquium (London, 18–21 October 2003)*, ed. Fahmida Suleman (London: Oxford University Press, 2007), xx.

38   Ibid., xxi.

39   Steigerwald., 386.

40   Ibid.

41   Ibid.

CHAPTER 5

1   Aga Khan IV, "Keynote Address at the Governor General's Canadian Leadership Conference on Leadership and Diversity" (address presented at the Canadian Museum of Civilization, Gatineau, Canada, May 19, 2004), http://www.iis.ac.uk/view_article.asp?ContentID=104233.

2   Aga Khan Development Network, http://www.akdn.org/.

3   Ibid.

4   A chart of the organizational structure of the AKDN, showing a list of its agencies, is included in the appendix.

5   Malise Ruthven, "The Aga Khan Development Network and Institutions," in *A Modern History of the Ismailis*, 190.

6   Aga Khan Development Network, "Frequent Questions," http://www.akdn.org/faq.asp.

7   Ibid.

8   Ruthven, 190.

9   Ibid.

10   Aga Khan Development Network, "Frequent Questions."

11   Ibid.

12   Ibid.

13   Ibid.

14   Institute of Ismaili Studies, "Aga Khan Development Network (AKDN): An Ethical Framework."

15   Steinberg, 3.

16   Ibid., 59.

17   Ibid.

18   Ibid., 88.

19   Ibid., 87.

20   Ibid., 91.

21   Ibid., 88.

22   Ibid., 91.

23   Ibid., 88.

24   Ibid., 208.

25   Ibid., 70–71.

26   Ibid., 71.

27   Ibid.

28   Ibid.

29   Ibid., 72.

30   Ibid.

31   Ibid., 59.

32   Ibid.

33   Ibid., 71.

34   Aga Khan Development Network, "Afghanistan," http://www.akdn.org/afghanistan.

35   Aga Khan IV, "Statement," Kabul Conference.

36   Aga Khan Development Network (AKDN), "Social Audits in Afghanistan: Making Local Governance More Transparent," *AKDN Development Blog*, June 8, 2009, http://www.akdn.org/blog.asp?id=765.

[37] Ibid.

[38] Anand Gopal, "$1,000 for a kebab? Afghan villages fight corruption," the *Christian Science Monitor*, March 25, 2009, http://www.csmonitor.com/World/Asia-South-Central/2009/0325/p01s02-wosc.html.

[39] Aga Khan IV, "Statement," Kabul Conference.

[40] Ibid.

[41] Ibid.

[42] Aga Khan IV, "Democracy, Pluralism and Civil Society," in *Where Hope Takes Root: Democracy and Pluralism in an Interdependent World* (Vancouver: Douglas & McIntyre, 2008), 87.

[43] Ibid., 88.

[44] Aga Khan IV, "Underwriting Human Progress," in *Where Hope Takes Root*, 67.

[45] Aga Khan Development Network (AKDN), "AKDN Civil Society Programme Afghanistan 2006–2008," www.akdn.org/publications/civil_society_afghanistan_programme.pdf.

[46] Aga Khan Development Network (AKDN), "Multi-Input Area Development," *AKDN Development Blog*, Arpril 29, 2009, http://www.akdn.org/Content/737.

[47] Caroline Arnold, personal interview (Geneva, Switzerland, October 7, 2010).

[48] Zahra Kassam Mamdani, "Education for Pluralism: Explorations & Avenues for Future Programming," draft concept note for Aga Khan Foundation (March 2006), 7.

[49] Ibid.

[50] Ibid.

[51] Ibid., 7–8.

[52] Ibid., 11.

[53] Government of Canada, "Girls' Education Support Programme," http://www.afghanistan.gc.ca/canada-afghanistan/projects-projets/serv2.aspx.

[54] Aga Khan Foundation Canada, 'Canada and Aga Khan Foundation in Afghanistan,' AKFC Press Brochure.

[55] Ibid.

[56] Ibid.

[57] Richard Phinney, *Change in the Making: A Journey in Afghanistan* (Aga Khan Foundation Canada, 2009).

[58] Ruthven, 191.

[59] Ibid.

[60] Steinberg, 16.

[61] Ruthven, 219. He concludes by recognizing that while this notion may not be palatable to all, its practical benefits should be "the esoteric theology that legitimizes that tradition is not accessible to everyone, but its value may be judged by its practical results, and the promise it holds for the future."

CHAPTER 6

1   Aga Khan IV, "Underwriting Human Progress," in *Where Hope Takes Root*, 61.

2   Aga Khan IV, "Renewing Democracy's Promise," in Ibid., 115.

3   Sajoo, *Muslim Ethics*, 87.

4   Ibid.

5   Aga Khan IV, "Underwriting Human Progress," 61.

6   According to Bassam Tibi (*Islam Between Culture and Politics* [New York, 2001], 2): "The notion of an Islamic system is an 'invention of tradition' pursued by the adherents of Islamism in contemporary Islam as much as the caliphate was an arbitrary addition to Islam in its classical period."

7   Carl Ernst, *Following Muhammad: Rethinking Islam in the Contemporary World* (Chapel Hill: University of North Carolina Press, 2003), 140.

8   José Casanova, "The Secular, Secularizations, Secularisms," in *Rethinking Secularism*, eds. Craig Calhoun et al (Oxford: Oxford University Press, 2011), 54. Also see his *Public Religions in the Modern World* (Chicago: University of Chicago Press, 1994).

9   Talal Asad, *Formations of the Secular: Christianity, Islam, Modernity* (Stanford: Stanford University Press, 2003), 16.

10   Casanova, "The Secular," 55.

11   Ibid., 58.

12   Charles Taylor, *A Secular Age* (Cambridge: Harvard University Press, 2007), 269.

13   Casanova, "The Secular," 58.

14   Ibid.

15   Abdolkarim Soroush, "Remarks" (address presented at Islam and Democracy, conference in Mashhad, Iran, December 1–2, 2004), http://www.drsoroush.com/English/By_DrSoroush/E-CMB-20041126-Islam_and_Democracy-conference_in_Mashhad.html.

16   Asghar Ali Engineer, "Interview: The Compatibility of Islam, Secularism and Modernity," in *New Voices of Islam*, ed. Farish A. Noor (Leiden: International Institute for the Study of Islam in the Modern World [ISIM], 2002), 30.

17   Abdulaziz Sachedina, *The Role of Islam in the Public Square: Guidance or Governance?*, ISIM Paper 5 (Amsterdam: Amsterdam University Press, 2006), 6.

18   Wilfred McClay, "Two Concepts of Secularism," in *Religion Returns to the Public Square: Faith and Policy in America*, eds. Hugh Heclo and Wilfred McClay (Baltimore: Johns Hopkins University Press, 2003), 53, citing Lewis's "What Went Wrong," the *Atlantic Monthly* (January 2002).

19   Sachedina, *Role of Islam*, 6.

20   Engineer, 33.

21   Ibid., 29.

22 Aga Khan Development Network (AKDN), "Aga Khan Speaks on Preventing the Failure of Democracy," AKDN Press Centre, http://www.akdn.org/Content/444.

23 Engineer, 33.

24 Abdou Filali-Ansary, "There is no Opposition Between Secularism and Islam," *Reset: Dialogues on Civilizations* (March 15, 2007), http://www.resetdoc.org/EN/Ansary-Rabat.php.

25 Ibid.

26 Ibid.

27 Abdou Filali-Ansary, "Muslims and Democracy," *Journal of Democracy* 10.3 (1999): 20.

28 Ibid., 21.

29 Ibid.

30 Filali-Ansary (Ibid., 26) argues that the favorable reception of democracy in many Muslim countries is reflective of its perception as another utopian ideology, just as nationalism and socialism were seen to be. The danger in this view is that, without the proper management of democratic machinery, democracy may come to be seen as another unattainable ideal, and thereby deepen the misunderstanding on the part of Muslims towards secularization and democracy as well as strengthen the opinion that Islam and democracy represent two irreconcilable outlooks.

31 Ibid.

32 Ibid., 28.

33 Ibid.

34 Abdullahi A. An-Na'im, "The Synergy and Interdependence of Human Rights, Religion and Secularism," *polylog: Forum for Intercultural Philosophy* 3 (2001), http://them.polylog.org/3/faa-en.htm.

35 Ibid.

36 Ibid.

37 Aga Khan IV, "Renewing Democracy's Promise," 120.

38 Ibid., 121.

39 Aga Khan IV, "What Makes Democracy Work?" in *Where Hope Takes Root*, 110.

40 Ibid., 111.

41 Charles Taylor, *The Malaise of Modernity*, 15.

42 Ibid., 4.

43 Sajoo, *Muslim Ethics*, 81.

44 Ibid.

45 The Institute of Ismaili Studies, "Aga Khan Development Network (AKDN): An Ethical Framework."

46 Mohamed Talbi, trans. Ronald L. Nettler, "Mohamed Talbi on understanding the Qur'an," in *Modern Muslim Intellectuals and the Qur'an*, ed. Suha Taji-Farouki

(Oxford: Oxford University Press in association with the Institute of Ismaili Studies 2004), 227.

47   Sajoo, *Muslim Ethics*, 76.

48   Aga Khan IV, 'Address,' Conference of German Ambassadors.

49   Filali-Ansary, 'Muslims and Democracy,' 26.

50   Robert W. Hefner, *Civil Islam: Muslims and Democratization in Indonesia* (Princeton: Princeton University Press, 2000), 11.

51   Ibid., 12.

52   Ibid.

53   Ibid., 13.

54   Ibid., 11.

55   George Marsden, "What has Athens to do with Jerusalem? Religious Commitment in the Academy" (plenary address presented at the annual meeting of the American Academy of Religion, Washington, DC, November 21,1993).

56   Canadian Survey of Giving and Volunteering, http://www.givingandvolunteering. ca/files/giving/en/csgvp_highlights_2007.pdf, 23.

57   Ibid., 9.

58   Robert Putnam, *Bowling Alone: The Collapse and Revival of American Community* (New York: Simon & Schuster, 2000), see chapter 4.

59   Ibid.

60   For a fuller explanation, see Will Kymlicka, *Multicultural Citizenship: A Liberal Theory of Minority Rights* (Oxford: Oxford University Press, 1995).

61   Tariq Modood, *Multicultural Politics: Racism, Ethnicity, and Muslims in Britain* (Minneapolis: University of Minnesota Press, 2005), 133.

62   Ibid., 103–4.

63   Ibid.

64   Ibid., 178.

65   Eva Schubert, "Modern Citizenship, Multiple Identities," in *Muslim Modernities*, 180.

66   Ibid., 181.

67   Ibid., 180–181.

68   Aga Khan IV, "What Makes Democracy Work?" in *Where hope takes root*, 107.

69   Ibid.

70   Ibid., 108.

71   Ibid.

72   Ibid., 109.

73   Ibid.

74   Ibid.

75   Ibid., 111.

76   Sajoo, *Muslim Ethics*, 81.

77   Ibid., 79.

78 Ibid., 78.

79 Ibid., 80.

80 Ibid., 85.

81 Ibid.

82 Ibid., 89.

83 Ibid.

84 Ibid., 87.

85 Ibid.

86 Edward Shils, "The Virtue of Civil Society," *Government and Opposition* 26:1 (Winter 1991): 11. Civility, Shils explains, means "regarding other persons, including one's adversaries, as members of the same society, even though they belong to different parties or to different religious communities or to different ethnic groups" (13).

87 Amyn B. Sajoo, "Civil Imagination after September 11, 2001," *The Ismaili United Kingdom* (March 2005), 39.

88 Ibid., 38

89 Ibid., 39.

90 Ibid.

91 Ibid.

92 Ibid., 40.

93 Bhiku Parekh, "British Commitments," *Prospect* 114 (September 25, 2005), http://www.prospectmagazine.co.uk/2005/09/britishcommitments/.

94 Tariq Modood, "Remaking multiculturalism after 7/7," *openDemocracy* (September 29, 2005), http://www.opendemocracy.net/debates/article.jsp?id=2&debateId=124&articleId=2879.

95 Parekh, "British Commitments."

96 Bruce B. Lawrence, "Scripture, History and Modernity: Readings of the Qur'an," in *Muslim Modernities*, 26.

97 Aga Khan, "Renewing Democracy's Promise," 122.

98 Aga Khan IV, "Address by His Highness the Aga Khan" (address presented to the Tutzing Evangelical Academy upon receiving the Tolerance Award, May 20, 2006), http://www.akdn.org/speeches/200506_Tutzing.htm.

99 Ibid.

100 Ibid.

CHAPTER 7

1 Martha C. Nussbaum, "Radical Evil in Liberal Democracies: The Neglect of the Political Emotions," in *Democracy and the New Religious Pluralism*, ed. Thomas Banchoff (Oxford: Oxford University Press, 2007), 171.

2 Thomas Banchoff, "Introduction," in Ibid., 5.

3   Abdou Filali-Ansary, "Introduction: Theoretical Approaches to Cultural Diversity," in *The Challenge of Pluralism: Paradigms from Muslim Contexts*, eds. Abdou Filali-Ansary and Sikeena Karmali Ahmed (Edinburgh: Edinburgh University Press Ltd/The Aga Khan University Institute for the Study of Muslim Civilisations, 2009), 2.

4   Ibid.

5   Diana Eck, "What is Pluralism?" *The Pluralism Project at Harvard University*, http://www.pluralism.org/pages/pluralism/what_is_pluralism.

6   Aga Khan IV, "Is Civil Society Bankable?" in *Where Hope Takes Root*, 25.

7   Aga Khan IV, "Democracy, Pluralism and Civil Society," in Ibid., 87.

8   Ashutosh Varshney, "Ethnic Conflict and Civil Society: India and Beyond," *World Politics* Vol. 53, No. 3 (April 2001): 365.

9   Ibid., 363. "Countervailing forces are created when organizations such as trade unions, associations of businessmen, traders, teachers, doctors and lawyers, and at least some cadre-based political parties (different from the ones that have an interest in communal polarization) are communally integrated. [...] Civic organizations, for all practical purposes, become the ears and arms of the administration. A synergy emerges between the local wings of the state and local civic organizations, making it easier to police the emerging situation and preventing it from degenerating into riots and killings.... In the end, polarizing politicians either do not succeed or eventually give up trying to provoke and engineer communal violence" (378).

10 Aga Khan IV, "Democracy, Pluralism and Civil Society," 90.

11 Ibid.

12 Ibid., 87.

13 Ibid.

14 Filali-Ansary, "Introduction," 3.

15 Aga Khan IV, "Is Civil Society Bankable?," 19.

16 Ibid., 25.

17 Aga Khan IV, "Underwriting Human Progress," in *Where Hope Takes Root*, 59.

18 As defined by the *Oxford English Dictionary*: "the existence or toleration of a diversity of ethnic groups or differing cultures and views within a society."

19 Aga Khan IV, "Is Civil Society Bankable?," 25.

20 Robert Hefner, "Introduction: Modernity and the Remaking of Muslim Politics," in *Remaking Muslim Politics: Pluralism, Contestation, Democratization*, ed. Robert W. Hefner (Princeton: Princeton University Press, 2005), 28.

21 Ibid.

22 Global Centre for Pluralism, "Defining Pluralism," *Pluralism Papers* No. 1 (January 2012), 1–2.

23 Ibid., 3.

24 Ibid., 2.

25 Ibid.

26 Ibid.

27 Ibid., 9–13 ff.

28 Shah-Kazemi, "Metaphysics," http://www.iis.ac.uk/view_article. asp?ContentID=101259.

29 Aziz al-Azmeh, "Pluralism in Muslim Societies," in *The Challenge of Pluralism*, 13.

30 Ibid., 14.

31 Ibid., 12.

32 Bernard Lewis, *The Jews of Islam* (London: Routledge & Kegan Paul, 1984), 8–9.

33 I thank Prof Piyo Rattansi (Emeritus Professor of History and Philosophy of Science at University College, London) for his valuable discussions with me on this score.

34 Abdulaziz Sachedina, *Islamic Roots of Democratic Pluralism* (New York: Oxford University Press, 2001), 69.

35 Institute of Ismaili Studies, "Aga Khan Development Network [AKDN]: An Ethical Framework."

36 Ibid.

37 Asad, 153–4, n. 66.

38 Ibid., 14, n. 50.

39 Ali S. Asani, "On Pluralism, Intolerance, and the Quran," *The American Scholar* 72:1 (Winter 2002): 55.

40 "Everything (that exists) will perish except His own Face."

41 In his note on verse 55:27, Asad writes: "the word 'face' or 'countenance'" is "a term used metonymically in classical Arabic to denote the 'self' or 'whole being' of a person - in this case, the essential Being, or Reality, of God."

42 Shah-Kazemi, "Metaphysics," http://www.iis.ac.uk/view_article.asp?ContentID= 101259.

43 Seyyed Hossein Nasr, *Ideals and Realities of Islam* (London: Allen & Unwin, 1966), 27.

44 According to Fazlur Rahman (*Major Themes of the Qur'an* [Minneapolis, 1980], 167–8), it is in the context of the rejection of exclusivism and salvational election that the Qur'an judges some doctrines of Jews and Christians, namely (1) the superiority of one community through divine election (Q. 2:111) and (2) the doctrine of divine incarnation, which sets Jesus, and therefore Jesus's community, apart from other prophets as unique (whereas "The son of Mary," says the Qur'an, "was but a Messenger" before whom had gone many messengers (Q. 5:72–75)). The Qur'an responds to these exclusivist claims by affirming the criteria of individual righteousness and asserting that no one community can lay claim to guidance or superiority. Such is the case in verse 2:124, where Abraham asks God if He would make of his progeny "leaders of men," to which God replies, "My promise does not extend to the unjust ones."

45   Asad notes that the application of the terms "Islam" and "muslim" to the followers of Muhammad is a post-Qur'anic development and cannot be applied when translating the Qur'an. He writes in *Message of the Qur'an,* p. 885, n. 17: "I have translated the terms 'muslim' and 'Islam' in accordance with the original connotation, namely, 'one who surrenders [or has surrendered] himself to God', and 'man's self surrender to God'…. It should be borne in mind that the 'institutionalised' use of the terms—that is, the exclusive application to the followers of Prophet Muhammad—represents a definitely post-Qur'anic development and hence must be avoided in a translation of the Qur'an."

46   Reza Shah-Kazemi, "The Metaphysics of Interfaith Dialogue: A Qur'anic Perspective," in *Paths to the Heart: Sufism and the Christian East,* ed. James S. Cutsinger (Bloomington: World Wisdom, 2002), 180.

47   Ibid.

48   Italics mine.

49   Aga Khan III, *Memoirs,* 174.

50   Asani, "On Pluralism," 55.

51   Ibid.

52   Ibid., 56.

53   Ibid., 53.

54   Ibid., 59.

55   Ibid., 57.

56   Shah-Kazemi, *Paths to the Heart,* 169.

57   Sajoo, *Muslim Ethics,* 76.

58   Ibid., 76.

59   Shah-Kazemi, *Paths to the Heart,* 173.

60   "And of His signs is the creation of the heavens and the earth, and the difference of your languages and colours."

61   Shah-Kazemi, *Paths to the Heart,* 180.

62   Asani, "On Pluralism," 56.

63   Azim Nanji, 'Beyond the Clash of Civilizations' (address at the University of Waterloo, 2001), http://iis.ac.uk/view_article.asp?ContentID=101122.

64   Ibid.

65   Ibid.

66   Amir Hussain, 'Muslims, Pluralism, and Interfaith Dialogue,' in *Progressive Muslims: On Justice, Gender and Pluralism,* ed. Omid Safi (Oxford: Oneworld, 2003), 258.

67   Montgomery Watt, *Muhammad at Medina* (Oxford: Oxford University Press, 1956), 223.

68   Sajoo, *Muslim Ethics,* 63.

69   Asani, "On Pluralism," 56–57.

70   Daftary, *The Isma'ilis,* 254.

71 Jiwa, "Religious Pluralism in Egypt."

72 Ibid.

73 Sajoo, *Muslim Ethics*, 50–51.

74 Ibid., 57.

75 Aga Khan IV, "Address," Conference of German Ambassadors.

76 Shils, "The Virtue of Civil Society," 11.

77 Ibid., 13.

78 Farhad Kazemi, "Perspectives on Islam and Civil Society," in *Islamic Political Ethics: Civil Society, Pluralism, and Conflict*, ed. Sohail H. Hashmi (Princeton: Princeton University Press, 2002), 40.

79 Amyn B. Sajoo, "Introduction: Civic Quests and Bequests," in *Civil Society in the Muslim World: Contemporary Perspectives*, ed. Amyn B. Sajoo (London: I.B. Tauris & Co Ltd, 2002), 1.

80 Aziz Esmail, "Self, Society, Civility and Islam," in Ibid., 66.

81 Sajoo, "Introduction," 3.

82 Ibid., 7.

83 Hasan Hanafi, "Alternative Conceptions of Civil Society: A Reflective Islamic Approach," in *Islamic Political Ethics*, 58.

84 John L. Esposito, "Islam and Civil Society," in *Modernizing Islam: Religion in the Public Sphere in Europe and the Middle East*, eds. John L. Esposito and François Burgat (London: C. Hurst & Co., 2003), 70.

85 Sajoo, "Introduction," 2.

86 Ibid., 15.

87 Kazemi, 38.

88 Ibid., 42–3.

89 Sajoo, "Introduction," 12.

90 Aga Khan IV, "Enhancing Pluralism," in *Where Hope Takes Root*, 9.

91 Ibid.

92 Ibid.

93 Ibid., 13.

94 Ibid.

95 Ibid., 14.

96 Global Centre for Pluralism, "Frequently Asked Questions," http://pluralism.ca/faqs.html.

97 Ibid.

98 Aga Khan IV, "Enhancing Pluralism," 10–11.

99 Ibid., 11.

100 Abdou Filali-Ansary, "Civil Society in the Maghreb" (presented at Civil Society in the Maghreb, conference at the Ismaili Centre, London, UK, June 2001), http://www.iis.ac.uk/view_article.asp?ContentID=103838.

101 Ibid.

102   Ibid.

CHAPTER 8

1   Navid Kermani, "Intellect," *Encyclopaedia of the Qur'an*, Online Edition, 2011, http://www.brillonline.nl/subscriber/entry?entry=q3_SIM-00224.
2   A. H. Mathias Zahniser, "Knowledge and Thinking," in *Blackwell Companion to the Qur'an*, ed. Andrew Rippin (Malden: Blackwell Pub., 2006), 295.
3   Franz Rosenthal, *Knowledge Triumphant* (Leiden: E.J. Brill, 1970), 2.
4   Azim A. Nanji, "Learning and Education," in *The Muslim Almanac*, 409.
5   Ibid.
6   Institute of Ismaili Studies, "Aga Khan Development Network (AKDN): An Ethical Framework."
7   Aga Khan IV, "Opening Address," in *Word of God, Art of Man*, xx.
8   Ibid.
9   The Institute of Ismaili Studies, "Aga Khan Development Network (AKDN): An Ethical Framework."
10   Dimitri Gutas notes in his *Greek Thought, Arabic Culture* (London, 1998) that there is little evidence and much debate as to who founded or established the Bayt al-Hikma; he gives preference to al-Rashid (r. 786–809) (54–60).
11   Ted Thornton, *History of the Middle East Database*, http://www.nmhtthornton.com/mehistorydatabase/abbasid_golden_age.php.
12   The Institute of Ismaili Studies, "Aga Khan Development Network (AKDN): An Ethical Framework."
13   Nanji, "Learning and Education," 410.
14   Ibid., 411.
15   Ibid.
16   Ibid.
17   Ibid.
18   Parvin S. Peerwani, "Pir Nasir Khusraw's Concept of Intellect and Theory of Intellectual Education (I)," http://simerg.com/literary-readings/pir-nasir-khusraws-concept-of-intellect-and-theory-of-intellectual-education/.
19   Nasir Khusraw, *Knowledge and Liberation*, 26.
20   Hunzai, "The Concept of Knowledge," 132. Here, Hunzai notes that al-Ghazali supported the Ismaili argument of the necessity for an infallible Imam, but with a twist: "Al-Ghazali, unlike his predecessors, realised the necessity for an infallible Imam and labelled his predecessors ignorant for their failure to realise this. However, his own arguments 'Our infallible teacher is Muhammad(s)' or 'Your teacher is hidden (*gha'ib*)' do not seem to refute in any way the necessity of the Imam…. Further, al-Ghazali cannot in any sense justify that Muhammad(s) belongs only to him and his party, for the Ismailis too, as is clear from the

above, claim that the perpetual necessity of an infallible Imam is to accomplish the Prophet's mission, which due to the spatial and temporal hindrances and limitations of human intellect, it was not possible to complete in the lifetime of the Prophet."

21 Ibid., 128.

22 Ibid., 129.

23 Ibid., 132.

24 al-Tusi, *Contemplation and Action*, 29.

25 Ibid., 30.

26 Ibid., 41.

27 Ibid.

28 Ibid.

29 Walker, *Abu Ya'qub al-Sijistani: Intellectual Missionary*, 27.

30 Ibid., 32.

31 Ibid., 39.

32 Ibid., 40.

33 Ibid., 43.

34 Ibid., 44.

35 Ibid., 48–49.

36 Ibid., 49.

37 Ibid., 52.

38 Ibid., 52–53.

39 Ibid., 53.

40 Ibid.

41 Ibid., 54.

42 Ibid., 57.

43 Ibid.

44 Ibid.

45 Ibid., 58.

46 Abu Ya'qub Sijistani, "Unveiling of the Hidden (from *Kashf al-mahjub*)," in *An Anthology of Philosophy in Persia (vol 2): Ismaili Thought in the Classical Age from Jabir ibn Hayyan to Nasir al-Din Tusi*, trans. Hermann Landolt, eds. S. H. Nasr and M. Aminrazavi (London: I.B. Tauris in association with The Institute of Ismaili Studies, 2008), 94.

47 Aga Khan IV, "Speech by His Highness the Aga Khan," (presented at the Foundation Stone Laying Ceremony of the Aga Khan Academy, Dhaka, Bangladesh, May 20, 2008), http://www.akdn.org/Content/661/Foundation-Stone-Laying-Ceremony-of-the-Aga-Khan-Academy-Dhaka.

48 Aga Khan IV, "Speech by His Highness the Aga Khan" (presented at the Centenary Celebration Meeting, Association of American Universities—Making a Difference: Reflections on Shared Problems,

Shared Opportunities and Shared Responsibilities in International Higher Education, Washington, DC, USA, April 22, 2001), http://www.akdn.org/Content/576/Centenary-Celebration-Meeting-Association-of-American-Universities.

49 Aga Khan Development Network (AKDN), "Focus Areas: Educational Activities," http://www.akdn.org/education.asp.

50 Aga Khan IV, 'Speech,' American Universities.

51 Ibid.

52 Aga Khan IV, 'Remarks,' Academy of Sciences, Lisbon.

53 Aga Khan IV, "The Peterson Lecture" (presented to the Annual Meeting of the International Baccalaureate, marking its fortieth anniversary, Atlanta, USA, April 18, 2008), http://www.akdn.org/Content/637/Annual-Meeting-of-the-International-Baccalaureate.

54 Aga Khan IV, "Speech," Academy of Sciences, Lisbon.

55 Aga Khan IV, "Peterson Lecture."

56 Aga Khan IV, "Speech," Academy of Sciences, Lisbon.

57 Aga Khan IV, "Peterson Lecture."

58 Ibid.

59 Aga Khan IV, "Speech at the Opening Ceremony of the Aga Khan School" (presented at the Opening Ceremony of the Aga Khan School, Osh, Kyrgyz Republic, October 30, 2002), http://www.akdn.org/Content/589/Opening-Ceremony-of-the-Aga-Khan-School-Osh.

60 Aga Khan IV, "Peterson Lecture."

61 Ibid.

62 Ibid.

63 Ibid.

64 Al-Mu'ayyad fi'l-Din al-Shirazi, "The Light of Intellect," in *Shimmering Light: An Anthology of Ismaili Poetry*, trans. Faquir M. Hunzai and ed. Kutub Kassam (London: I.B. Tauris in association with the Institute of Ismaili Studies, 1996), 47.

CHAPTER 9

1 "The In-Between World of Vikram Lall," *RandomHouse.ca*, http://www.randomhouse.ca/catalog/display.pperl?isbn=9780385659918.

2 Ibid.

3 Karim H. Karim, "At the Interstices of Tradition, Modernity and Postmodernity: Ismaili Engagements with Contemporary Canadian Society," in F. Daftary, ed., *A Modern History of the Ismailis*, 279.

4 Ibid.

5 Ibid.

6   Aly Kassam-Remtulla, "Chapter Five: Global Ismailism: Rethinking Diaspora, Nation and Religion," in "(Dis)placing Khojahs: Forging Identities, Revitalizing Islam and Crafting Global Ismailism" (AB honors thesis, Department of Anthropology, Stanford University, 1998), http://ismaili.net/Source/1121b/05. html.

7   Karim, "Interstices," 279.

8   Aga Khan IV, "Address by His Highness The Aga Khan" (presented at the Foundation Ceremony of The Delegation of the Ismaili Imamat, Ottawa, Canada, June 6, 2005), http://www.akdn.org/Content/121/Aga-Khan-and-Governor-General-of-Canada-Initiate-the-Delegation-of-the-Ismaili-Imamat.

9   Ibid.

10 Karim, "Interstices," 274.

11 Ibid., 273.

12 Ibid.

13 Ibid.

14 Ibid.

15 Steinberg, 59.

16 Ibid., 3.

17 Stephen Harper, "Peace, Prosperity and Equality Through Pluralism," Ottawa, Canada (December 6, 2008), http://www.pm.gc.ca/eng/media.asp?id=2346.

18 Karim, "Interstices," 286.

19 Ibid., 287.

20 Ibid., 286.

21 Ibid.

22 Ibid., 285.

23 Ibid.

24 Zahra Jamal, "Embodying Ethics, Performing Pluralism: Volunteerism among Ismailis in Houston, TX," *The Pluralism Project at Harvard University*, http://pluralism.org/reports/view/200.

25 Ibid.

26 Karim, "Interstices," 286.

27 Ibid., 287.

28 Ibid.

29 Ibid.

30 Steinberg, 102.

31 Ibid.

32 Ibid.

33 Ibid., 104–5.

34 Khalil Andani, "Shi`a Ismai`ili Islam," (lecture delivered at the University of Toronto, Canada, November 2, 2011), http://www.youtube.com/watch?v=XcpDOSMDhYM&mid=546501.

35 S. H. Nasr, *Ideals and Realities of Islam* (London: Allen & Unwin, 1966), 162.

36 Aga Khan III, Foreword to *Muhammad: A Mercy To all the Nations*, by Kasim-
    'Ali Jairaz-Bhai (London: Luzac, 1937).

37 Steinberg, 193.

38 Ibid., 198.

39 Ibid., 198.

40 Kassam-Remtulla, "(Dis)placing Khojahs," http://ismaili.net/Source/1121b/05.
    html.

41 Ibid.

42 Ibid.

43 Ibid.

44 Ibid.

45 Ibid.

46 Ibid.

47 Ibid.

48 Karim, "Interstices," 289.

49 Ibid.

50 Ibid.

51 Ibid.

BIBLIOGRAPHY[*]

Aga Khan Development Network (AKDN). "Afghanistan." http://www. akdn.org/afghanistan.

———. "Aga Khan Speaks on Preventing the Failure of Democracy." AKDN Press Centre. http://www.akdn.org/Content/444.

———. "AKDN Civil Society Programme Afghanistan 2006–2008." www.akdn.org/publications/civil_society_afghanistan_programme.pdf.

———. "Focus Areas: Educational Activities." http://www.akdn.org/education.asp.

———. "Frequent Questions." http://www.akdn.org/faq.asp.

———. "Multi-Input Area Development." *AKDN Development Blog*, April 29, 2009. http://www.akdn.org/Content/737.

———. "Social Audits in Afghanistan: Making Local Governance More Transparent." *AKDN Development Blog*, June 8, 2009. http://www. akdn.org/blog.asp?id=765.

Aga Khan Foundation Canada. "Canada and Aga Khan Foundation in Afghanistan." AKFC Press Brochure.

Aga Khan III. Foreword to *Muhammad: A Mercy To all the Nations*, by Kasim-'Ali Jairaz-Bhai. London: Luzac, 1937.

———. *The Memoirs of Aga Khan: World Enough and Time*. New York: Simon and Schuster, 1954.

Aga Khan IV, "His Highness the Aga Khan"s Statement" (presented at the London Conference on Afghanistan, January 28, 2010), http://www.akdn.org/Content/955/Statement-Issued-at-the-London-Conference-on-Afghanistan.

---

[*] The bibliography does not include all the works cited in the notes.

————. "Address by His Highness the Aga Khan." Address presented at the Annual Conference of German Ambassadors, Berlin, Germany, September 6, 2004. http://www.akdn.org/Content/583/Annual-Conference-of-German-Ambassadors.

————. "Address by His Highness the Aga Khan." Address presented to the Tutzing Evangelical Academy Upon Receiving the Tolerance Award, May 20, 2006. http://www.akdn.org/speeches/200506_Tutzing.htm.

————. "Address by His Highness The Aga Khan." Presented at the Foundation Ceremony of The Delegation of the Ismaili Imamat, Ottawa, Canada, June 6, 2005. http://www.akdn.org/Content/121/Aga-Khan-and-Governor-General-of-Canada-Initiate-the-Delegation-of-the-Ismaili-Imamat.

————. "Keynote Address at the Governor General's Canadian Leadership Conference on Leadership and Diversity." Address presented at The Canadian Museum of Civilization, Gatineau, Canada, May 19, 2004. http://www.iis.ac.uk/view_article.asp?ContentID=104233.

————. "Message to the International Islamic Conference." Read at the International Islamic Conference: True Islam and Its Role in Modern Society," Amman, Jordan, July 4–6, 2005. http://ammanmessage.com/index.php?option=com_content&task=view&id=57&Itemid=42.

————. "Opening Address." In *Word of God, Art of Man: The Qur'an and its Creative Expressions: Selected Proceedings from the International Colloquium (London, 18–21 October 2003)*, edited by Fahmida Suleman, xix–xxi. London: Oxford University Press, 2007.

————. "Remarks by His Highness the Aga Khan." Presented at the Academy of Sciences, Lisbon, Portugal, May 8, 2009. http://www.akdn.org/Content/741/Remarks-by-His-Highness-the-Aga-Khan-at-Portugals-Academy-of-Sciences.

————. "Speech at the Graduation Ceremony of the University of Alberta." Presented at the University of Alberta, Edmonton, Canada, June 9, 2009. http://www.akdn.org/Content/767/Speech-by-His-Highness-the-Aga-Khan-at-the-Graduation-Ceremony-of-the-University-of-Alberta.

————. "Speech at the Opening Ceremony of the Aga Khan School." Presented at the Opening Ceremony of the Aga Khan School,

Osh, Kyrgyz Republic, October 30, 2002. http://www.akdn.org/Content/589/Opening-Ceremony-of-the-Aga-Khan-School-Osh.

———. "Speech by His Highness the Aga Khan." Presented at the Foundation Stone Laying Ceremony of The Aga Khan Academy, Dhaka, Bangladesh, May 20, 2008. http://www.akdn.org/Content/661/Foundation-Stone-Laying-Ceremony-of-the-Aga-Khan-Academy-Dhaka.

———. "Speech by His Highness the Aga Khan." Presented at the Centenary Celebration Meeting, Association of American Universities—Making a Difference: Reflections on Shared Problems, Shared Opportunities and Shared Responsibilities in International Higher Education, Washington, DC, USA, April 22, 2001. http://www.akdn.org/Content/576/Centenary-Celebration-Meeting-Association-of-American-Universities.

———. "Speech by His Highness the Aga Khan." Statement presented at the Nobel Institute on Democratic Development, Pluralism and Civil Society, Oslo, Norway, April 7, 2005. http://www.akdn.org/Content/599.

———. "Speech On Acceptance of the 2009 Nouvel Economiste Philanthropic Entrepreneur of the Year 2009 Award." Presented at the Cour des Comptes, Palais Cambon, December 17, 2009. http://www.akdn.org/Content/924/Speech-by-His-Highness-the-Aga-Khan-at-the-Cour-des-Comptes-Court-of-Accounts-Palais-Cambon.

———. "Statement by His Highness the Aga Khan." Statement presented at the Kabul Conference on Afghanistan, July 20, 2010. http://www.akdn.org/Content/1003.

———. "The LaFontaine-Baldwin Lecture." Presented at the LaFontaine-Baldwin Symposium, Toronto, Canada, October 15, 2010. http://www.akdn.org/Content/1018.

———. "The Peterson Lecture." Presented to the Annual Meeting of the International Baccalaureate, marking its fortieth anniversary, Atlanta, USA, April 18, 2008. http://www.akdn.org/Content/637/Annual-Meeting-of-the-International-Baccalaureate.

———. *Where Hope Takes Root: Democracy and Pluralism in an Interdependent World.* Vancouver: Douglas & McIntyre, 2008.

Al-Azmeh, Aziz. "Pluralism in Muslim Societies." In *The Challenge of Pluralism: Paradigms from Muslim Contexts*, edited by Abdou Filali-Ansary and Sikeena Karmali Ahmed, 9–15. Edinburgh: Edinburgh University Press Ltd/The Aga Khan University Institute for the Study of Muslim Civilisations, 2009.

Al-Shirazi, Al-Mu'ayyad fi'l-Din. "The Light of Intellect." In *Shimmering Light: An Anthology of Ismaili Poetry*, translated by Faquir M. Hunzai and ed. Kutub Kassam, 47. London: I.B. Tauris in association with the Institute of Ismaili Studies, 1996.

Al-Tusi, Nasir al-Din. "Sayr wa Suluk." In *Contemplation and Action: The Spiritual Autobiography of a Muslim Scholar*, edited and translated by S. J. Badakhchani. London: I.B. Tauris in association with Institute of Ismaili Studies, 1998.

Amir-Moezzi, Mohammad Ali. *The divine guide in early Shi'ism: The Sources of Esotericism in Islam*. Albany: State University of New York Press, 1994.

An-Na'im, Abdullahi A. "The Synergy and Interdependence of Human Rights, Religion and Secularism." *polylog: Forum for Intercultural Philosophy* 3 (2001). http://them.polylog.org/3/faa-en.htm.

Asad, Muhammad. *Message of the Qur'an: Translated and Explained*. Gibraltar: Dar al-Andalus, 1984.

Asad, Talal. *Formations of the Secular: Christianity, Islam, Modernity*. Stanford: Stanford University Press, 2003.

Asani, Ali S. "On Pluralism, Intolerance, and the Quran," *The American Scholar* 72:1 (Winter 2002): 52–60.

———. "From Satpanthi to Ismaili Muslim: The Articulation of Ismaili Khoja Identity in South Asia," In *A Modern History of the Ismailis: Continuity and Change in a Muslim Community*, edited by Farhad Daftary, 95–128. London: I.B. Tauris in association with The Institute of Ismaili Studies, 2011.

Aziz, K. K. "Introduction." In *Aga Khan III: Selected Speeches and Writings of Sir Sultan Muhammad Shah*, edited by K. K. Aziz, 1–198. London: Kegan Paul International, 1998.

Banchoff, Thomas. "Introduction." In *Democracy and the New Religious Pluralism*, edited by Thomas Banchoff, 3–18. Oxford: Oxford University Press, 2007.

Barton, Adriana. "Ismaili Success: Made in Vancouver." *BCBusiness,* July 2, 2006. http://www.bcbusinessonline.ca/2006/07/01/ ismaili-success-made-vancouver.

Birt, M. Yahya. "The Message of Fazlur Rahman." *Newsletter of the Association of Muslim Researchers,* June 27, 1996. http://www. freerepublic.com/focus/fr/531762/posts.

Brett, Michael. "The Realm of the Imam: The Fatimids in the Tenth Century." *Bulletin of the School of Oriental and African Studies* 59:3 (1996): 431–449.

———. Review of *Fatimid History and Ismaili Doctrine,* by Paul E. Walker. *Journal of the American Oriental Society* 128.3 (2008): 574

———. *The Rise of the Fatimids: The World of the Mediterranean and the Middle East in the fourth century of the Hijra, tenth century CE.* Leiden: Brill, 2001.

Canadian Survey of Giving and Volunteering. http://www. givingandvolunteering.ca/files/giving/en/csgvp_highlights_2007.pdf.

Canard, M. "al-Hakim Bi-amr Allah." In *Encyclopaedia of Islam, Second Edition,* Online Edition, 2011. http://www.brillonline.nl/subscriber / entry?entry=islam_SIM-2637.

Casanova, José. "The Secular, Secularizations, Secularisms." In *Rethinking Secularism,* edited by Craig Calhoun, Mark Juergensmeyer, and Jonathan van Antwerpen, 54–74, Oxford: Oxford University Press, 2011.

Clarkson, Adrienne. "Introduction." Presented at the LaFontaine-Baldwin Symposium, Toronto, Canada, October 15, 2010. http://www.akdn. org/Content/1019.

Daftary, Farhad. "Hasan-i Sabbah and the Origins of the Nizari Isma`ili Movement." In *Mediaeval Isma'ili History and Thought,* edited by Farhad Daftary, 181–204. New York: Cambridge University Press, 1996.

———. "Intellectual Life among the Ismailis: An Overview." In *Intellectual Traditions in Islam,* edited by Farhad Daftary, 87–111. London: I.B. Tauris in association with The Institute of Ismaili Studies, 2000.

———. *Ismailis in Medieval Muslim Societies.* London: I.B. Tauris in association with The Institute of Ismaili Studies, 2005.

————. *The Assassin Legends: Myths of the Isma'ilis*. London: I.B. Tauris & Co Ltd., 1995.

————. *The Isma'ilis: Their History and Doctrines*. Cambridge: Cambridge University Press, 1990.

Eck, Diana. "What is Pluralism?." *The Pluralism Project at Harvard University*. http://www.pluralism.org/pages/pluralism/what_is_pluralism.

Edwards, Anne. *Throne of Gold: The Lives of the Aga Khans*. London: William Morrow & Co, 1996.

El-Bizri, Nader. "Prologue." In *The Ikhwan al-Safa' and their Rasa'il: An Introduction*, edited by Nader el-Bizri, 1–33. Oxford: Oxford University Press in association with the Institute of Ismaili Studies, 2008.

Enayat, Hamid. "An Outline of the Political Philosophy of the *Rasa'il* of the Ikhwan al-Safa'." In *Isma'ili Contributions to Islamic Culture*, edited by Seyyed Hossein Nasr, 23–50. Tehran: Imperial Iranian Academy of Philosophy, 1977.

Engineer, Asghar Ali. "Interview: The Compatibility of Islam, Secularism and Modernity." In *New Voices of Islam*, edited by Farish A. Noor, 29–34. Leiden: International Institute for the Study of Islam in the Modern World (ISIM), 2002.

Ernst, Carl. *Following Muhammad: Rethinking Islam in the Contemporary World*. Chapel Hill: University of North Carolina Press, 2003.

Esmail, Aziz. "Islam and Modernity: Intellectual Horizons." In *The Muslim Almanac: A reference work on the history, faith, culture, and peoples of Islam*, edited by Azim A. Nanji, 483–487. Detroit: Gale Research, 1996.

————. "Self, Society, Civility and Islam." In *Civil Society in the Muslim World: Contemporary Perspectives*, edited by Amyn B. Sajoo, 61–94. London: I.B. Tauris & Co Ltd, 2002.

————. "The Role of the Institute of Ismaili Studies." the *Ismaili UK* (2000). http://www.iis.ac.uk/view_article.asp?ContentID=101010.

————. "Why History?" *Africa Ismaili* (1970): 20–27. http://www.iis.ac.uk/view_article.asp?ContentID=100996

Esposito, John L. "Islam and Civil Society." In *Modernizing Islam: Religion in the Public Sphere in Europe and the Middle East*, edited by John L. Esposito and François Burgat, 69–100. London: C. Hurst & Co., 2003.

Filali-Ansary, Abdou. "Civil Society in the Maghreb." Presented at Civil Society in the Maghreb, conference at the Ismaili Centre, London, UK, June 2001. http://www.iis.ac.uk/view_article.asp?ContentID=103838.

———. "Introduction: Theoretical Approaches to Cultural Diversity." In *The Challenge of Pluralism: Paradigms from Muslim Contexts*, edited by Abdou Filali-Ansary and Sikeena Karmali Ahmed, 1–8. Edinburgh: Edinburgh University Press Ltd/The Aga Khan University Institute for the Study of Muslim Civilisations, 2009.

———. "Muslims and Democracy." *Journal of Democracy* 10.3 (1999): 18–32.

———. "There is no Opposition Between Secularism and Islam." *Reset: Dialogues on Civilizations* (March 15, 2007). http://www.resetdoc.org/EN/Ansary-Rabat.php.

Gellner, Ernest. *Muslim Society*. Cambridge: Cambridge University Press, 1981.

Glassé, Cyril. *The New Encyclopedia of Islam*. Walnut Creek: AltaMira Press, 2001.

Global Centre for Pluralism. "Defining Pluralism." *Pluralism Papers* No. 1 (January 2012).

———. "Frequently Asked Questions." http://pluralism.ca/faqs.html.

Gopal, Anand. "$1,000 for a kebab? Afghan villages fight corruption." the *Christian Science Monitor*, March 25, 2009. http://www.csmonitor.com/World/Asia-South-Central/2009/0325/p01s02-wosc.html.

Government of Canada, "Girls' Education Support Program." http://www.afghanistan.gc.ca/canada-afghanistan/projects-projets/serv2.aspx.

Halm, Heinz. "The cosmology of the pre-Fatimid Isma`iliyya." In *Mediaeval Isma'ili History and Thought*, edited by Farhad Daftary, 75–84. New York: Cambridge University Press, 1996.

———. "The Isma`ili Oath of Allegiance (`ahd) and the 'Sessions of Wisdom' (*majalis al-hikma*) in Fatimid Times." In *Mediaeval Isma`ili History and Thought*, edited by Farhad Daftary, 91–116. New York: Cambridge University Press, 1996.

———. *The Fatimids and Their Traditions of Learning*. London: I.B. Tauris in association with The Institute of Ismaili Studies, 1997.

Hanafi, Hasan. "Alternative Conceptions of Civil Society: A Reflective Islamic Approach." In *Islamic Political Ethics: Civil Society, Pluralism, and Conflict*, edited by Sohail H. Hashmi, 56–76. Princeton: Princeton University Press, 2002.

Harper, Stephen. "Peace, Prosperity, and Equality Through Pluralism." Presented at the Opening Ceremony of the Delegation of the Ismaili Imamat, Ottawa, Canada, December 6, 2008), http://www.pm.gc.ca/eng/media.asp?id=2346.

Hefner, Robert W. *Civil Islam: Muslims and Democratization in Indonesia*. Princeton: Princeton University Press, 2000.

———. "Introduction: Modernity and the Remaking of Muslim Politics." In *Remaking Muslim Politics: Pluralism, Contestation, Democratization*, edited by Robert W. Hefner, 1–36. Princeton: Princeton University Press, 2005.

Hodgson, Marshall G. S. *The Order of Assassins*. New York: AMS Press, 1980.

Hunzai, Faquir Muhammad. "*Ta'wil* of the Qur'an and the *Shari'a* according to Hakim Nasir-i Khusraw." Paper presented at Nasir Khusraw: Yesterday, Today and Tomorrow, conference, Khorog, Tajikistan, September 2–4, 2003.

———. "The Concept of Knowledge According to al-Kirmani (d. after 411/1021)." In *Reason and Inspiration in Islam: Theology, Philosophy and Mysticism in Muslim Thought*, edited by Todd Lawson, 127–141. London: I.B. Tauris & Co Ltd in association with The Institute of Ismaili Studies, 2005.

Hussain, Amir. "Muslims, Pluralism, and Interfaith Dialogue." In *Progressive Muslims: On Justice, Gender and Pluralism*, edited by Omid Safi, 251–269. Oxford: Oneworld, 2003.

Institute of Ismaili Studies. "Aga Khan Development Network (AKDN): An Ethical Framework." 2000. http://www.iis.ac.uk/view_article.asp?ContentID=101094.

———. "The Ismaili Imamat." http://iis.ac.uk/view_article.asp?ContentID=110993.

Ivanow, Wladimir. *Ismaili Tradition Concerning the Rise of the Fatimids*. London: Islamic Research Association in association with Oxford University Press, 1942.

Jamal, Zahra. "Embodying Ethics, Performing Pluralism: Volunteerism among Ismailis in Houston, TX." *The Pluralism Project at Harvard University.* http://pluralism.org/reports/view/200.

Jiwa, Shainool. "Religious Pluralism in Egypt: The Ahl al-kitab in Early Fatimid Times." Paper delivered at the annual meeting of the Middle Eastern Studies Association of North America, November 19, 2001. http://www.iis.ac.uk/view_article.asp?ContentID=101208.

Karim, Karim H. "At the Interstices of Tradition, Modernity and Postmodernity: Ismaili Engagements with Contemporary Canadian Society." In *A Modern History of the Ismailis: Continuity and Change in a Muslim Community,* edited by Farhad Daftary, 265–296. London: I.B. Tauris in association with The Institute of Ismaili Studies, 2011.

Kassam, Tazim R. *Songs of Wisdom and Circles of Dance: Hymns of the Satpanth Isma`ili Muslim Saint, Pir Shams.* Albany: State University of New York Press, 1995.

Kassam-Remtulla, Aly. "(Dis)placing Khojahs: Forging Identities, Revitalizing Islam and Crafting Global Ismailism." AB Honors thesis, Department of Anthropology, Stanford University, 1998. http://ismaili.net/Source/1121b/05.html.

Kassamali, Sumayya. "Why Canada Doesn't Need an Islamic Art Museum." *Islamic Insights,* June 8, 2010. http://www.islamicinsights.com/news/opinion/why-canada-doesn-t-need-an-islamic-art-museum.html.

Kazemi, Farhad. "Perspectives on Islam and Civil Society." In *Islamic Political Ethics: Civil Society, Pluralism, and Conflict,* edited by Sohail H. Hashmi, 38–54. Princeton: Princeton University Press, 2002.

Kenney, Jason. "Statement—Minister Kenney issues statement to recognize Canada's Ismaili Muslim Community as they celebrate Navroz." Ottawa, Canada, March 19, 2011. http://www.cic.gc.ca/english/department/media/statements/2011/2011-03-19a.asp.

Kermani, Navid. "Intellect." *Encyclopaedia of the Qur'an,* Online Edition, 2011. http://www.brillonline.nl/subscriber/entry?entry=q3_SIM-00224.

Lafaye, Jean-Jacques. "Interview with His Highness Prince Karim Aga Khan IV: The Power of Wisdom." *Politique Internationale* (Spring 2010). http://www.politiqueinternationale.com/revue/article.

php?id_revue=127&id=909&content=synopsis, trans. Ismaili.net, http://ismaili.net/heritage/node/30502.

Lalani, Arzina R. *Early Shi`i thought: the teachings of Imam Muhammad al-Baqir.* London: I.B. Tauris in association with the Institute of Ismaili Studies, 2000.

Lawrence, Bruce B. "Scripture, History and Modernity: Readings of the Qur'an." In *Muslim Modernities: Expressions of the Civil Imagination*, edited by Amyn B. Sajoo, 25–50. London: I.B. Taurus, 2008.

Lewis, Bernard. *The Assassins: A Radical Sect in Islam.* London: Weidenfeld and Nicolson, 1967.

———. *The Jews of Islam.* London: Routledge & Kegan Paul, 1984.

Mamdani, Zahra Kassam. "Education for Pluralism: Explorations & Avenues for Future Programming." Draft Concept Note for Aga Khan Foundation (March 2006).

Mansur al-Yaman, Ja'far b. 'Kitab al-'Alim wa'-l-Ghulam." In *The Master and the Disciple: An Early Islamic Spiritual Dialogue*, translated by James W. Morris. London: I.B. Tauris in association with The Institute of Ismaili Studies, 2001.

McClay, Wilfred. "Two Concepts of Secularism." In *Religion Returns to the Public Square: Faith and Policy in America,* edited by Hugh Heclo and Wilfred McClay, 31–62. Baltimore: Johns Hopkins University Press, 2003.

Modood, Tariq. "Remaking multiculturalism after 7/7." *openDemocracy* (September 29, 2005). http://www.opendemocracy.net/debates/article.jsp?id=2&debateId=124&articleId=2879.

———. *Multicultural Politics: Racism, Ethnicity, and Muslims in Britain.* Minneapolis: University of Minnesota Press, 2005.

Moussalli, Ahmad S. *The Islamic Quest for Democracy, Pluralism, and Human Rights.* Gainesville: University Press of Florida, 2001.

Nanji, Azim A. "Learning and Education." In *The Muslim Almanac: A reference work on the history, faith, culture, and peoples of Islam*, edited by Azim A. Nanji, 409–419. Detroit: Gale Research, 1996.

———. "Beyond the Clash of Civilizations." Address at the University of Waterloo, 2001. http://iis.ac.uk/view_article.asp?ContentID=101122.

————. "Isma`ilism xvii. The Imamate in Isma`ilism." In *Encyclopaedia Iranica*, Online Edition, December 15, 2007. http://www.iranicaonline. org/articles/ismailism-xvii-the-imamate-in-ismailism.

————. "Khojas." *Encyclopaedia of Islam and Muslim World*, Vol. II, edited by Richard C. Martin, 393. New York: MacMillan Reference Books, 2003.

————. "Rethinking our World: the Search for a Pluralistic Vision." Peterson Lecture, May 2003, Geneva. International Baccalaureate Association, 2004.

————. "Shi`i Ismaili Interpretations of The Holy Qur'an." *Selected Proceedings of the International Congress for the Study of the Qur'an* (1980): 39–49. http://www.iis.ac.uk/view_article.asp?ContentID=111705.

Nasr, Seyyed Hossein. "Introduction." In *Isma`ili Contributions to Islamic Culture*, edited by Seyyed Hossein Nasr, 1–5. Tehran: Imperial Iranian Academy of Philosophy, 1977.

————. *Ideals and Realities of Islam*. London: Allen & Unwin, 1966.

Nettler, Ronald L. "Mohamed Talbi on understanding the Qur'an." In *Modern Muslim Intellectuals and the Qur'an*, edited by Suha Taji-Farouki, 225–240. Oxford: Oxford University Press in association with the Institute of Ismaili Studies 2004.

Netton, Ian Richard. "The Rasa'il Ikhwan al-Safa' in the History of Ideas in Islam." In *The Ikhwan al-Safa' and their Rasa'il: An Introduction*, edited by Nader el-Bizri, 123–138. Oxford: Oxford University Press in association with the Institute of Ismaili Studies, 2008.

Nu`man ibn Muhammad, Abu Hanifah. *The Pillars of Islam: Da`a'im al-Islam of al-Qadi al-Nu`man*, translated by Asaf A.A. Fyzee; completely revised and annotated by Ismail Kurban Husein Poonawala. New Delhi: Oxford University Press, 2002.

Nussbaum, Martha C. "Radical Evil in Liberal Democracies: The Neglect of the Political Emotions." In *Democracy and the New Religious Pluralism*, edited by Thomas Banchoff, 171–202. Oxford: Oxford University Press, 2007.

Parekh, Bhiku. "British Commitments." *Prospect* 114 (September 25, 2005). http://www.prospectmagazine.co.uk/2005/09/britishcommitments/.

Peerwani, Parvin S. "Pir Nasir Khusraw's Concept of Intellect and Theory of Intellectual Education (I)." http://simerg.com/literary-readings/

pir-nasir-khusraws-concept-of-intellect-and-theory-of-intellectual-education/.

Phinney, Richard. *Change in the Making: A Journey in Afghanistan*. Aga Khan Foundation Canada, 2009.

Pickthall, Marmaduke. *The glorious Koran: a bi-lingual edition with English translation, introduction and notes*. London: Allen & Unwin, 1976.

Putnam, Robert. *Bowling Alone: The Collapse and Revival of American Community*. New York: Simon & Schuster, 2000).

Rahman, Fazlur. *Major Themes of the Qur'an*. Minneapolis, 1980.

Ramachandran, Sudha. "Ismailis in deadly education spat." *Asia Times*, March 11, 2005. http://www.atimes.com/atimes/South_Asia/GC11Df06.html.

Rosenthal, Franz. *Knowledge Triumphant*. Leiden: E.J. Brill, 1970.

Ruthven, Malise. "The Aga Khan Development Network and Institutions." In *A Modern History of the Ismailis: Continuity and Change in a Muslim Community*, edited by Farhad Daftary, 189–220. London: I.B. Tauris in association with The Institute of Ismaili Studies, 2011.

Sachedina, Abdulaziz. *Islamic Roots of Democratic Pluralism*. New York: Oxford University Press, 2001.

———. *The Role of Islam in the Public Square: Guidance or Governance?*. ISIM Paper 5. Amsterdam: Amsterdam University Press, 2006.

Sajoo, Amyn B. "Beyond The Exotic: The Pleasures of 'Islamic' Art." the *Ismaili United Kingdom* No. 42 (July 2001): 16–18. http://www.iis.ac.uk/view_article.asp?ContentID=101171.

———. "Civil Imagination after September 11, 2001." the *Ismaili United Kingdom* (March 2005): 38–40.

———. "Introduction." In *Muslim Modernities: Expressions of the Civil Imagination*, edited by Amyn B. Sajoo, 1–24. London: I.B. Taurus, 2008.

———. "Introduction: Civic Quests and Bequests." In *Civil Society in the Muslim World: Contemporary Perspectives*, edited by Amyn B. Sajoo, 1–34. London: I.B. Tauris & Co Ltd, 2002.

———. "Introductory Remarks." Presented at The "Good" Society: An Ethical Perspective, conference at the Institute of Ismaili Studies, London, UK, April 2001. http://www.iis.ac.uk/view_article.asp?ContentID=103808.

———. *Muslim Ethics: Emerging Vistas*. London: I.B. Tauris, 2004.

Schubert, Eva. "Modern Citizenship, Multiple Identities." In *Muslim Modernities: Expressions of the Civil Imagination*, edited by Amyn B. Sajoo, 161–182. London: I.B. Taurus, 2008.

Shah-Kazemi, Reza. "The Metaphysics of Interfaith Dialogue: A Qur'anic Perspective." Paper presented at Paths to the Heart: Sufism and the Christian East, conference, University of South Carolina, USA, October 18–20, 2001. http://www.iis.ac.uk/view_article. asp?ContentID=101259.

———. "The Metaphysics of Interfaith Dialogue: A Qur'anic Perspective." In *Paths to the Heart: Sufism and the Christian East*, edited by James S. Cutsinger, 140–189. Bloomington: World Wisdom, 2002.

———. *Justice and Remembrance: Introducing the Spirituality of Imam 'Ali*. London: I.B. Tauris in association with The Institute of Ismaili Studies, 2006.

Shah, Bulbul. "Al-Qadi al-Nu'man and the Concept of *Batin*." In *Reason and Inspiration in Islam: Theology, Philosophy and Mysticism in Muslim Thought*, edited by Todd Lawson, 117–126. London: I.B. Tauris & Co Ltd in association with The Institute of Ismaili Studies, 2005.

Shils, Edward. "The Virtue of Civil Society." *Government and Opposition* 26:1 (Winter 1991): 3–20.

Sijistani, Abu Ya'qub. "Unveiling of the Hidden (from *Kashf al-mahjub*)." In *An Anthology of Philosophy in Persia (vol 2): Ismaili Thought in the Classical Age from Jabir ibn Hayyan to Nasir al-Din Tusi*, translated by Hermann Landolt, edited by S. H. Nasr and M. Aminrazavi, 83–128. London: I.B. Tauris in association with the Institute of Ismaili Studies, 2008.

Soroush, Abdolkarim. "Remarks." Address presented at Islam and Democracy, conference in Mashhad, Iran, December 1–2, 2004. http:// www.drsoroush.com/English/By_DrSoroush/E-CMB-20041126-Islam_and_Democracy-conference_in_Mashhad.html.

Stackhouse, John and Patrick Martin. "Canada: 'A model for the world.'" the *Globe and Mail*, February 2, 2002.

Steigerwald, Diana. "Isma'ili *Ta'wil*." In *The Blackwell Companion to the Qur'an*, edited by Andrew Rippin, 386–400. Malden: Blackwell Pub., 2006.

Steinberg, Jonah. *Isma`ili Modern: Globalization and Identity in a Muslim Community.* Chapel Hill: The University of North Carolina Press, 2011.

Taylor, Charles. *A Secular Age.* Cambridge: Harvard University Press, 2007.

———. *The Malaise of Modernity.* Concord: Anansi, 1991.

The Institute of Ismaili Studies. "Graduate Programme in Islamic Studies and Humanities." http://www.iis.ac.uk/view_article. asp?ContentID=104478.

———. "IIS Overview." http://www.iis.ac.uk/view_article.asp?ContentID= 104413.

Thornton, Ted. *History of the Middle East Database.* http://www. nmhtthornton.com/mehistorydatabase/abbasid_golden_age.php.

Today. MSNBC.com, December 13, 2010. http://today.msnbc.msn.com/ id/26184891/vp/40639864#40639864.

Vaglieri, L. Veccia. "Ghadir Khumm." In *The Encyclopedia of Islam*, CD-ROM Edition.

Valpy, Michael. "The World of the Aga Khan." the *Globe and Mail*, February 2, 2002. http://www.theglobeandmail.com/focus/ the-world-of-the-aga-khan/article443054/.

Varshney, Ashutosh. "Ethnic Conflict and Civil Society: India and Beyond." *World Politics* Vol. 53, No. 3 (April 2001): 362–398.

Virani, Shafique N. *The Ismailis in the Middle Ages: A History of Survival, A Search for Salvation.* Oxford: Oxford University Press, 2007.

Walker, Paul E. "Fatimid Institutions of Learning." *Journal of the American Research Center in Egypt* 34 (1997): 179–200.

———. "The Institute of Ismaili Studies." *Encyclopaedia Iranica*, Online Edition, December 15, 2004. http://www.iranicaonline.org/articles/ institute-of-ismaili-studies.

———. *Early Philosophical Shiism: The Ismaili Neoplatonism of Abu Ya`qub al-Sijistani.* Cambridge: Cambridge University Press, 1993.

Watt, Montgomery. *Muhammad at Medina.* Oxford: Oxford University Press, 1956.

Yusuf Ali, Abdullah. *The holy Qur'an: Arabic text with an English translation and commentary.* Delhi: Kitab Pub. House, 1973.

Zahniser, A. H. Mathias. "Knowledge and Thinking." In *Blackwell Companion to the Qur'an*, edited by Andrew Rippin, 282–297. Malden: Blackwell Pub., 2006.

Acknowledgements

I am grateful to all those at McGill University who were involved with the successful completion of this study in 2012. At the time, it was the first significant study to map the contours of contemporary Ismaili thought. For this reason, it remains relevant and is therefore being published in its original form.

I am also grateful to the coterie of individuals who have been a buttress and an encouragement throughout the years, and from whom I have learned much.

Finally, I am grateful to my family for their continual support. To my parents and grandparents, especially, I am grateful for their unwavering encouragement and guidance. It is to them that this work is dedicated.

Printed in the United States
By Bookmasters